S0-ANN-578

# 1993

# ZAGAT
# NEW YORK CITY
# RESTAURANT
# SURVEY

Published and Distributed by

ZAGAT SURVEY
4 Columbus Circle
New York, N.Y. 10019
212-977-6000

# CONTENTS

# TO ORDER

**ZAGAT U.S. HOTEL, RESORT, SPA SURVEY**

**ZAGAT SURVEY: AMERICA'S
TOP RESTAURANTS**

**ZAGAT SURVEY: AMERICA'S
BEST VALUE RESTAURANTS**

**ZAGAT RESTAURANT SURVEYS**
Atlanta; Atlantic City; Boston; Chicago;
Dallas–Fort Worth; Hawaii; Houston; Kansas City;
London; Los Angeles–Southern California;
Miami–Southern Florida; Montreal; New Orleans;
New York City; Orlando–Central Florida;
Pacific Northwest; Philadelphia;
San Francisco; Southwest; St. Louis;
Tri-State–CT/NJ/NY; Washington, D.C.–Baltimore

**ZAGAT NYC MARKETPLACE SURVEY**
covering food, wine and entertaining sources

**ZAGAT/AXXIS CityGuides™**
for desktop, notebook and handheld computers.
Comprehensive mapping software fully integrated
with Zagat restaurant and hotel ratings; available
by city on disk or nationwide on CD-ROM.

Call (212) 977-6000 • (800) 333-3421

or Write to:

Zagat Survey
4 Columbus Circle
New York, New York 10019

**Regarding
Corporate Gifts and
Deluxe Editions, call
(212) 977-6000
or (800) 333-3421**

# INTRODUCTION

Here are the final results of our *1993 New York City Restaurant Survey*, covering 1,248 restaurants in what we believe is the best and most varied dining scene in the world.

By annually surveying large numbers of regular restaurant-goers, we think we have achieved a uniquely current and reliable guide. We hope you agree. This year, over 8,300 people participated in our *Survey*, up 19 percent from last year. Since the participants dined out an average of 3.1 times per week, this *Survey* is based on over 3,700 meals per day (seven times what a single critic eating two meals a day five days a week can cover in a full year) and roughly 1,350,000 meals per year.

Knowing that the quality of this *Survey* is the direct result of their thoughtful voting and commentary, we thank each one of our participants. This is really "your book."

To help guide our readers to NYC's best meals and best buys, we have prepared a number of lists. See, for example, New Yorkers' Favorites (page 9), Top Ratings (pages 10–14) and Best Buys (pages 15–20). On the assumption that most people want a "quick fix" on the places at which they are considering eating, we have also tried to be concise and to provide handy indexes.

**We invite you to be a reviewer in our next *Survey*.** To do so, simply send a stamped, self-addressed, business-size envelope to ZAGAT SURVEY, 4 Columbus Circle, New York, NY 10019. This will permit us to contact you next summer. Each participant will receive a free copy of our *1994 New York City Restaurant Survey* when it is published.

Your comments, suggestions and criticisms of this year's *Survey* are also solicited. There is always room for improvement – with your help.

New York, New York          Nina and Tim Zagat
November 25, 1992

# FOREWORD

While the recession, now in its third year, has been hard on many restaurants, the flipside is that New York is now clearly "an eater's market." As one surveyor summed it up, the high-flying restaurants of the 1980s have "returned to earth".

A major development favoring consumers has been an explosion of bargain prix fixe menus. This phenomenon followed the success of a $19.92 lunch promotion in which most of the city's top restaurants participated in connection with this past summer's Democratic National Convention. The enthusiastic response of New Yorkers led many of these restaurants to extend their prix fixe menus and convinced many other restaurants to jump onto the bandwagon. We've listed the more important of these menus at pages 19 to 20.

Focusing on the economy, we asked our surveyors how they felt the recession has affected the restaurant scene. Most replied that restaurants have become "friendlier" and "more accessible", offering "more extras" and "reduced prices" and, even producing "better food." Our numerical ratings confirm these observations: the average ratings for food, decor and service over the entire 1,240-plus restaurants that we surveyed increased slightly, while the average price of a meal dropped by $1.25 – a cost reduction of 4 percent. The decline in average price may be due to the fact that most of the new restaurants that we surveyed are value-oriented ethnics, pasta places, bistros and grills. However, "good value" has become a hallmark of dining out in New York. Accordingly, we have listed over 200 value-oriented restaurants at pages 15 to 18.

Given the economy, we've been surprised that significant openings are still outrunning closings by 145 to 45. The restaurant industry clearly retains great vitality. The fact is that, despite the sour economy, new restaurants are opening daily and, for the most part, these newcomers (e.g. Banana Cafe, Becco, Boca Chica, Brasserie des Theatres, Follonico, Gabriel's, Grange Hall, Manhattan Plaza Cafe, Oceana, Park Avenue Cafe, Snaps, Stick to Your Ribs BBQ, Trois Jean and Zoe) seem to be delivering better food and more variety at lower prices. Only a handful of the closed restaurants (e.g. Eze, Maxim's, Mondrian, Phoenix Garden and Raga) will really be missed.

Several other factors augur well for the long-term vigor of the New York City restaurant scene:

- The continuing arrival of thousands upon thousands of immigrants from around the world, enriching our dining choices by bringing their diverse national cuisines with them.

- The flow into the industry of highly motivated and well-educated young people from professional training institutions such as The Culinary Institute of America.

- The rise to dominance of dynamic, young American chefs, e.g. David Bouley (Bouley), Terry Brennan (Prix Fixe), Andrew D'Amico (Sign of the Dove), Bobby Flay (Mesa Grill), Michael Lomonaco ("21" Club), John Loughran (River Cafe), Waldy Malouf (Hudson River Club), Charlie Palmer (Aureole), Deborah Ponzek (Montrachet), Alfred Portale (Gotham), Michael Romano (Union Square), Michael Ronis (Carmine's), Anne Rosensweig (Arcadia), Tom Valenti (Alison on Dominick Street), David Waltuck (Chanterelle), David Walzog (Arizona 206), Barry Wine (Quilted Giraffe) and many others who run the City's most popular kitchens.

- Improving sources of fresh, often organic, ingredients (from bread to exotic fruits, vegetables, game and fish) demanded by the new, young star chefs and their immigrant peers.

- A dining public that is committed, both by choice and by necessity, to dining out – witness the 19 percent increase in our surveyor base.

In sum, 1992 may have been a tough and competitive year for restaurants, but it has emerged as a vintage year for restaurant-going, with the future promising even better dining here in the Restaurant Capital of the World.

New York, New York          Nina and Tim Zagat
November 25, 1992

# EXPLANATION OF RATINGS AND SYMBOLS

**FOOD, DECOR** and **SERVICE** are each rated on a scale of 0 to 30 in columns marked **F, D** and **S**:

       0–9   = poor to fair
      10–19 = good to very good
      20–25 = very good to excellent
      26–30 = extraordinary to perfection

The **COST** column, headed by a **C**, reflects the estimated price of a dinner with one drink and tip. As a rule of thumb, lunch will cost 25 percent less.

An **Asterisk (\*)** after a restaurant's name means the number of persons who voted on the restaurant is too low to be statistically reliable; **L** for late means the restaurant serves after 11 PM; **S** means it is open on Sunday; **X** means no credit cards are accepted; **(92)** means the numerical ratings and comments are based on our *1992 Survey*.

By way of **Commentary**, we attempt to summarize the comments of the *Survey* participants, occasionally retaining a prior year's comment where appropriate. The prefix **U** means comments were uniform; **M** means they were mixed.

The names of the restaurants with the highest overall ratings and greatest popularity are printed in solid capital letters, e.g., "**BOULEY**."

If we do not show ratings on a restaurant, it is either an important **newcomer** or a popular **write-in**; however, comments are included and the estimated cost, including one drink and tip, is indicated by the following symbols:

        **I** = below $15
      **M** = $15 to $30
       **E** = $30 to $50
    **VE** = $50 or above

# NEW YORKERS' FAVORITE RESTAURANTS

Each of our reviewers has been asked to name his or her five favorite restaurants. The 50 spots most frequently named, in order of their popularity, are:

| | |
|---|---|
| 1. Bouley | 26. Mesa Grill |
| 2. Aureole | 27. Da Umberto |
| 3. Union Square Cafe | 28. Hudson River Club |
| 4. Four Seasons | 29. Periyali |
| 5. Gotham Bar & Grill | 30. Lespinasse |
| 6. La Cote Basque | 31. Terrace |
| 7. Lutece | 32. Provence |
| 8. Le Bernardin | 33. Dock's Oyster Bar |
| 9. Cafe des Artistes | 34. Quilted Giraffe |
| 10. Le Cirque | 35. Capsouto Freres |
| 11. Peter Luger | 36. Sparks Steak House |
| 12. River Cafe | 37. Trattoria dell'Arte |
| 13. Chanterelle | 38. Alison on Dominick |
| 14. Il Mulino | 39. Prix Fixe |
| 15. La Grenouille | 40. John Clancy's |
| 16. Manhattan Ocean Club | 41. La Caravelle |
| 17. One If by Land, TIBS | 42. Smith & Wollensky |
| 18. Aquavit | 43. Cellar in the Sky |
| 19. Sign of the Dove | 44. Arcadia |
| 20. Carmine's | 45. Shun Lee Palace |
| 21. Rainbow Room | 46. Le Perigord |
| 22. Jo Jo | 47. Coco Pazzo |
| 23. Palm | 48. Le Madri |
| 24. Montrachet | 49. Oyster Bar |
| 25. Box Tree | 50. Remi |

It's obvious that most of the restaurants on the above list are among the City's most expensive, but New Yorkers are notorious bargain hunters. Fortunately, our city has an abundance of wonderful ethnic restaurants and other inexpensive spots that fill the bill. Thus, we have listed over 200 "Best Buys" on pages 15–18, and identified Prix Fixe and Pre-Theater Bargains at some of the city's major restaurants on pages 19 and 20.

# TOP RATINGS*

## TOP 50 FOOD RATINGS

**28** – Bouley
Aureole
**27** – Le Cirque
Lutece
Le Bernardin
La Cote Basque
Peter Luger
La Grenouille
Il Mulino
**26** – Gotham Bar & Grill
Chanterelle
Four Seasons
Union Square Cafe
Les Celebrites
**25** – La Caravelle
Sushisay
Quilted Giraffe
Lespinasse
Montrachet
Arcadia
Manhattan Ocean Club
Patsy's Pizza (Bklyn)
Le Regence
Le Perigord
La Reserve
Terrace

Da Umberto
Primavera
March
**24** – Sparks Steak House
Periyali
River Cafe
Il Nido
Lafayette
Il Giglio
Parioli Romanissimo
Palm
Hatsuhana
Felidia
Tse Yang
Sonia Rose
Shun Lee Palace
Canton
Jo Jo
Oceana
Cellar in the Sky
Aquavit
**23** – Rosemarie's
Paola's
Alison

## TOP SPOTS BY CUISINE

**Top American**
**28** – Aureole
**26** – Gotham Bar & Grill
Union Square Cafe
**25** – Quilted Giraffe
Arcadia
March

**Top Brunch**
**24** – River Cafe
**23** – Box Tree
Sign of the Dove
Cafe des Artistes
Hudson River Club
Capsouto Freres

**Top Breakfast**
**22** – Carlyle Dining Rm.
**21** – Cafe Pierre
**20** – Regency
"44"
Sarabeth's
**19** – Edwardian Room

**Top Cafes**
**26** – Gotham Bar & Grill
Union Square Cafe
**24** – River Cafe
**23** – Sign of the Dove
Cafe des Artistes
Duane Park Cafe

---

*Excluding restaurants with voting too low to be reliable.

## Top Chinese
24 – Tse Yang
 Shun Lee Palace
 Canton
23 – Szechuan Kitchen
 Chin Chin
22 – Shun Lee West

## Top Continental
26 – Four Seasons
24 – Cellar in the Sky
23 – Box Tree
 One if by Land, TIBS
 Sign of the Dove
22 – Leopard

## Top Delis
21 – Second Avenue Deli
20 – Carnegie Deli
17 – Ratner's
16 – Katz's Deli
 Stage Deli
15 – Wolf's Deli

## Top French
28 – Bouley
27 – Le Cirque
 Lutece
 Le Bernardin
 La Cote Basque
 La Grenouille

## Top French Bistros
25 – Montrachet
24 – Jo Jo
23 – Alison
 La Metairie
22 – Capsouto Freres
 Park Bistro

## Top Greek/Mideast
24 – Periyali
21 – Karyatis
20 – Pamir
 Roumeli Taverna
19 – Cafe Crocodile
 Khyber Pass

## Top Hotel Dining
27 – Le Cirque/Mayfair
26 – Les Celebrites/Essex
25 – Lespinasse/St. Regis
 Le Regence/Athenee
24 – Lafayette/Drake
23 – Box Tree/Box Tree

## Top Indian
23 – Dawat
21 – Darbar
 Jewel of India
20 – Mitali East/West
19 – Haveli
 Akbar

## Top Italian
27 – Il Mulino
25 – Da Umberto
 Primavera
24 – Il Nido
 Il Giglio
 Parioli Romanissimo

## Top Japanese
25 – Sushisay
24 – Hatsuhana
 Iso
23 – Sushi Zen
 Japonica
 Omen

## Top Mex/Tex-Mex
22 – Zarela
21 – Mi Cocina
20 – Rosa Mexicana
19 – Bright Food Shop
 Pedro Paramo
 Benny's Burritos

## Top Miscellaneous
24 – Sonia Rose
 Aquavit
23 – Hudson River Club
 Solera
22 – Tropica
20 – Boca Chica

## Top Newcomers/Rated
26 – Les Celebrites
25 – Lespinasse
24 – Oceana
22 – Cafe Botanica
Park Avenue Cafe
21 – Manhattan Plaza Cafe

## Top Newcomers/Unrated
— Banana Cafe
— Becco
— Brasserie des Theatres
— Grange Hall
— Snaps
— Trois Jean

## Top Old New York
27 – Peter Luger
24 – Palm
23 – Cafe des Artistes
22 – Oyster Bar
20 – Gage & Tollner
19 – "21" Club

## Top People-Watching
27 – Le Cirque
La Grenouille
26 – Four Seasons (lunch)
23 – Rao's
22 – Remi
21 – Elio's

## Top Pizza
25 – Patsy's Pizza (Bklyn)
23 – John's Pizzeria
22 – Patsy's (1st Ave.)
20 – Vinnie's Pizza
19 – Mezzogiorno
— Totonno (Bklyn)†

## Top Pub Dining
23 – Rao's
22 – Oyster Bar Saloon
21 – Chefs & Cuisiniers
20 – Wollenksy's Grill
Frank's
19 – "21" Club

## Top Seafood
27 – Le Bernardin
25 – Manhattan Ocean Club
24 – Oceana
22 – Wilkinson's
Oyster Bar
Sea Grill

## Top South by SW
23 – Mesa Grill
21 – Coach House
Miracle Grill
20 – Gage & Tollner
Lola
19 – Arizona 206

## Top Steakhouses
27 – Peter Luger
24 – Spark's Steakhouse
Palm
22 – Post House
Christ Cella
Smith & Wollenksy

## Top Tasting Menus
28 – Bouley
Aureole
27 – Le Cirque
26 – Chanterelle
25 – Quilted Giraffe
24 – River Cafe

## Top Thai
22 – Thailand Restaurant
Jai Ya Thai
21 – Thai House Cafe
Thai Chef
Tommy Tang's
Shaliga Thai

## Top Trips to Country*
— Jean-Louis, Greenwich
— La Panetiere, Rye NY
— Mirabelle, St. James LI
— Saddle River Inn, NJ
— Xaviar's, Garrison NY
— Xaviar's, Piermont NY

---

\* See *Zagat Tri-State Restaurant Survey* for ratings.
†Voting too low to be rated.

# TOP 50 OVERALL DECOR
## (In order of rating)

**28** – Les Celebrites
    Rainbow Room
    Bouley
**27** – Four Seasons
    Temple Bar
    River Cafe
    La Grenouille
    Lespinasse
    Le Regence
    One if by Land, TIBS
    Windows on the World
    Aureole
    La Cote Basque
**26** – Cafe des Artistes
    Terrace
    Sign of the Dove
    Box Tree
    Le Bernardin
    Palio
    Hudson River Club
    Edwardian Room
    Cellar in the Sky
    Tavern on the Green
    Cafe Botanica
    Water's Edge

    Carlyle Dining Room
**25** – Aquavit
    Le Cirque
    Jezebel
    View
    Halcyon
    Mark's
    Oak Room
    La Reserve
**24** – Water Club
    La Caravelle
    Tse Yang
    Chanterelle
    Lutece
    Quilted Giraffe
    Stanhope
    Lafayette
    44
    March
    Eldorado Petit
    Adrienne
    Petrossian
    Gotham Bar & Grill
    Cafe Pierre
    Laura Belle

# TOP VIEWS
## (In alphabetical order)

Cellar in the Sky
Giando
Harbour Lights
Hudson River Club
Parker's Lighthouse
Rainbow Room
River Cafe

Terrace
Top of the Sixes
View
Water Club
Water's Edge
Windows on the World
World Yacht Cruises

# TOP ROOMS

Aquavit
Aureole
Bouley
Cafe des Artistes
Cafe Nicholson
Carlyle Dining Room
Edwardian Room
Eldorado Petit
Four Seasons
Jezebel
La Cote Basque
La Grenouille

Le Bernardin
Les Celebrites
Mark's
Oak Room
One if by Land, TIBS
Palio
Quilted Giraffe
Rainbow Room
Sign of the Dove
Tavern on the Green
Temple Bar

# TOP 50 OVERALL SERVICE
## (In order of rating)

26 – Aureole
Four Seasons
Lutece
Chanterelle
Le Regence
25 – Bouley
La Cote Basque
La Grenouille
Le Bernardin
Les Celebrites
Lespinasse
La Caravelle
Le Cirque
24 – Lafayette
Cellar in the Sky
Box Tree
Le Perigord
Quilted Giraffe
March
Carlyle Dining Room
La Reserve
Oceana
23 – Terrace
Gotham Bar & Grill
Union Square Cafe

Leopard
Montrachet
Aquavit
Mark's
One if by Land, TIBS
Sonia Rose
River Cafe
22 – Arcadia
Chiam
Le Chantilly
Primavera
Tse Yang
Cafe Botanica
Chez Michallet
Cafe Pierre
Cafe des Artistes
Il Mulino
Grifone
Manhattan Ocean Club
Rainbow Room
Sign of the Dove
DeGrezia
Il Tinello
Edwardian Room
Erminia

# BEST BUYS

## TOP 100 BANGS FOR THE BUCK

This list reflects the best dining values in our *Survey*. It is produced by dividing the cost of a meal into the combined ratings for food, decor and service.

1. McDonald's (160 B'way)
2. Papaya King
3. Gray's Papaya
4. Amir's Falafel
5. Vinnie's Pizza
6. Orig. Cal. Taq. (Bklyn)
7. Cafe Lalo
8. Cupcake Cafe
9. Chicken Chef
10. Patisserie Lanciani
11. Freddie & Pepper
12. Patsy's Pizza (Bklyn)
13. Caffe Vivaldi
14. Angelica Kitchen
15. Denino's (S.I.)
16. John's Pizzeria
17. Manhattan Plaza Cafe
18. Veselka
19. Benny's Burritos
20. Corner Bistro
21. Viand
22. La Caridad
23. Szech. Hunan Cottage
24. Manganaro's Hero-Boy
25. El Pollo
26. Atomic Wings
27. Chez Brigitte
28. Szechuan Kitchen
29. EJ's Luncheonette
30. Anglers & Writers
31. Sotto Cinque
32. Pasta Place (S.I.)
33. Harriet's Kitchen
34. Old Town Bar
35. Ludlow Street Cafe
36. Totonno Pizzeria (Bklyn)
37. Arturo's Pizzeria
38. Two Boots
39. Westside Cottage
40. Bo Ky
41. Silk Road Palace
42. Burger Heaven
43. Edison Cafe
44. Kiev
45. Bali Burma
46. Aggie's
47. Eighteenth & Eighth
48. Patsy's Pizza (1st Ave.)
49. Stick to Ribs BBQ (Qns)
50. Boca Chica
51. Passage to India
52. Ed Debevic's
53. Lupe's East L.A.
54. Pandit
55. Pedro Paramo
56. Tartine
57. Afghan Kebab House
58. Bright Food Shop
59. Menchanko-Tei
60. Cucina della Fontana
61. Serendipity 3
62. Boogies
63. Frutti di Mare
64. Wong Kee
65. Christine's
66. Whole Wheat 'n Berrys
67. Bubby's
68. Cafe S.F.A.
69. Lai Lai West
70. Antico Caffee
71. Teresa's
72. Lamarca
73. Marnie's Noodle Shop
74. Haveli
75. Bella Donna
76. Cloister Cafe
77. Cucina Stagionale
78. Katz's Deli
79. Hunan Balcony
80. Pizzeria Uno
81. Good Enough to Eat
82. Cucina di Pesce
83. Colombia Cottage
84. Brother's BBQ
85. Ollie's
86. Angels
87. Thailand Restaurant
88. Urban Grill
89. Popover Cafe
90. Cucina & Co.
91. Dallas BBQ
92. Khyber Pass
93. Hunan Garden
94. Jackson Hole
95. Dosanko
96. Fanelli
97. Pizzapiazza
98. Indian Cafe
99. La Boulangere
100. Iso

# TOP BANGS FOR THE BUCK
## BY CUISINE
### (In order of ranking)

**American**
Manhattan Plaza Cafe
Anglers & Writers
Cafe S.F.A.
Good Enough to Eat

**Bar-B-Q**
Stick to Ribs BBQ
Brother's BBQ
Dallas BBQ
Brother Jimmy's BBQ

**Breakfast/Brunch**
Friend of a Farmer
Royal Canadian
Good Enough to Eat
Sarabeth's

**Burgers & Dogs**
McDonald's (160 B'way)
Papaya King
Gray's Papaya
Corner Bistro

**Cafes**
Manhattan Plaza Cafe
Edison Cafe
Cafe S.F.A
Cloister Cafe

**Caribbean/So. Amer.**
La Caridad
El Pollo
Day-O
Boca Chica

**Cent./Eastern Europe**
Veselka
Kiev
Christine's
Teresa's

**Chicken**
Chicken Chef
El Pollo
Atomic Wings
Harriett's Kitchen

**Chinese**
La Caridad
Szechuan Hunan
Szechuan Kitchen
Westside Cottage

**Coffee Houses**
Cafe Lalo
Cupcake Cafe
Patisserie J. Lanciani
Caffe Vivaldi

**Delis**
Katz's
Second Avenue Deli
Carnegie Deli
N.Y. Deli

**Diners/Coffee Shops**
Viand
EJ's Luncheonette
Edison Cafe
Aggie's

**French**
Chez Brigitte
Tartine
La Boulangere
La Bonne Soup

**Health Food**
Angelica Kitchen
Whole Wheat 'n Berry's
Bubby's
Zen Palate

**Hotels**
Cafe Botanica/Essex Hse.
Nicole Brasserie/Omni Pk.
Lexington Ave. Grill/Loews
Russell's/Sheraton Pk.

**Indian†**
Passage to India
Pandit
Haveli
Indian Cafe

---

† Virtually every Indian restaurant serves an all-you-can-eat buffet lunch for $15 or less.

16

## Indonesian/Burmese
Bali Burma
Mingala West/Burmese
Road to Mandalay
Nusantara

## Italian
Sotto Cinque
Cucina della Fontana
Frutti di Mare
Antico Caffee

## Japanese
Mechenko-Tei
Marnie's Noodle Shop
Dosanko
Iso

## Mexican/Tex-Mex
Benny's Burritos
Lupe's East L.A.
Pedro Paramo
Bright Food Shop

## Middle Eastern
Amir's Falafel
Afghan Kebab House
Khyber Pass
Marti Kebab

## Newcomers/Rated
Manhattan Plaza Cafe
Bali Burma
Eighteenth & Eighth
Boca Chica

## Oddballs, Etc.
Manganaro's Hero-Boy
Ludlow Street Cafe
Jekyl & Hyde
Tibetan Kitchen

## Outta Boro
Original Taqueria (Bklyn)
Dennino's (S.I.)
Pasta Place (S.I.)
Stick to Ribs BBQ (Qns)

## Pastarias
Lamarca
Angels
Ecco-La
Tutta Pasta

## Pizza
Vinnie's Pizza
Freddie & Pepper Pizza
Patsy's Pizza (Bklyn)
John's Pizzeria

## Pubs
Corner Bistro
Old Town Bar
Fanelli
Chumley's

## Seafood
Jane St. Seafood
Oriental Town Seafood
Hosteria Fiorello
Dock's Oyster Bar

## Southern
Two Boots
Great Jones Cafe
Sylvia's
Miracle Grill

## Spanish
Cafe Español
Sevilla
Rio Mar
El Faro

## Steakhouses
Embers (Bklyn)
L'Entrecote
Wollensky's Grill
Steak Frites

## Thai
Thailand Restaurant
Boonthai
Thai House Cafe
Mueng Thai

# 100 MORE GOOD VALUES
### (A bit more expensive, but worth every penny)

Akadi
Artepasta
Aspen Cafe
Barney Greengrass
Bellisimo
Bendix Diner
Bertha's
Bloom's Delicatessen
Broadway Diner*
Broome Street Bar
Brother Jimmy's BBQ
BTI*
Cafe Andrusha
Cafe Buon Gusto
Canyon Road
Carmine's*
Carnegie Deli
Chef Ho's
Chumley's
Ci Vediamo*
Coming or Going
Copeland's
Cowgirl Hall of Fame
Day-O
Do Da's
Ecco-La
El Charro*
Empire Diner
Empire Szechuan*
1st Wok
44 Southwest
Friend of a Farmer
Garibaldi Ristorante
Grand Dairy
Grange Hall
Great Shanghai
Great Amer. Health Bar
Groceries
Hard Rock Cafe
Hwa Yuan Szechuan
Il–Corallo Trattoria
India Pavillion*
Island Spice
Iso
Jekyll & Hyde
John's of 12th Street
Kan Pai
Kodnoi
La Bonne Soupe
La Fondue

La Taza De Oro
Levee
Little Poland
Manhattan Chili Co.
Mappamondo*
Mary Ann's*
Meridiana
Mingala Burmese
Mingala West
Mitali East/West
Mr. Tang's
Mueng Thai
Nawab
NoHo Star
Perk's Fine Cuisine
Pete's Place
Phoebe's
Pie, The
Planet Hollywood
Pongsri Thai
Road to Mandalay
Rocking Horse Cafe
Royal Canadian Pancake*
Sabra
Sambuca
2nd Avenue Brasserie
Second Avenue Deli
Shabu Tatsu
Shark Bar
Soup Burg*
Sugah's
Sultan
Sylvia's
Tai Hong Lau
Tang Tang*
Tatany
Thai Chef
Thai House Cafe
Thompkins Park
Tibetan Kitchen
Tony's Di Napoli
Tortilla Flats
Tutta Pasta*
Uskudar
Walker's
Westside Cafe
White Horse Tavern
Woo Chon
Zen Palate

*Has multiple locations.

# PRIX FIXE MENUS BELOW $40
# AT MAJOR RESTAURANTS*†

## • Lunch •

| | | | |
|---|---|---|---|
| Adrienne | $28.00 | Le Cirque | $34.00 |
| Akbar | 12.95 | L'Ecole | 16.00 |
| Ambassador Grill | 19.93 | Le Pistou | 19.93 |
| American Harvest | 22.00 | Lespinasse | 38.00 |
| Arcadia | 19.93 | Les Pyrenees | 17.50 |
| Arizona 206 | 19.93 | Les Sans Culottes | 11.00 |
| Ballroom | 18.50 | Levana | 21.90 |
| Barbetta | 19.93 | Lutece | 38.00 |
| Becco | 19.00 | Manhattan Cafe | 14.00 |
| Bellini by Cipriani | 19.93 | Mark's | 24.00 |
| Bombay Palace | 11.95 | Montrachet | 19.93 |
| Bouley | 32.00 | Nirvana | 12.95 |
| Cafe des Artistes | 19.50 | Nusantara | 17.50 |
| Cafe Pierre | 32.00 | Oceana | 26.00 |
| Capsouto Freres | 19.93 | Odeon | 14.50 |
| Carlyle Dining Rm.† | 27.00 | Palm | 19.93 |
| Chanterelle | 30.00 | Paul & Jimmy's | 14.50 |
| Darbar† | 12.95 | Peacock Alley | 19.50 |
| Dawat | 11.95 | Petrossian | 29.00 |
| Eldorado Petit | 25.00 | Prix Fixe | 18.50 |
| Fu's | 19.93 | Quatorze | 11.50 |
| Gage & Tollner | 18.95 | Quatorze Bis | 11.95 |
| Girafe | 20.75 | Rene Pujol | 23.00 |
| Gotham Bar/Grill | 19.93 | Sal Anthony's | 9.95 |
| Halcyon | 19.93 | San Domenico | 19.93 |
| Harry Cipriani | 19.93 | Sardi's | 22.95 |
| Hudson River Club | 19.93 | Second Ave. Deli† | 19.93 |
| Jean Lafitte | 20.00 | Shun Lee Palace | 19.93 |
| Jewel of India† | 11.95 | Sonia Rose | 18.50 |
| J. Sung Dynasty | 18.00 | Tavern on Green | 15.50 |
| La Caravelle | 33.00 | Terrace | 25.00 |
| La Cote Basque | 28.00 | "21" Club | 19.93 |
| La Grenouille | 39.50 | Urban Grill | 12.95 |
| La Reserve | 31.00 | Windows on World | 23.00 |
| Le Chantilly | 25.00 | World Yacht | 27.50 |

---

*Prices as we go to press. Since prix fixe prices may change, or be cancelled at anytime, the only way to be sure is to call the restaurant before going.
†All you can eat.

# • Dinner •

| | | | |
|---|---|---|---|
| Adrienne* | $28.50 | Le Pistou | $30.00 |
| Akbar | 21.25 | Lespinasse | 38.00 |
| Alison* | 26.00 | Les Pyrenees | 26.00 |
| Ambassador Grill** | 20/25 | Les Sans Culottes | 19.95 |
| American Harvest | 22.00 | Le Steak | 22.95 |
| An American Place | 29.95 | Levana | 27.00 |
| Anche Vivolo* | 17.50 | Manhattan Cafe* | 14.00 |
| Aquavit* | 39.00 | Marylou's* | 15.95 |
| Arcadia* | 24.93 | Montrachet | 25.00 |
| Arizona 206* | 24.93 | Nirvana | 21.95 |
| Barbetta* | 39.00 | Nusantara | 25.00 |
| Becco | 19.00 | Oceana | 36.00 |
| Bellini by Cipriani* | 29.50 | Paul & Jimmy's* | 19.50 |
| Bombay Palace | 11.95 | Petrossian* | 38.00 |
| Cafe Botanica** | 24/29 | Pierre au Tunnel | 26.00 |
| Cafe des Artistes | 32.50 | Poiret* | 19.95 |
| Cafe Luxembourg* | 26.50 | Prix Fixe | 24.00 |
| Cafe Pierre* | 34.00 | Rainbow Room* | 38.50 |
| Dawat | 21.95 | Regency | 27.50 |
| Eldorado Petit | 28.00 | Rene Pujol | 32.00 |
| Ferrier* | 19.95 | Russian Tea Room | 39.75 |
| Florent** | 15/17 | Sal Anthony's* | 15.95 |
| Four Seasons – Grill | 26.50 | San Domenico | 24.93 |
| Fu's | 24.93 | Sardi's* | 32.95 |
| Gage & Tollner | 21.95 | Scarlatti* | 32.00 |
| Girafe* | 29.75 | Sfuzzi* | 29.50 |
| Halcyon* | 24.93 | Shun Lee Palace* | 24.93 |
| Harry Cipriani | 38.00 | Snaps* | 24.93 |
| Hudson River Club* | 31.00 | Sonia Rose | 29.50 |
| Il Menestrello | 29.50 | Stanhope | 35.00 |
| Jean Lafitte | 24.00 | Supper Club* | 27.00 |
| Jewel of India | 22.95 | Symphony Cafe | 18.50 |
| Jockey Club* | 24.93 | Tavern on Green* | 21.50 |
| J. Sung Dynasty** | 20/25 | Terrace | 36.00 |
| La Caravelle* | 37.00 | "21" Club* | 37.50 |
| La Colombe d'or* | 24.50 | Vivolo* | 17.50 |
| La Reserve* | 39.00 | Water Club | 24.93 |
| L'Ecole | 26.00 | Windows on World** | 34/36 |

---

*Pre-theater only.
**Prices separated by a slash are for pre-theater and for normal dinner hours, respectively.

# ALPHABETICAL
# DIRECTORY
# OF RESTAURANTS

|   | F | D | S | C |
|---|---|---|---|---|

### Abe's Steak House/S
**18 | 13 | 17 | $42**

1568 First Ave. (bet. 81st & 82nd Sts.), 879-0900
*M – If not in the steakhouse big leagues, this Eastsider
satisfies with "huge" portions and "good quality", plus a
"homey" atmosphere; critics brand it "stodgy" and say
"wear a gray wig" to blend in.*

### Acme Bar & Grill/LS
**14 | 11 | 13 | $21**

9 Great Jones St. (bet. B'way & Lafayette), 420-1934
*M – "Killer hot sauces" and "deadly" drinks are served at
this "down 'n' dirty" NoHo version of a Dixie truckstop;
both decor and service "leave much to be desired", but
"good music" keeps the "noisy college crowd" happy.*

### Adrienne/S
**21 | 24 | 21 | $53**

The Peninsula Hotel, 700 Fifth Ave. (55th St.), 903-3918
*U – With its "comfortable" setting, fine Mediterranean
fare and "attentive" service, this classy hotel restaurant
should be more popular; that it's often "too quiet" (i.e.
empty) may be due to its high prices and chef changes.*

### Afghan Kebab House
**18 | 7 | 14 | $16**

764 Ninth Ave. (bet. 51st & 52nd Sts.), 307-1612/X
1345 Second Ave. (bet. 70th & 71st Sts.), 517-2776
155 W. 46th St. (bet. 6th & 7th Aves.), 768-3875
*U – Despite decor from the "Afghan Salvation Army",
these BYO ethnics have lots of fans for their "juicy"
kebabs that fill you up without skewering your wallet.*

### Aggie's/SX
**17 | 10 | 11 | $15**

146 W. Houston St. (MacDougal St.), 673-8994
*M – The resident cat is "friendlier than the waiters" at
this "new age coffee shop"; it's a favorite Village
hangout thanks to its "solid, down-home grub with
eccentric twists", laid-back prices and "groovy" crowd.*

### Aglio e Olio (92)
**17 | 18 | 17 | $31**

145 W. 55th St. (bet. 6th & 7th Aves.), 582-9589
*M – "Bright and attractive", this Italianized cafe offers
pastas, sandwiches and rich desserts at fair prices that
customers applaud; critics say it's "unremarkable."*

### Akadi
**– | – | – | M**

186 Eighth Ave. (bet. 19th & 20th Sts.), 929-1110
*Self-described as "the only restaurant in NYC serving
African-French cuisine" (from the Ivory Coast), this mod
Chelsea newcomer is worth a try, especially since it's
hard to spend $20 for a meal.*

|   | F | D | S | C |
|---|---|---|---|---|

**Akbar**/S · · · · · · · · · · · · · · · 19 | 18 | 18 | $29
475 Park Ave. (bet. 57th & 58th Sts.), 838-1717
*U – "You almost can't go wrong" at this "upscale" North
Indian known for its "well-spiced" food, including
vegetarian dishes, and "pleasant", "quiet" dark setting;
its $11.95–$13.95 prix fixe lunches can't be beat – at
least not on Park Avenue.*

**Albuquerque Eats**/LS · · · · · · · · · 13 | 14 | 13 | $22
375 Third Ave. (27th St.), 683-6500
*M – The "Amerimex" food is mostly "substandard", but
that's never stopped this lively dive from drawing a
rowdy young crowd for "killer" margaritas and live, late,
rafter-rattling rockabilly music.*

**Al Bustan** /S (92) · · · · · · · · · · · 18 | 18 | 18 | $32
827 Third Ave. (bet. 50th & 51st Sts.), 759-5933
*U – There aren't many Middle Easterners in Midtown,
so this rather bright, mid-priced Lebanese yearling is
welcome; however, while it pleases most, it excites few.*

**Alcala**/S · · · · · · · · · · · · · · · 17 | 17 | 17 | $33
349 Amsterdam Ave. (bet. 76th & 77th Sts.), 769-9600
*U – "Tasty tapas" are the top touts at this "upscale"
West Side Spaniard; though there's debate over the rest
of the menu, the "casually elegant" setting, "good wines"
and "attentive" staff win general approval.*

**Algonquin Hotel, The**/LS · · · · · · · 14 | 19 | 17 | $40
59 W. 44th St. (bet. 5th & 6th Aves.), 840-6800
*U – "They continually find good cabaret acts, so why
can't they find a chef?" is the key question regarding
this lengendary Theater District dowager out of a
Hirschfeld cartoon; however, it remains a favorite for
drinking in nostalgia along with cocktails or tea in the
wood-paneled lobby, before going elsewhere to eat.*

**Alison on Dominick Street**/S · · · · · 23 | 20 | 22 | $49
38 Dominick St. (bet. Varick & Hudson Sts.), 727-1188
*U – It isn't easy to find, but owner Alison Price's warm
welcome and chef Tom Valenti's "delicious and daring"
French-Mediterranean fare have both foodies and
romantics heading to SoHo for "first-class" candlelit dining.*

**Allegria**/LS · · · · · · · · · · · · · · 15 | 16 | 12 | $31
MGM Bldg., 1350 Ave. of Americas (55th St.), 956-7755
*M – This "lively" Midtown Italian serves "solid" pizza,
pastas and the like in a "cheery" setting, but some call it
a "cookie-cutter" Italian with food that "ain't Allegria."*

| | F | D | S | C |
|---|---|---|---|---|

### Alo Alo/LS
**14 | 17 | 14 | $31**

1030 Third Ave. (61st St.), 838-4343
*M – The Northern Italian food is merely "ok ok", but the bar scene is still "hot hot" at this slick, "pseudo-Euro" Eastsider; stick to basics if dining, or better yet, just have drinks and watch the "beautiful people in black."*

### Amazon Village/S
**8 | 19 | 9 | $24**

Pier 25, West St. (bet. Canal & Chambers Sts.), 227-2900
*M – "Club Med on Hudson", this open-air complex on a Downtown pier provides an instant summer vacation with sand, volleyball, disco, "wild partying" and an "amazing view" "of Joisey"; P.S. "don't eat" and BYO.*

### Ambassador Grill/S
**20 | 21 | 21 | $42**

U.N. Plaza – Park Hyatt Hotel, One U.N. Plaza, 44th St.
(bet. 1st & 2nd Aves.), 702-5014
*U – This "elegant and dignified" U.N. neighbor offers "consistently good" American grill fare, "smooth" service and a "dramatic" mirrored decor; it's a "great price performer" with weekend brunch a "sybaritic delight."*

### America/LS
**13 | 15 | 13 | $24**

9 E. 18th St. (bet. 5th Ave. & B'way), 505-2110
*M – "Oh, say can you hear?" is the anthem at this ear-splitting, mod "airplane hangar" with America's longest menu and singles bar; the food is less than star-spangled, but where else can you get anything from lobster to peanut butter sandwiches?; it's a favorite with kids and Kansas cousins – and only a few NYers.*

### American Festival Cafe/LS
**14 | 19 | 15 | $33**

Rockefeller Skating Rink, 20 W. 50th St. (bet. 5th & 6th Aves.), 246-6699
*M – A festival for the eye – viewing the skating rink in winter, expanding into it for alfresco in summer – this Americana-filled American cafe is still no festival for the taste buds; though, some say the kitchen's "improving."*

### American Harvest/S
**18 | 19 | 18 | $39**

Vista Int'l Hotel, West St. (bet. Liberty & Vesey), 432-9334
*U – Recently refurbished, this "elegant" Downtown dining room offers a seasonal menu based on American produce; "nicely presented" food and a "deluxe" setting make it "a natural for business lunches"; $22 prix fixe.*

### Amici Miei/LS
**16 | 17 | 14 | $29**

475 W. Broadway (Houston St.), 533-1933
*M – The "SoHo scene surpasses" the "so-so" food and so-slow service at this "noisy and trendy" Milanese; we hear new management is improving things, but the young, beautiful Downtown crowd could care less.*

| | F | D | S | C |

### Amir's Falafel/SX
| | 16 | 7 | 13 | $10 |

2911-A Broadway (bet. 113th & 114th Sts.), 749-7500
*M – Critics contend that this Columbia favorite "lost its
edge" after moving to "less funky" quarters, but most
still commend it for quick, "tasty and cheap" meals of
falafel and other "savory" Middle Eastern fare.*

### Amsterdam's/LS
| | 15 | 11 | 14 | $23 |

428 Amsterdam Ave. (bet. 80th & 81st Sts.), 874-1377
454 Broadway (bet. Grand & Howard Sts.), 925-6166
*U – Fans flock to these "informal and reasonable"
rotisseries for "dependable" grills served in a "noisy",
"convivial" ambiance; the decor isn't much, but the bar
crowd is an eyeful.*

### An American Place
| | 22 | 19 | 20 | $45 |

2 Park Ave. (32nd St.), 684-2122
*M – To his many devotees, nationally renowned chef
Larry Forgione is "a genius" whose sprawling cafe gets
"better and better with age", serving récherché
American cuisine that's an "epicurean adventure"; critics
feel it "misses the top" and can be "precious."*

### Anche Vivolo/L
| | 19 | 18 | 17 | $33 |

222 E. 58th St. (bet. 2nd & 3rd Aves.), 308-0112
*U – With "reliable" Northern Italian cooking, "helpful"
service and a "comfortable" pastel setting, this Eastsider
has no trouble attracting fans; on top of that, its prix fixe
dinners are "one of the best deals in town."*

### Andiamo/LS
| | 19 | 19 | 17 | $42 |

1991 Broadway (bet. 67th & 68th Sts.), 362-3315
*M – A "soaring", art-filled setting and live jazz are
attractions, but a growing chorus of critics say this
Lincoln Center Italian has "slipped"; still, it's easily
"better than most on the West Side."*

### Angelica Kitchen/SX
| | 19 | 14 | 15 | $16 |

300 E. 12th St. (bet. 1st & 2nd Aves.), 228-2909
*U – "Back-to-nature" types groove on this bargain East
Village organic Vegetarian which serves a "delicious,
satisfying macrobiotic" seasonal menu that "changes
each equinox and solstice"; the setting is "Zen-like" and
"tranquil" despite staff bent on "educating the public."*

### Angelo's of Mulberry St./LS
| | 19 | 12 | 16 | $32 |

146 Mulberry St. (bet. Hester & Grand), 966-1277
*M – This "roll-up-your-sleeves" old-timer (circa 1902) is
"what Little Italy is all about": "good, basic" red-sauce
fare with "lots of garlic" served in "crowded", "tacky" digs.*

| | F | D | S | C |

**Angels**/S      | 18 | 12 | 15 | $20 |
1135 First Ave. (bet. 62nd & 63rd Sts.), 980-3131
*U – The lines and seating at this tiny East Side heart-
healthy Italian may try an angel's patience, but the
reward is "heavenly" homemade bread and pastas at
merciful prices.*

**Anglers & Writers**/LSX    | 17 | 22 | 17 | $21 |
420 Hudson St. (St. Lukes Pl.), 675-0810
*U – This "cozy" West Villager resembles a Wisconsin
"country cottage" decorated with books and fishing gear;
raves go to its home-baked pies, cakes and breads,
"special preserves", soups and "low-key high tea."*

**Antico Caffee**/LSX    | 17 | 13 | 14 | $19 |
1477 Second Ave. (77th St.), 879-4824
*M – "Interesting pasta combos" and "designer pizzas" at
low prices keep this "colorful" Eastsider jumping with a
noisy, "just-out-of-college" crowd.*

**Antolotti's**/S    | 16 | 13 | 16 | $38 |
337 E. 49th St. (bet. 1st & 2nd Aves.), 688-6767
*M – A dated Eastsider that "still has a following" for its
"no surprises, good basic Italian" food and "courteous,
helpful servers" who cook at the table; critics say, that
while "nothing's wrong, nothing's right, either."*

**Aperitivo**    | 19 | 15 | 18 | $40 |
29 W. 56th St. (bet. 5th & 6th Aves.), 765-5155
*M – If this Midtown Italian old-timer "never changes",
that's how regulars like it; they count on "solid" cooking
(e.g. "best veal chops in town"), "pleasant service" and
"homey" decor; dissenters simply say "old."*

**Appetito***\*    | 18 | 17 | 17 | $42 |
47 W. 39th St. (bet. 5th & 6th Aves.), 391-5286
*U – Garmentos crown this their "new Italian champion"
with "good" salads, pasta and other basics making it
"wonderful for lunch"; it's over by 9 PM.*

**AQUAVIT**    | 24 | 25 | 23 | $53 |
13 W. 54th St. (bet. 5th & 6th Aves.), 307-7311
*U – A "breath of cool Arctic air", this "Scandinavian
stunner" inspires superlatives for both its "knockout"
looks and "rarified" food: "exceptional and different",
"Nordic bliss", "how Swede it is"; to avoid "Rockefeller
prices", try the cheaper, equally good, upstairs cafe.*

**ARCADIA**    | 25 | 22 | 22 | $58 |
21 E. 62nd St. (bet. 5th & Madison Aves.), 223-2900
*U – This "stylish", "intimate" East Side "jewel box"
overflows with admirers who "can't get enough" of
Anne Rosenzweig's American cuisine: "inventive and
delicious", "as beautiful to look at as it is to eat."*

26

|   | F | D | S | C |
|---|---|---|---|---|

**Arcobaleno** (92)  | 16 | 16 | 18 | $36 |
21 E. 9th St. (bet. 5th Ave. & University Pl.), 473-2215
*M – For "solid" Italian fare and "courteous" service,*
*Villagers enjoy this "slightly worn, but warm", "retreat."*

**Aria**  | 20 | 18 | 19 | $40 |
253 E. 52nd St. (2nd Ave.), 888-1410
*M – "Very good" food and service, plus a "peaceful" setting,*
*cause most to sing the praises of this Midtown Northern*
*Italian, but some say it's "not remarkable or unique."*

**Arizona 206 and Cafe**/LS  | 19 | 18 | 16 | $35 |
206 E. 60th St. (bet. 2nd & 3rd Aves.), 838-0440
*M – "Crowded" and "noisy as a cattle stampede", this*
*Eastsider contends for "NYC's best SW"; chef David*
*Walzog's "adventurous" fare has local pepper-lovers*
*putting up with "narcissistic" service and "tables and*
*chairs for midgets"; P.S. the cafe's a "real deal."*

**Arlecchino**/LS  | 18 | 17 | 19 | $30 |
192 Bleecker St. (bet. 6th Ave. & MacDougal), 475-2355
*U – "Cramped but cute", this harlequin-motif trattoria*
*has "well-prepared" food and a "convivial" feel; "grab a*
*window seat and watch the Village in action."*

**Arqua**  | 23 | 18 | 19 | $44 |
281 Church St. (White St.), 334-1888
*U – A "favorite Downtowner", this TriBeCa Tuscan wins*
*praise for its "unusual and wonderful" pastas and other*
*"authentic" fare, plus its amber setting is "pretty in a*
*spare way"; there's "major noise" at prime evening hours.*

**Arriba Arriba**  | 12 | 10 | 13 | $19 |
1463 Third Ave. (bet. 82nd & 83rd Sts.), 249-1423
484 Amsterdam Ave. (bet. 83rd & 84th Sts.), 580-8206
762 Ninth Ave. (51st St.), 489-0810
*M – "Very cheap", this trio of "beans and cheese"*
*Mexicans is another example of margaritas needed to*
*face "very ordinary" food and "smug and surly" service.*

**Artepasta**/S  | – | – | – | I |
81 Greenwich Ave. (Bank St.), 229-0234
*You don't get this crowded without being good or cheap;*
*this simple West Village Italian newcomer is both.*

**Arturo's Pizzeria**/LS  | 18 | 9 | 12 | $15 |
106 W. Houston St. (Thompson St.), 677-3820
*U – This popular brick-oven pie joint is known for its*
*thin-crust pizzas, cold beer, hot jazz and "nicely worn-in"*
*("dark and divey") setting; it's a real "Village experience."*

|  | **F** | **D** | **S** | **C** |

**Asia**/S                              | 17 | 20 | 17 | $31 |
1155 Third Ave. (bet. 67th & 68th Sts.), 879-5846
*M – "A bold attempt at Pan Asian cuisine", this hand-some wood-paneled Eastsider wins praise for "interesting concept" but mixed reviews for execution.*

**Aspen Cafe**                          | – | – | – | I |
2274 Broadway (82nd St.), 799-0578
*A fresh face on the West Side, this easygoing New American cafe feels like a mountain breeze – here's hoping it can cook for the local cliff-dwellers.*

**Assembly, The**                       | 17 | 14 | 17 | $40 |
16 W. 51st St. (bet. 5th & 6th Aves.), 581-3580
*M – Fans contend, and ratings confirm, this Midtown steakhouse is "making a comeback"; it may be "dark, smoky and noisy", but it treats regulars right.*

**Asti**/LS                             | 12 | 16 | 17 | $35 |
13 E. 12th St. (bet. 5th Ave. & University Pl.), 741-9105
*M – Red sauce and Rigoletto are the hallmarks of this Village institution where diners sing opera along with unabashedly hammy waiters and "Chef Boy Ar Dee" in the kitchen; it's "crazy NY fun" – "once in a lifetime."*

**Atomic Wings**/LSX                    | 18 | 6 | 10 | $12 |
1644 Third Ave. (92nd St.), 410-3800
1446 First Ave. (bet. 75th & 76th Sts.), 772-8400
2794 Broadway (108th St.), 316-2300
2180 Broadway (77th St.), 877-1010
179 W. 4th St. (bet. 6th & 7th Aves.), 627-9500
*M – "Burn, baby, burn" could be the motto of these wing joints that operate out of a series of Star Wars bars around town; they dish up good, "atomically hot" wings and waffle fries that require lots of brew to cool off.*

**Au Cafe**                             | – | – | – | M |
1700 Broadway (53rd St.), 757-2233
*From breakfast beignets and cafe au lait to late-supper steak frites, salad or crab cakes, this handsome new Theater District cafe has it all; plenty of outdoor seats make it ideal for fair weather lingering or people-watching.*

**Au Mandarin**/S                       | 20 | 18 | 18 | $29 |
World Financial Ctr., 200-250 Vesey St., 385-0313
*U – "Light, fresh and tasty" Chinese cuisine efficiently served in this "elegant", "tranquil" food court place; busy at lunch, it's like Outer Mongolia at night.*

**Aunt Sonia's** (Brooklyn)/S           | 19 | 15 | 18 | $29 |
1123 Eighth Ave. (12th St.), 718-965-9526
*M – Popular Park Slope "hangout" with "interesting" updates of homestyle cooking in a "friendly", "laid-back" ambiance; if the food is "unpredictable", try Sunday brunch.*

| F | D | S | C |
|---|---|---|---|

## AUREOLE
| 28 | 27 | 26 | $65 |

34 E. 61st St. (bet. Madison & Park Aves.), 319-1660
*U – Chef Charlie Palmer's French-accented American
ranks No. 2 overall in our Survey and inspires
paroxysms of praise: "luminous", "poetry in motion",
"magical"; service rates No. 1 in the city, and both the
flowers and townhouse setting are "gorgeous"; in sum,
"going to heaven should be this good."*

## Automatic Slim's/LS
| 14 | 15 | 13 | $22 |

733 Washington St. (Bank St.), 645-8660
*U – "Wear black and carry a motorcycle helmet" to
blend in at this "hip" West Villager; the burgers, spuds,
etc. are a diversion from the real attraction: "an amazing
late-night scene" fueled by "cool music" and margaritas.*

## Au Troquet/S
| 21 | 20 | 19 | $42 |

328 W. 12th St. (Greenwich St.), 924-3413
*M – Like going to Paris, this West Villager offers "very
good" bistro fare in a "tiny but warm" setting; high prices
may account for an often low turnout.*

## Azzurro/S
| 19 | 17 | 17 | $39 |

245 E. 84th St. (bet. 2nd & 3rd Aves.), 517-7068
*U – "Well-prepared pasta" and "fresh, tasty" Sicilian
dishes keep this Upper East Side "family-run affair"
bustling; it's "noisy" but "sympatico", with "friendly,
prompt" service and new, "pretty" quarters.*

## Bacchus
| – | – | – | E |

27 W. 24th St. (bet. 5th & 6th Aves.), 633-0123
*Whether this sprawling stylish Italian cafe can cook is too
soon to say, but they sure had a good decorator and as
the name suggests drink, not food, is the priority here.*

## Baci/SX
| 19 | 12 | 14 | $30 |

412 Amsterdam Ave. (bet. 79th & 80th), 496-1550
*U – "Cramped" and "cacophonous", this popular
"thimble-sized" West Side storefront has "fine" pastas
and other Northern Italian food at fair prices; you "get to
know your neighbor" since you sit so close together.*

## Back Porch/S
| 13 | 13 | 14 | $25 |

488 Third Ave. (33rd St.), 685-3828
*M – Though "nothing to rave about", this Midtowner is
"good" for the likes of pasta, quiche and salad; it stays
busy by affording "a quick bite at a fair price."*

## Bali Burma
| 17 | 12 | 16 | $18 |

651 Ninth Ave. (bet 45th & 46th Sts.), 265-9868
*M – There aren't many Indonesian-Burmese spots, that's
why this simple Westsider is "interesting" and "unfamiliar";
critics dismiss it as "ok, but not exciting" – it's "cheap",
so you can "bring friends" and decide for yourself.*

| | F | D | S | C |

### Ballato's
| 18 | 13 | 18 | $31 |

55 E. Houston St. (bet. Mott & Mulberry), 274-8881
*U – Don't let the funky location deter you – this "cozy"
Neapolitan storefront offers "tasty Italian home cooking",
"friendly service" and a "family atmosphere" – not to
mention a modest check.*

### Ballroom, The/LS
| 18 | 18 | 17 | $39 |

253 W. 28th St. (bet. 7th & 8th Aves.), 244-3005
*U – At this festive restaurant-cum-cabaret, taste-
tempting tapas are the top performers, but watch out –
those tiny tidbits can total up to a tremendous tab; still,
it's "lots of fun" and the buffet lunch is a great deal.*

### Banana Cafe
| – | – | – | E |

111 E. 22nd St. (bet. Park Ave. So. & Lexington), 995-8500
*Just opened, this "must-see" Brazilian has become an
overnight "hot spot" with some really interesting food;
the pulsating high-ceilinged space looks like a Brazilian
banana plantation during Carnaval; it's one of the most
important new arrivals of the year.*

### Bangkok Cuisine/LS
| 19 | 14 | 16 | $25 |

885 Eighth Ave. (bet. 52nd & 53rd Sts.), 581-6370
*U – "Tingling, tasty Thai" dishes come "as spicy as you
want" at this Midtowner, handy for pre-/post- theater
dining; it offers "courteous" service and "tacky" comfort.*

### Bangkok House
| 20 | 14 | 17 | $25 |

1485 First Ave. (bet. 77th & 78th Sts.), 249-5700
*U – Turn on your taste buds at this "terrific Thai", rated
one of the "city's best" for its "fresh", "fiery" flavors; it's
"upscale" as Thais go, and the staff is "pleasant."*

### Barbetta/L
| 17 | 22 | 18 | $47 |

321 W. 46th St. (bet. 8th & 9th Aves.), 246-9171
*M – With its "gorgeous garden" and "lovely" townhouse
setting, this Northern Italian Theater District grande
dame has decor that historically has outscored its food
and service; this year, rising food ratings suggest that
the kitchen is "back on track"; give it a try.*

### Barney Greengrass/SX
| 22 | 7 | 12 | $20 |

541 Amsterdam Ave. (bet. 86th & 87th Sts.), 724-4707
*U – At this West Side deli you feel like you're back in the
'40s; the smoked salmon and other delights are perfect.*

### Barocco/LS
| 20 | 16 | 16 | $39 |

301 Church St. (bet. Walker & White Sts.), 431-1445
*U – "Still hip", this TriBeCa Tuscan "remains fresh"
thanks to "uncomplicated, well-prepared food", a "cool",
"artsy" ambiance and a late-night, celeb crowd ("I saw
Liza!"); "wear black for better service."*

| | F | D | S | C |
|---|---|---|---|---|

**Barolo**/LS — 16 | 22 | 14 | $41
398 W. Broadway (bet. Spring & Broome), 226-1102
*U – With its "stunning" garden and "flashy" clientele, this "slick" SoHo Piedmontese offers plenty for the eyes; as for food and service, the ratings speak for themselves.*

**Basta Pasta** — 17 | 15 | 16 | $28
37 W. 17th St. (bet. 5th & 6th Aves.), 366-0888
*U – It's a mind-bending concept, a Japanese-owned Italian, but "what a surprise", "it works", thanks to "fresh pastas" and a blond-wood, open-kitchen setting that's "efficient and stylish."*

**Bayamo**/LS — 14 | 16 | 13 | $23
704 Broadway (bet. W. 4th & Washington Pl.), 475-5151
*M – A "very NYU" crowd enjoys this Chino-Latino's "surreal" tropical decor, "party" ambiance and drinks that "can kill a horse"; it's like "eating in a Disney ride."*

**Beach Cafe**/LS — 12 | 11 | 13 | $23
1326 Second Ave. (70th St.), 988-7299
*M – Budget East Side Italian-American standby that fills the local "hunger need"; critics say its "Miracle-Whip-on-white-bread" cuisine is not worth a walk.*

**Becco**/LS — – | – | – | M
355 W. 46th St. (bet. 8th & 9th Aves.), 397-7597
*A "breath of life" on Restaurant Row, this handsome newcomer from the Bastianich family (of Felidia fame) has a new approach to Italian dining: automatically serving a choice of antipasti and pastas to all diners for $19; if you still have room, all entrees are only a few bucks more.*

**Beijing Duck House**/S — 19 | 10 | 14 | $26
144 E. 52nd St. (bet. Lexington & 3rd), 759-8260
22 Mott St. (Columbus Sq.), 227-1810
1 Herald Ctr., 34th St. & Broadway, 736-3280/X
*U – Stick to the duck or "you're outta luck" at this low-rent Chinese minichain; while the duck is all it's quacked up to be, all else is à la duck pond.*

**Bella Donna**/LSX — 19 | 9 | 13 | $18
307 E. 77th St. (bet. 1st & 2nd Aves.), 535-2866
*U – "Bargains don't get better" than at this Eastsider which sells "amazingly cheap", "fab" pastas and pizzas ($5.95 for lunch!); but you pay in other ways – i.e. lines, crowds, "Mussolini-esque" service.*

**Bella Luna**/S — 18 | 15 | 16 | $26
584 Columbus Ave. (bet. 88th & 89th Sts.), 877-2267
*U – "Decent, well-priced food", "pleasant" decor and "nice people" make this West Side Italian a local standby for families and friends.*

|   | F | D | S | C |
|---|---|---|---|---|

**Bella Mama** (S.I.)/S            | 17 | 14 | 16 | $25 |

266 Morning Star Rd. (Walker St.), 718-891-0545
*M – "Lusty" Southern Italian that provides "huge
portions" of "real food" at "great prices"; the "long wait"
proves Mama's doing something right.*

**Bell Caffe\***/LS (92)          | 17 | 18 | 18 | $23 |

310 Spring St. (bet. Greenwich & Hudson), 334-BELL
*M – For "cheap", "crunchy granola–style fare", this
SoHo Vegetarian rings the bell; its "pleasant" staff and
old-shoe comfort are best enjoyed if you're in no hurry.*

**Bellevues**/LS                 | 19 | 13 | 16 | $28 |

496 Ninth Ave. (bet. 37th & 38th Sts.), 967-7850
*U – The name's "ironic" given the anything-but-belle 9th
Avenue locale, but the basic bistro food is "solid" at this
Parisian outpost with its slicked-up coffee house decor
and late-night "MTV crowd."*

**Bellini by Cipriani**/LS        | 20 | 19 | 19 | $51 |

Michelangelo Hotel, 777 Seventh Ave. (bet. 50th & 51st
Sts.), 265-7770
*M – Bellini-boosters praise this Venetian's "excellent
pastas and risottos", namesake cocktails and "slick
ambiance"; Bellini-bashers say this ex–hot spot is
"overbearing, overpriced and should be overlooked."*

**Bellisimo**                    | – | – | – | I |

274 Third Ave. (bet. 22nd & 23rd Sts.), 254-3641
*In the attractive space formerly occupied by Brandywine,
NYC has just one more pasta place; it's the formula of
lotsa food at low, low prices, which works since there's
usually a full house.*

**Ben Benson's**/S               | 21 | 16 | 18 | $46 |

123 W. 52nd St. (bet. 6th & 7th Aves.), 581-8888
*U – "Macho meals" and business deals are the game at
this "textbook" Midtown steakhouse, where the hefty
steaks, chops, etc. are very good; the Americana-filled
setting is "clubby" and popular, i.e. "loud" and "crowded."*

**Bendix Diner**                 | – | – | – | I |

219 Eighth Ave. (21st St.), 366-0560
*Open from 7 AM to 11 PM, with a menu that covers
everything under the sun – from Swedish pancakes to
granola to American entrees to Thai dishes – this bright
yellow, funky, home cookin' specialist is "made for the '90s."*

**Benihana of Tokyo**/S (92)     | 14 | 15 | 17 | $29 |

120 E. 56th St. (bet. Park & Lexington), 593-1627
47 W. 56th St. (bet. 5th & 6th Aves.), 581-0930
*U – At this national chain of Japanese steakhouses, the
grilled food may not win any culinary awards, but the
showmen Samurai chefs slice and dice so dramatically
that kids and tourists love these spots.*

|  F | D | S | C |
| --- | --- | --- | --- |

### Benito I/S
| 19 | 11 | 16 | $27 |

174 Mulberry St. (bet. Grand & Broome Sts.), 226-9171
*M – In the battle of the Benitos, this "tiny", frenetic, Little Italy Sicilian wins a slight edge for its "solid", "gutsy" cooking and "cozy" storefront setting.*

### Benito II/SX
| 18 | 10 | 16 | $27 |

173 Mulberry St. (bet. Grand & Broome Sts.), 226-9012
*M – The "smell of garlic lures you" to this "crowded" "homey" Little Italy joint and odds are you'll be glad it did; for "simple" Sicilian food, there are few better.*

### Benny's Burritos/LSX
| 19 | 10 | 13 | $14 |

93 Ave. A (6th St.), 254-2054
113 Greenwich Ave. (Jane St.), 727-0584
*U – High-octane margaritas and "fresh","delicious" "burritos the size of Baja" – at baja prices – explain the "endless lines", noise and young crowds at these "funky and tacky" Cal-Mexicans.*

### Benvenuti Ristorante
| 18 | 15 | 17 | $37 |

162 W. 36th St. (bet. 6th Ave. & B'way), 736-0178
*M – This Garment Center Italian is cut from the right cloth according to diners who welcome its "good food", "wonderful service" and reasonable prices (lets you "save for an Armani"); some disagree: "past its prime."*

### Bertha's/LS
| – | – | – | ı |

2160 Broadway (76th St.), 362-2500
*Bertha is Benny's sister – Benny Burritos, that is; opened at press time, its low-priced, hearty Cal-Mex has already raised the voltage on the young West Side circuit.*

### Bice/LS
| 21 | 21 | 17 | $47 |

7 E. 54th St. (bet. 5th & Madison Aves.), 688-1999
*U – "La Dolce Vita Milanese-style" shows no signs of abating at this trattoria, which delivers both scene and cuisine: it has an "ultrachic", "look-at-me" crowd and food that's "too good for a restaurant this trendy."*

### Bienvenue Restaurant
| 18 | 14 | 17 | $29 |

21 E. 36th St. (bet. 5th & Madison Aves.), 684-0215
*U – The name means "welcome", and that's just the feeling that this "cozy and inviting" Midtown bistro conveys; besides being "an excellent value", it offers solid "cuisine bourgeoise" and "Gallic charm."*

### Bill's Gay 90s/L
| 11 | 13 | 15 | $28 |

57 E. 54th St. (bet. Madison & Park Aves.), 355-0243
*M – Admirers of this turn-of-the-century themed Midtowner cite decent, simple food, old-time decor and a piano bar; critics say it's in "the right decade, wrong century" and wrong city – "move it to Peoria."*

| | F | D | S | C |
|---|---|---|---|---|

### Billy's/LS
16 | 13 | 17 | $34

948 First Ave. (bet. 52nd & 53rd Sts.), 753-1870
*U – This "classic" Sutton Place pub has comforted regulars for many years with its good "down-to-earth" fare (steaks, burgers, etc.), "friendly" service and "mellow", "old-NYC" atmosphere.*

### Bimini Twist/LS
15 | 13 | 16 | $28

345 Amsterdam Ave. (bet. 76th & 77th Sts.), 362-1260
*M – A "laid-back", low-budget Westsider that dishes up Caribbean-accented fare that's "a nice change of pace"; you may have to "twist and shout for service."*

### Bistro Bamboche (92)
20 | 14 | 19 | $39

1582 York Ave. (bet. 83rd & 84th Sts.), 249-4002
*U – Way over on the East Side, this narrow storefront bistro has a reputation for good cooking and modest prix fixe dinners; don't miss the soufflé.*

### Bistro du Nord/LS
18 | 17 | 16 | $40

1312 Madison Ave. (93rd St.), 289-0997
*M – Imagine "Paris in a box" – a small, stylish box – and you get an idea of this chic, Carnegie Hill bistro; "cozy" to most, "cramped" to others, the food is "good" to all.*

### Bistro 790*/LS
18 | 16 | 14 | $27

Sheraton Manhattan Hotel, 790 Seventh (51st St.), 621-8537
*U – "Surprisingly good food" – "try the soups and desserts" – at low prices make this bistro a good choice in Midtown for "a quick lunch" or for pre-/post-theater.*

### Bistro 36* (Brooklyn)/S
19 | 13 | 17 | $32

36 Joralemon St. (Columbia Pl.), 718-596-2968
*U – A boon for the Heights, this "pleasant" lace-curtained bistro provides "fresh and simple" food at fair prices; it "needs practice", but is still worth a try.*

### Bistrovia
– | – | – | M

1278 Third Ave. (bet. 73rd & 74th Sts.), 288-7076
*Handsome new East Side French bistro – it looks the look, but can it cook the look?; one thing's for sure, the menu has all the bistro standards.*

### Black Sheep, The/S
19 | 20 | 19 | $38

344 W. 11th St. (Washington St.), 242-1010
*U – Hard to top for "rustic charm", this "cozy" Village bistro, with a fire blazing in winter, is the perfect spot for a "casual romantic evening"; brunch is a best bet.*

### Bloom's Delicatessen
– | – | – | I

350 Lexington Ave. (40th St.), 922-3663
*NY delis aren't supposed to look good, but this new one breaks the rule without sacrificing quality; though it serves many items that are "typical coffee shop", happily the core deli dishes, i.e. pastrami sandwiches, are "the real thing."*

| F | D | S | C |
|---|---|---|---|

### Blue Light, The    | 18 | 14 | 20 | $29 |
242 E. 58th St. (bet. 2nd & 3rd Aves.), 758-1715
*U – Admirers give the "green light" to this low-budget East Side American "find", citing its "original" menu, "helpful" staff and "quiet", "comfortable" setting.*

### Blue Moon Mexican Cafe/LS (92)    | 12 | 10 | 12 | $21 |
150 Eighth Ave. (bet. 17th & 18th Sts.), 463-0560
1444 First Ave. (75th St.), 288-9811
287 Columbus Ave. (bet. 73rd & 74th Sts), 721-2701
*M – "Cheap and cheerful", this Mexican minichain is popular with Ranger fans since it's partly owned by Ron Greshner; diners face off: some calling it "lovely", others preferring to eat a hockey puck.*

### Boathouse Cafe/S    | 12 | 22 | 13 | $29 |
Central Park, East Park Dr. & 73rd St., 517-3623
*U – Sitting next to Central Park Lake, you'd best focus on the "enchanting", "Monet-like" scenery and try to ignore the "tasteless" Italian food and "inept" service.*

### Boca Chica/LS    | 20 | 14 | 15 | $20 |
13 First Ave. (1st St.), 473-0108
*U – "Besides the Brazilian drinks, there's much to enjoy" at this "funky" East Villager, from its "hearty", "tasty", "Pan-Latino" cooking to its "cute campy" setting; it's a "madhouse on weekends" when you can "dance your socks off" to the hot salsa music.*

### Bo Ky/SX    | 19 | 4 | 11 | $13 |
80 Bayard St. (Mott St.), 406-2292
*U – If you can stand the "soup-kitchen decor" and "fast, if not so friendly" service, you'll enjoy dirt-cheap and "delicious" soups and noodles at this Chinese-Vietnamese storefront.*

### Bombay Palace/S    | 16 | 15 | 16 | $27 |
30 W. 52nd St. (bet. 5th & 6th Aves.), 541-7777
*M – All agree that this Midtown Indian's lunch buffet is a "bargain", but beyond that, surveyors debate whether it's "decent", "dependable" and "courteous", or simply "dreary."*

### Bondini (92)    | 17 | 17 | 17 | $37 |
62 W. 9th St. (bet. 5th & 6th Aves.), 777-0670
*U – One of NY's "amazingly undiscovered" spots, this Village "oldie-but-goodie" Northern Italian is "an oasis of calm and quiet" in an area that lacks both qualities.*

### Boogies Diner/S    | 11 | 16 | 13 | $17 |
711 Lexington Ave. (bet. 57th & 58th Sts.), 355-1001
*M – "A riot of kitsch", there's a "funky" clothing store downstairs (for "Madonna wanna-bes") and a "fun, casual, cheap '50s-style luncheonette" upstairs.*

### Boom/LS
| 16 | 18 | 16 | $38 |

152 Spring St. (bet. Wooster St. & W. B'way), 431-3663
U – Explosively "hot", this SoHo newcomer is a
front-runner for the "scene-of-the-year" award; the
International menu is "quite good", but "who cares?"

### Boonthai*/S
| 17 | 16 | 16 | $22 |

1393-A Second Ave. (bet. 72nd & 73rd Sts.), 249-8484
M – This East Side newcomer is still experiencing some
"ups and downs", but given its low prices, "fresh", tasty
food and "caring service", it's a "welcome" arrival.

### Bora*
| 23 | 15 | 21 | $32 |

179 Madison Ave. (bet. 33rd & 34th Sts.), 725-3282
U – Chef-owner Nicola Jovic, formerly of Il Nido, cooks
up a storm at this new Murray Hill Northern Italian,
where smiling comes naturally for both host and guest.

### Borsalino/S
| 19 | 15 | 18 | $27 |

255 W. 55th St. (bet. B'way & 8th Ave.), 246-0710
U – Off to a fast start in Midtown, this "quiet", "cozy"
simple Italian has "'60s prices and '90s choices."

### Boulevard/LS
| 13 | 12 | 13 | $24 |

2398 Broadway (88th St.), 874-7400
M – This "relaxed" Westsider has a "diverse" American
menu that's "not bad for a cheap, informal meal"; on a
nice day, sit outside and watch the Broadway parade.

### BOULEY
| 28 | 28 | 25 | $70 |

165 Duane St. (bet. Greenwich & Hudson), 608-3852
U – Again No. 1 for both food and popularity, this "divine"
TriBeCa French organic leaves dazzled diners wondering
"where do you go from here?" – chef David Bouley's
cooking, best showcased by his $70 tasting menu, is
"inspired" and the "beautiful" setting is as "romantic
as the South of France"; all in all, it's an "intoxicating
experience", sobered only by "slow" service and "waits";
P.S. don't miss the $32 lunch.

### Boxers
| – | – | – | I |

190 W. 4th St. (Barrow St.), 633-BARK
Brew and blondes, or brunettes, are the draws at this
big "old-fashioned feeling" West Village barroom; the
pub fare is just good enough not to interfere with the
socializing that's going on indoors and out.

### Box Tree, The/LS
| 23 | 26 | 24 | $65 |

250 E. 49th St. (bet. 2nd & 3rd Aves.), 758-8320
M – One of NY's priciest and "most romantic" eateries,
this "intimate" Midtowner has a lovely art nouveau
setting; less inspiring is the good, but dated, Continental
cuisine; critics say "recherché", "hoity-toity."

**Braque**/LS | – | – | – | M |
775 Washington St. (W. 12th St.), 255-0709
*A limited, rustic, hearty Italian menu with daily specials
makes this Far West Village newcomer one to watch.*

**Brasserie**/LS | 15 | 14 | 15 | $29 |
100 E. 53rd St. (bet. Park & Lexington), 751-4840
*M – Early birds, night owls and everyone in between
use this 24-hour Midtown French "pit stop" for "reliable"
repasts ranging from business breakfasts to "onion soup
at 5 AM"; it's "there when you need it."*

**Brasserie des Theatres** | – | – | – | M |
Paramount Hotel, 245 W. 46th St. (bet. B'way & 8th), 719-5588
*Finally a real honest-to-goodness brasserie; this
choucroute specialist, run by the folks from Les Halles
and Park Bistro, is open for breakfast, lunch and dinner;
it has the right light mood and prices to star on B'way.*

**Bravo Gianni**/LS (92) | 20 | 16 | 17 | $49 |
230 E. 63rd St. (bet. 2nd & 3rd Aves.), 752-7272
*M – Regulars say bravo for first-rate Northern Italian
food and "special treatment" from its namesake owner-
host; others may feel slighted, especially given the tab.*

**Brazilian Pavilion**/S (92) | 16 | 14 | 16 | $31 |
316 E. 53rd St. (bet. 1st & 2nd Aves.), 758-8129
*U – The cool green-tile setting at this bright but simple
Brazilian affords a nice change of pace in Midtown, but
lest one be confused, "it's not Rio."*

**Bridge Cafe**/LS | 19 | 16 | 18 | $32 |
279 Water St. (Dover St.), 227-3344
*U – "Hidden away" near the Brooklyn Bridge, this pub/
cafe provides "solid American" fare in an "authentic
old-NY setting"; lunch packs in an office crowd, while
dinner, "quiet early", picks up after 9 PM.*

**Bright Food Shop**/X | 19 | 11 | 16 | $19 |
216 Eighth Ave. (21st St.), 243-4433
*M – This "quirky" Chelsean serves "Mexican-Oriental"
food that's "inventive", "tasty and cheap"; the
luncheonette decor is "cool" to some, "sterile" to others.*

**Brighton Grill & Oyster Bar**/LS | 16 | 14 | 15 | $31 |
1313 Third Ave. (bet. 75th & 76th Sts.), 988-6663
*U – "Upbeat" and "airy", this Eastsider "delivers what it
promises" – "good grilling", "terrific salads" and other
"simple, wholesome" fare in a "casual" setting.*

**Brio**/LS | 18 | 16 | 16 | $35 |
786 Lexington Ave. (bet. 61st & 62nd Sts.), 980-2300
*U – An often "overlooked" Bloomie's neighbor that has
"first-rate", "homelike" Italian cooking, an attractive,
wood-paneled setting and efficient service.*

|   | F | D | S | C |
|---|---|---|---|---|

**Broadway Diner**/SX  | 14 | 10 | 13 | $17 |

590 Lexington Ave. (52nd St.), 486-8838
1726 Broadway (55th St.), 765-0909
*M – With "'50s-diner ambiance and prices" and "'90s American" cooking, these "upscale" coffee shops serve fast "fill-er-up fare" that's "fun" for a meal "on the run."*

**Broadway Grill**/L  | 15 | 13 | 14 | $29 |

Holiday Inn, 1605 Broadway (48th St.), 315-6161
*M – Try this Times Square American for its "tasty" grills, thin-crust pizzas and desserts, all at reasonable prices; but some critics say it "feels like Kansas City."*

**Broome Street Bar**/LSX  | 14 | 13 | 14 | $19 |

363 W. Broadway (Broome St.), 925-2086
*U – "A great hangout", this "laid-back" SoHo pub is best for burgers and beer, brunch and other basics, served in a "cozy", "lived-in" setting; weekdays it's locals' territory, but on Saturday it's suburban tourists.*

**Brother Jimmy's BBQ**/LS  | 15 | 11 | 13 | $18 |

1461 First Ave. (76th St.), 288-0999
*M – For "spicy ribs" and other "sloppy, finger-lickin' good" Southern grub, there's always this "down 'n' dirty" Eastsider; cold beer, good tunes and "frat-house-basement decor" attract a party-animal bar crowd.*

**Brother's Bar-B-Q**/LS  | 15 | 11 | 13 | $17 |

228 Houston St. (bet. 6th Ave. & Varick), 727-2775
*M – Carolina cravings are quelled by this "funky" SoHo BBQ's ribs, greens and other "artery-hardening" eats; of course it's "a dive", but it has "great music" and a "hick-meets-hip" crowd.*

**Bruno Ristorante**/L  | 21 | 19 | 21 | $46 |

240 E. 58th St. (bet. 2nd & 3rd Aves.), 688-4190
*U – Whether in the formal dining room downstairs or the lively piano bar up, this pricey East Side standby pleases with "good", Classic Italian food and caring service.*

**B. Smith's**/LS  | 18 | 17 | 16 | $35 |

771 Eighth Ave. (47th St.), 247-2222
*U – As "stylish" and "upbeat" as its vivacious owner, model Barbara Smith, this "sassy" Theater District spot features "imaginative", Southern-accented cooking, a "roomy", "airy" setting and a high-energy crowd, plus a large party room upstairs.*

**BTI**  | – | – | – | I |

1712 Second Ave. (bet. 88th & 89th Sts.), 427-1488
250 W. 86th St. (bet. B'way & West End Ave.), 875-0460
*The "B" stands for Burmese, the "T" for Thai and the "I" for Indonesian; the combo stands for good food at low prices, e.g. $4.50 for the weekday lunch special – that doesn't leave much for decor.*

### Bubby's/S
| 17 | 9 | 13 | $17 |

120 Hudson St. (N. Moore St.), 219-0666
*M – Bubby-boosters like the "great desserts" ("oh, those pies"), sandwiches and other health-aware fare served at this TriBeCa dive; Bubby-bashers say it isn't the same since it's been discovered.*

### Buckaroo's/LS
| 14 | 11 | 13 | $14 |

1431 First Ave. (74th St.), 861-8844
*M – This hokey Eastsider wins "yippies" from a "young crowd" for its "cheap", "decent" American bar menu; to older 'pokes, it's "totally ordinary."*

### Bull & Bear/LS
| 16 | 18 | 17 | $40 |

Waldorf-Astoria Hotel, 301 Park Ave. (49th St.), 872-4900
*M – "Ticker-tape" types are bullish on this "clubby, macho" Waldorf watering hole, where the American fare is as "businesslike" (read "stodgy") as the crowd.*

### Buona Sera/S
| 17 | 11 | 14 | $24 |

94 University Pl. (12th St.), 627-9200
*M – By most reports, this low-budget Village Italian is a good "relaxed" place for pizza, pasta, etc., but others say it's "merely ok" and "inattentive."*

### Burger Heaven
| 13 | 6 | 12 | $12 |

804 Lexington Ave. (62nd St.), 838-3580/SX
536 Madison Ave. (54th St.), 753-4214/X
9 E. 53rd St. (bet. 5th & Madison Aves.), 752-0340/S
20 E. 49th St. (bet. 5th & Madison Aves.), 755-2166/X
291 Madison Ave. (bet. 40th & 41st Sts.), 685-6250/X
*M – "You can count on" these coffee shops for "decent burgers" and tuna or chicken salad sandwiches; there's "no decor", but they're quick and cheap; critics ask, "what's burger 'hell' if this is 'heaven' ?"*

### Busby's/LS
| 16 | 15 | 14 | $33 |

45 E. 92nd St. (Madison Ave.), 360-7373
*M – To some, this Carnegie Hill American is a "standby" with "good, simple food", a "pleasant", airy setting and well-heeled crowd; to others it's proof that "WASP cooking is an oxymoron."*

### Cabana Carioca/S
| 18 | 10 | 14 | $23 |

123 W. 45th St. (bet. 6th & 7th Aves.), 581-8088
133 W. 45th St. (bet. 6th & 7th Aves.), 730-8375
*M – "Nobody leaves hungry or poor" from these Theater District Brazilians; if you ignore the "seedy", "cramped quarters" and "sweaty waiters", you'll enjoy good, "solid fare" in "Gulliverian portions at Lilliputian prices"; 123 is the "original", 133 specializes in Brazilian-style grills.*

|   | F | D | S | C |
|---|---|---|---|---|

**Cafe**/LS          | 18 | 19 | 15 | $37 |

210 Spring St. (6th Ave.), 274-0505
M – "Delicious when it's on", this SoHo "scene" bistro is
"packed with Eurotypes in black"; the outdoor terrace
and hostmanship of Richard Widmaier-Picasso get high
marks, but the service doesn't.

**Cafe Andrusha**/S      | 19 | 14 | 18 | $26 |

1742 Second Ave. (bet. 90th & 91st Sts.), 360-1128
U – At this "tiny" Yorkville Eastern European, you'll find
home cooking "as authentic as the people who serve it";
it's an "unbelievable value" for "superb" borscht,
blintzes, pierogies, kreplach, etc. served with a smile.

**Cafe Bel Canto**/S (92)    | 15 | 11 | 10 | $18 |

1991 Broadway (bet. 67th & 68th Sts.), 362-4642
U – Near Lincoln Center, this Spartan atrium is one of
the few "unhurried" places where you can linger over a
salad, sandwich and drink.

**Cafe Botanica**/LS      | 22 | 26 | 22 | $45 |

Essex House, 160 Central Park S. (bet. 6th & 7th Aves.),
484-5120
U – The "best upscale brunch in town", a "superbuy"
luncheon buffet and "excellent" prix fixe menus –
all in a "lovely space" that's "a veritable flower garden" –
combine to make this Californian one of NYC's best
new restaurants on all accounts.

**Cafe Buon Gusto**/LSX   | 19 | 10 | 16 | $21 |

236 E. 77th St. (bet. 2nd & 3rd Aves.), 535-6884
U – "Unpretentious food" at "1960 prices" is the draw at
this aptly named "neighborhood Italian" that's "homey
and hearty", but also "cramped and rushed."

**Cafe Crocodile**        | 19 | 17 | 19 | $40 |

354 E. 74th St. (bet. 1st & 2nd Aves.), 249-6619
M – For "imaginative" Mediterranean fare in a setting
that "feels like home", try this often "superb" Eastsider;
despite occasional off-nights, it's "special."

**Cafe de Bruxelles**/LS   | 20 | 18 | 18 | $35 |

118 Greenwich Ave. (W. 13th St.), 206-1830
M – For the "best french fries this side of anywhere",
head for this "charming" lace-curtained West Village
Belgian, where the "hearty, satisfying" food and brew
are "tops on a cold winter's night."

**CAFE DES ARTISTES**/LS   | 23 | 26 | 22 | $49 |

1 W. 67th St. (bet. CPW & Columbus), 877-3500
U – This "perfect valentine" near Lincoln Center
combines "crisp service", a "romantic" setting filled with
lovely murals of gamboling nymphs, and Contemporary
French cooking that keeps getting "better and better";
it's always among the most popular in our Survey.

|   | **F** | **D** | **S** | **C** |

### Cafe des Sports/S
18 | 14 | 18 | $32
329 W. 51st St. (bet. 8th & 9th Aves.), 581-1283
U – A Theater District standby that "aims to please" and usually does, this "honest bistro" specializes in "fresh, unfancy French food" at "moderate prices"; though its decor is a bit tired, it's perfect for pre-theater.

### Cafe Español/LS
19 | 14 | 17 | $25
172 Bleecker St. (1 block east of 6th Ave.), 505-0657
63 Carmine St. (off 7th Ave.), 675-3312
U – With these busy and noisy Village Spanish siblings, you know exactly what you're getting – "ample portions" of "always good" garlic-intensive low-priced food.

### Cafe Europa (92)
17 | 16 | 17 | $36
347 E. 54th St. (bet. 1st & 2nd Aves.), 755-0160
U – Despite being a bit "seedy" and "bumbling", this basic bistro has become an Eastside standby thanks to its "reassuring" qualities: good food, charming, if dated, decor and "fair" prices by Midtown standards.

### Cafe Greco/S
17 | 17 | 17 | $31
1390 Second Ave. (bet. 71st & 72nd Sts.), 737-4300
M – Early-bird specials make this "dependable" East Side Mediterranean "one of the best buys in town"; its "wholesome" cooking, "pleasant" room and "variable service" add up to "enjoyable" but "unmemorable."

### Cafe Lalo/LSX
19 | 16 | 13 | $13
201 W. 83rd (bet. Amsterdam & B'way), 496-6031
M – "Prepare to be scrunched" at this West Side coffee house that draws hordes for "scrumptious desserts" and cappuccino served by an "uptight staff."

### Cafe Loup/LS
18 | 18 | 17 | $34
105 W. 13th St. (bet. 6th & 7th Aves.), 255-4746
M – Though "nothing to howl at the moon about", this Village French bistro offers "sprightly, consistent" cooking in a "clean and cozy" setting with "admirable taste in art" but "dispassionate" service.

### Cafe Lucas/LS
14 | 11 | 13 | $19
1307 Third Ave. (bet. 74th & 75th Sts.), 744-4978
M – What this "banal" "neighborhood joint" has going for it are "reasonable" prices for decent pasta and pizzas; supporters insist it has "lots of character", but others shrug, "I'd rather eat in a school cafeteria."

### Cafe Luxembourg/LS
20 | 17 | 16 | $42
200 W. 70th (bet. Amsterdam & West End), 873-7411
M – A clear majority aver that this "brassy and sassy", off-white Lincoln Center French perennial "stands the test of time" with its "cultured crowd", "hearty" bistro fare and "lively staff"; dissenters deem it "sterile", with "ditzy waiters" serving "not-so-hot" food.

**Cafe Metairie**/S | 18 | 19 | 17 | $36 |

1442 Third Ave. (82nd St.), 988-1800
*M – Most call this French Eastsider "an unexpected pleasure" with loads of "country charm" and "good" cooking; foes feel its best days are past.*

**Cafe Nicholson** | 18 | 23 | 20 | $48 |

323 E. 58th St. (bet. 1st & 2nd Aves.), 355-6769
*U – When this "most romantic" East Side limited-menu American cafe will be open depends on its eccentric owner's mood, but if you want a perfect place for a small party or a tryst, don't miss this beauty.*

**Cafe Pierre**/LS | 21 | 24 | 22 | $52 |

The Pierre Hotel, 61st St. & Fifth Ave., 940-8185
*U – "Luxurious in all aspects", from its "relaxing", "elegant" gray satin decor to its refined French fare served by a "very professional" staff; about the only criticism to be heard is that it's "a little stuffy."*

**Cafe San Martin**/LS | 17 | 15 | 17 | $37 |

1458 First Ave. (bet. 75th & 76th Sts.), 288-0470
*M – Maybe it's "not quite what it should be", but this "middle-aged" Eastsider is "still a good choice" for that NY rarity, "good Spanish food"; once owner-maitre d' Ramon gets to know you, the service is warm.*

**Cafe S.F.A.**/S | 17 | 19 | 16 | $22 |

Saks Fifth Ave., 611 Fifth (bet. 49th & 50th), 940-4092
*U – "Relaxing after a shopping spree", this eighth-floor "roomy" cafe has a "nice view" of Rockefeller Center's rooftop gardens; its menu of soups, salads and other light dishes is "savory and well-priced."*

**Cafe St. John**/S | 18 | 16 | 17 | $26 |

500 West 110th (bet. B'way & Amsterdam), 932-8420
*M – Featuring a "respectable" "European menu with a French emphasis", this "pleasant" Morningside Heights cafe is seen by most as "a boon to the neighborhood"; detractors say it "promises more than it delivers."*

**Cafe Tabac**/LS | 14 | 15 | 11 | $32 |

232 E. 9th St. (bet. 2nd & 3rd Aves.), 674-7072
*M – "The '80s live" at this East Village bistro that's "good for celebrity sightings", but not so hot if you're hungry; the bar is where it's at, though you may "need a tattoo to fit in" and service is so bad it's "beyond belief."*

**Cafe Trevi**/LS | 22 | 17 | 21 | $43 |

1570 First Ave. (bet. 81st & 82nd Sts.), 249-0040
*U – "Steady" and "low-key", this East Side Northern Italian has "reliable, fresh" cooking, "unobtrusive service" and "warm" "intimate" ambiance; it's a "favorite" in an area that has better Italian food than Rome.*

|  F  |  D  |  S  |  C  |

**Cafe Un Deux Trois**/LS    | 15 | 14 | 14 | $32 |
123 W. 44th St. (bet. 6th & 7th Aves.), 354-4148
*M – It's love-it-or-hate-it at this big Times Square bistro;
critics call it a "French Horn & Hardart", but it's packed
with those who call it "festive" and "endearing."*

**Cafe Word of Mouth**/S    | 18 | 14 | 15 | $24 |
1012 Lexington Ave. (bet. 72nd & 73rd Sts.), 249-5351
*M – This famed East Side caterer now serves eat-in
with comments from "sinfully good" to "mediocre", and
from "obliging" to "not yet organized."*

**Caffe Bianco**/SX (92)    | 16 | 14 | 14 | $21 |
1486 Second Ave. (bet. 77th & 78th Sts.), 988-2655
*U – Sidewalk seating and the backyard garden are the
highlights of this "charming and relaxing" East Side
cafe; it's a favorite for coffee and desserts but has a
broad menu of other items that also work well.*

**Caffe Biondo**\*/LSX    | 18 | 14 | 13 | $23 |
141 Mulberry St. (bet. Grand & Hester), 226-9285
*U – A little brick-walled "cappuccino pit stop" thought by
some to be "Little Italy's finest for desserts."*

**Caffe Bondi**/S    | 18 | 17 | 17 | $30 |
7 W. 20th St. (bet. 5th & 6th Aves.), 691-8136
*U – This Flatiron District cafe "has the right mix of good
food and informality"; the "simple yet exquisite Italian
dishes" and "nice" staff make it "always pleasant."*

**Caffe Cefalu** /SM    | – | – | – | M |
259 W. 4th St. (bet. Charles & Perry Sts.), 989-7131
*Mainly it's pasta! pasta! pasta! but fish, veal and chicken
are also on the menu at this homey West Village Italian
where the tin-ceilinged chintz-tablecloth decor matches
the modest prices; dinner only except weekends.*

**Caffe Cielo**/S    | 18 | 17 | 17 | $34 |
881 Eighth Ave. (bet. 52nd & 53rd Sts.), 246-9555
*M – Though the "staff tries hard", the reliably good
Northern Italian menu you've seen before draws mostly
shrugs; the attractive "decor includes sky and clouds,
but don't expect heaven."*

**Caffe Florence**    | – | – | – | M |
9 Jones St. (bet. Bleecker & W. 4th Sts.), 989-1220
*Chef Georgine Caviola returns to the restaurant scene
with this mid-priced, checked-tablecloth, white-walled
West Village Tuscan cafe that's a cause for celebration.*

**Caffe La Strada**\*/LS    | 20 | 15 | 18 | $29 |
78 E. 4th St. (bet. 2nd & 3rd Aves.), 353-8026
*U – "One of the better East Village Northern Italians";
"small and appealing", its "solid food", "comfortable
seating" and "gracious management" all win plaudits.*

| F | D | S | C |
|---|---|---|---|

**Caffe Rosso\*/LS**     | 18 | 17 | 19 | $28 |

284 W. 12th St. (W. 4th St.), 633-9277
*U – A small winner, this "charming" Village stop employs
"good Northern Italian food", a "subdued" setting and a
"winning" staff to produce a "romantic dinner."*

**Caffe Vivaldi/LSX**     | 16 | 19 | 14 | $16 |

32 Jones St. (bet. Bleecker & W. 4th Sts.), 929-9384
*U – Reflecting "the old Village at its best", this Viennese-
style coffee house with its "fireside coziness" and
"excellent desserts" served to the strains of a Callas aria
is perfect "for a romantic tête-à-tête."*

**Caliente Cab Co./LS**     | 11 | 12 | 11 | $20 |

21 Waverly Pl. (Greene St.), 529-1500
61 Seventh Ave. S. (Bleecker St.), 243-8517
*U – These "not-so-caliente" Village Tex-Mexes proffer
pre-fab parties with "dreary" food, "dreadful service",
"frozen margaritas" and a bridge-and-tunnel crowd.*

**Cal's/S**     | 20 | 19 | 18 | $34 |

55 W. 21st St. (bet. 5th & 6th Aves.), 929-0740
*U – Diners wonder why this Flatiron District "hidden gem"
with an "innovative" American kitchen, a "beautiful" bar
and "comfortable" setting remains undiscovered when it
deserves to be packed; see for yourself.*

**Camelback and Central/S**     | 12 | 11 | 13 | $25 |

1403 Second Ave. (73rd St,), 249-8380
*M – This East Side pub has long been a local choice for
"plain eats" "when you've run out of ideas"; recent
diners say the new menu is "a big improvement."*

**Cameos/LS**     | 18 | 18 | 18 | $40 |

169 Columbus Ave. (bet. 67th & 68th Sts.), 874-2280
*M – An "elegant but subdued" American with "soothing
pastel decor" that's reachable up a flight of stairs, and is
"holding up well"; critics say "edible but not memorable."*

**Campagnola/LS**     | 19 | 18 | 18 | $42 |

1382 First Ave. (bet. 73rd & 74th Sts.), 861-1102
*M – To the faithful, this East Side "country-style"
Northern Italian sets "a standard" with "outstanding"
food, "charming decor" and a personable staff; the
unconverted have trouble telling it from its competitors.*

**Can/S**     | 20 | 20 | 19 | $41 |

482 W. Broadway (Houston St.), 533-6333
*M – Some think SoHo's "stylish" French-Vietnamese
hybrid "belongs in LA"; while most rave about the
"imaginative" cuisine and modern decor, conservative
diners find the place "weird" and "cold."*

|   | F | D | S | C |
|---|---|---|---|---|

**Canastel's**/LS   | 16 | 17 | 15 | $33 |

233 Park Ave. S. (19th St.), 677-9622
*M – With its "hipper-than-thou" attitude, "glossy"
postmodern decor and "predictable" Northern Italian
fare, this Flatiron fixture has '80s written all over it,
however, it's still popular because it's predictably good.*

**Cantina**/LS   | 11 | 10 | 12 | $22 |

221 Columbus Ave. (70th St.), 873-2606
*M – "About par for the genre", this West Side
Tex-Mexican has a "run-of-the-mill" "microwave" menu,
lethal margaritas, young crowds, noise and low prices.*

**Canton**/SX   | 24 | 12 | 19 | $33 |

45 Division St. (bet. Bowery & Market Sts.), 226-4441
*U – The food is "Chinatown's best by a mile", say the
customers of this "sophisticated Cantonese"; not even a
"sterile dining room", service that "can be slow" and high
prices deter regulars from the risk-free ritual of allowing
owner Eileen to order for them.*

**Canyon Road**   | – | – | – | M |

1470 First Ave. (bet. 76th & 77th Sts.), 734-1600
*"Santa Fe comes to NYC" via this upscale, low key
successor to Albuquerque Eats; it's a good bet for
affordable SW fare, and now you can even hear each other.*

**Capriccio**   | 19 | 18 | 19 | $45 |

33 E. 61st St. (bet. Madison & Park Aves.), 759-6684
*M – Despite "good" North Italian fare, "caring service"
and a "pretty garden room", many feel this Eastsider
"needs new energy" and is "slightly expensive."*

**Capriccioso**\*/S   | 17 | 15 | 17 | $30 |

373 Amsterdam Ave. (bet. 77th & 78th Sts.), 877-7818
*M – Some already call it a "welcome addition" to the
West Side, but this Italian newcomer may be too green
to judge; still, surveyors say it "has potential."*

**Capsouto Freres**/S   | 22 | 22 | 21 | $43 |

451 Washington St. (Watts St.), 966-4900
*U – "Tough to find and tougher to forget", this TriBeCa
French bistro's "outstanding food", "gracious service"
and "lofty Downtown feel" make it "a solid favorite";
"don't miss the soufflés" or the "delectable brunch."*

**Captain's Table, The** (92)   | 18 | 14 | 16 | $42 |

860 Second Ave. (46th St.), 697-9538
*M – This Midtown seafood standby allows you to select
your fish from large platters before it's cooked; this
place exists because of its "well-prepared" results;
charges of "piracy" may one day bring it to account.*

|   | F | D | S | C |
|---|---|---|---|---|

### Caribe/SX
| | 15 | 16 | 13 | $22 |

117 Perry St. (Greenwich St.), 255-9191
*M – For its young crowd, "the food is secondary to the Caribbean feel" at this "overspiced but not overpriced" Villager with "killer drinks and island music", "jungle decor and funky staff"; "it's like going to Jamaica."*

### Carino/S
| | 19 | 12 | 18 | $27 |

1710 Second Ave. (bet. 88th & 89th Sts.), 860-0566
*U – "Sicilian home cooking with a smile" gives this Eastsider "a family feeling" that's "short on pretension but long on value"; though the decor "is nothing to speak of", it's hard to speak with your mouth full.*

### Carlyle Dining Room/S
| | 22 | 26 | 24 | $55 |

Carlyle Hotel, 983 Madison (bet. 76th & 77th), 744-1600
*U – "Immensely improved", this dining room is now "superb in every way", from its "recently redone" decor to its "classy" Continental fare; though "pricey", it's "one of the most civilized spots in the city"; try the prix fixe brunch.*

### Carmine's/S
| | 19 | 15 | 16 | $24 |

2450 Broadway (bet. 90th & 91st Sts.), 362-2200
200 W. 44th St. (bet. B'way & 8th Ave.), 221-3800
*U – "Go with a group" and "eat till you drop" at these "gutsy", "garlicky" red-sauce Italians; the bargain food is served family-style by the ton in a turn-of-the-century setting; there's no reserving (for less than six), "long waits" and "more noise than a JFK runway."*

### CARNEGIE DELI/LSX
| | 20 | 7 | 12 | $19 |

854 Seventh Ave. (bet. 54th & 55th Sts.), 757-2245
*U – This "Hirschfeld cartoon come to life" is "just what a deli should be" – i.e. "seriously huge" sandwiches, theatrically "abusive" servers and elbow-to-elbow dining; expect lines at this "shrine" to pastrami.*

### Carosello
| | – | – | – | M |

227 E. 50th St. (bet. 2nd & 3rd Aves.), 750-5315
*Too new to call, this mid-priced Midtown Italian has a warm rose-toned decor and seasoned management that make it worth checking out.*

### Casa Colombia* (Queens)/LSX
| | 19 | 9 | 13 | $23 |

86-23 Roosevelt Ave., Jackson Heights, 718-779-6459
*U – Some ask if Colombian food differs from its Latin neighbors, but one thing's for sure: this Jackson Heights "sleeper" can be counted on for lots of "fine" cooking if you're willing to forgo decor and service.*

### Casa Di Pre/X
| | 15 | 13 | 17 | $24 |

283 W. 12th St. (W. 4th St.), 243-7073
*M – A real oldie, this bargain Village haven of "home-cooked Italian" is "gracious" and "low-key"; to some, it's "only fair to good."*

|   | F | D | S | C |
|---|---|---|---|---|

### Casa La Femme/LS
`17 | 20 | 15 | $30`
150 Wooster St. (bet. Houston & Prince Sts.), 505-0005
M – "From the ashes of 150 Wooster" has sprung this
"stylish", spaced-out Mediterranean; word is the food's
"good", but "you need more than looks to succeed."

### Casalone/LS
`18 | 21 | 13 | $33`
1675 Third Ave. (bet. 93rd & 94th Sts.), 369-1944
U – Many welcome this charming, rustic East Side
Tuscan newcomer, praising its "terrific" garden, "good"
food and bargain prix fixe menus, but for reports of poor
service, it would be a homer.

### Castellano/S (92)
`17 | 17 | 18 | $44`
138 W. 55th St. (bet. 6th & 7th Aves.), 664-1975
M – Opposite City Center and near Carnegie Hall, this
honest Venetian should be a major draw, but despite
good pasta and fish dishes, solid service and an elegant
setting, it's no longer fashionable.

### Cavaliere/S
`17 | 18 | 17 | $37`
108 W. 73rd (bet. Columbus & Amsterdam), 799-8282
M – "If the Italian food was as good as the warm pastel
decor" at this "comfortable" West Side "hideaway", "it
would be a winner"; however, its kitchen and staff, while
"better-than-average", have "no special spark."

### Cedars of Lebanon/S
`16 | 12 | 16 | $27`
39 E. 30th St. (bet. Madison & Park Aves.), 725-9251
M – "Once a year" this "unhurried", "never-crowded"
Lebanese "gray lady" merits a trip; despite having
become "seedy" with food that's just "standard", the fact
that it has survived so long says something.

### CELLAR IN THE SKY
`24 | 26 | 24 | $90`
1 World Trade Ctr., 107th fl., West St. (bet. Liberty &
Vesey Sts.), 938-1111
U – "Brilliantly matching wine with food", this "truly
memorable" seven-course prix fixe extravaganza at the
top of the world is "an experience not to be missed"; the
only sticking point is the $90 tab before tax and tip.

### Cent' Anni/S
`23 | 14 | 19 | $41`
50 Carmine St. (bet. Bleecker & Bedford), 989-9494
U – There are "no gimmicks" at this Village Northern
Italian, just "solid, honest food" and "professional"
service in a "plain setting"; "it's a notch below the best",
but it doesn't miss by much.

### Century Cafe/L
`15 | 14 | 15 | $28`
132 W. 43rd St. (bet. 6th Ave. & B'way), 398-1988
U – Toned down and tuned up, this Theater District cafe
may look like it's out of the 21st century, but its
improved simple grill food is "good" late 20th century;
P.S. "to get the waiter's attention, shout, 'casting call'."

|   | F | D | S | C |
|---|---|---|---|---|

**Cesarina**  | 18 | 19 | 19 | $42 |

36 W. 52nd St. (bet. 5th & 6th Aves.), 582-6900
*M – "Good" Northern Italian fare and an attractive
setting across from The "21" Club make this Midtown
yearling "nice for business lunch", even if it's "pricey."*

**Chantal Cafe**  | 17 | 16 | 18 | $31 |

257 W. 55th St. (bet. B'way & 8th Ave.), 246-7076
*U – In a "cruddy" area, this "tiny", "pretty bistro" with
"civilized" dining on a budget is a "real find" – the price
is right, the people "friendly" and the "accents are
authentic"; not fabulous, but "felicitous."*

**CHANTERELLE**  | 26 | 24 | 26 | $70 |

2 Harrison St. (Hudson St.), 966-6960
*U – "Pure magic", "always a delight" and "sublime" typify
reactions to David and Karen Waltuck's "austere but so
elegant" TriBeCa French where both food and service
are "top-notch"; only the high tab and "stark" setting give
surveyors pause; the $30 prix fixe lunch is a good intro.*

**Chao Chow***/SX  | 17 | 8 | 11 | $21 |

111 Mott St. (bet. Canal & Hester Sts.), 226-2590
*M – "Wonderful" with soups that are called "the best in
town", but ratings for decor and service show that this is
just another Chinatown joint.*

**Charley O's**  | 10 | 11 | 11 | $25 |

9 Penn Plaza (bet. 7th & 8th Aves.), 630-0343
218 W. 45th St. (bet. B'way & 8th Ave.), 626-7300
*M – Handy to Madison Square Garden and Broadway
theaters, this dwindling pub chain is still ok for drinks,
sandwiches and burgers, however it gets lots of zingers:
"never again", "bad and getting worse", "only in a pinch."*

**Charlotte***/LS  | 19 | 21 | 18 | $40 |

Macklowe Hotel, 145 W. 44th (bet. 6th & B'way), 789-7508
*U – "Trying hard", this modern American near Times
Square offers "warm service", "dishes of quality",
"elegant" ambiance and bargain prix fixes; it's a "great
pre-theater" and brunch find.*

**Chef Ho's**/S  | 19 | 14 | 17 | $24 |

1720 Second Ave. (bet. 89th & 90th Sts.), 348-9444
*M – Way "above ordinary", this East Side Hunan-
Szechuan standby shines in its "new digs"; some say
it's "not as tangy as before" and is "a little pricey."*

**Chefs & Cuisiniers Club**/LS  | 21 | 15 | 18 | $38 |

36 E. 22nd St. (bet. Park Ave. S. & B'way), 228-4399
*M – A Flatiron "local favorite", this "mellow" place has
"one of the better Eclectic menus" in NY, but some find
the "sparse decor" and TV, above the bar, "distracting."*

| | F | D | S | C |
|---|---|---|---|---|

### Chelsea Commons/LS (92)          | 13 | 13 | 14 | $19 |

242 Tenth Ave. (24th St.), 929-9424
*U – Burgers, nachos and beers combine with "pleasant" pub ambiance and low prices to assure the longevity of this local standby; the garden in summer and fireplace in winter outshine the kitchen.*

### Chelsea Trattoria          | 20 | 16 | 18 | $36 |

108 Eighth Ave. (bet. 15th & 16th Sts.), 924-7786
*M – "Best of the Chelsea strip", this brick-walled Northern Italian has "well-prepared" fare that's "good if you're in the neighborhood", but not worth a detour.*

### Chez Brigitte/X          | 16 | 8 | 16 | $15 |

77 Greenwich Ave. (bet. Bank & 7th Ave.), 929-6736
*M – With only 12 stools, this West Village lunch counter is adored for its "honest home cooking" (soups, stews and desserts), "homey" service and low prices; critics say it's "a French truck stop" – "quel horreur, tant pis!"*

### Chez Jacqueline/S          | 19 | 17 | 17 | $36 |

72 MacDougal (bet. W. Houston & Bleecker), 505-0727
*U – This "casual" Village bistro offers "a solid value in Provençal cuisine", plus a "warm" "French-speaking" ambiance and "pretty" room; criticism is mild.*

### Chez Josephine/L          | 17 | 19 | 18 | $38 |

414 W. 42nd St. (bet. 9th & 10th Aves.), 594-1925
*U – Expect a "spirited" feeling and food that's "always pretty good" at this "campy", "colorful" French bistro dedicated to the great Josephine Baker, by her son Jean Claude; Josephine would be proud.*

### Chez Ma Tante/LS          | 19 | 18 | 17 | $35 |

189 W. 10th St. (bet. W. 4th & Bleecker), 620-0223
*U – Best in summer when its doors open to the street, this "tiny" French bistro may be "cramped", but that can't spoil its rustic charm or "reliable" French cooking.*

### Chez Michallet/S          | 22 | 21 | 22 | $40 |

90 Bedford St. (Grove St.), 242-8309
*U – Though some say "overrated in '92 Zagat", ratings are up across the board for this "très cute", "très petit" Village version of a "French country inn."*

### Chez Napoleon          | 19 | 12 | 19 | $32 |

365 W. 50th St. (bet. 8th & 9th Aves.), 265-6980
*U – "Quite a dump", this "unphoney", "underrated" Theater District "classic" of "French bourgeois cooking" "delivers the goods" at "bargain prices"; "no glamour, no glitz", but "everyone is satisfied."*

|   | F | D | S | C |
|---|---|---|---|---|

### Chiam/LS                     | 21 | 21 | 22 | $37 |

160 E. 48th St. (bet. Lexington & 3rd Aves.), 371-2323
U – This pricey Midtown Chinese yearling *"makes you
feel special"* with its *"Architectural Digest setting"*,
*"first-rate"* food and *"gracious service"*; sure, it's a bit
*"show biz"*, but just about everyone likes the show.

### Chicken Chef/SX               | 15 | 5 | 12 | $10 |

301 E. 80th St. (2nd Ave.), 517-8350
1177 Second Ave. (62nd St.), 308-9400
128 W. 10th St. (Greenwich Ave.), 929-1100
U – *"For those nights when you're too tired to cook"*,
these *"pleasant and economical"* grilled-chicken–
to–goers are a *"juicy"* *"staple."*

### Chikubu                       | 21 | 14 | 17 | $36 |

12 E. 44th St. (bet. 5th & Madison Aves.), 818-0715
U – The reason most surveyors admire this *"expensive"*
Grand Central–area Japanese is that it's a culinary
*"adventure"*; let the chef or one of the *"obliging waiters"*
guide your choices to *"a delightful"* meal.

### China Grill/S                 | 21 | 21 | 17 | $41 |

CBS Bldg., 60 W. 53rd St. (6th Ave.), 333-7788
M – A product of the '80s, this *"fast-paced"*, *"sleek and
satisfying"* Midtown Cal-Chinese modeled on LA's
Chinois on Main is said to be putting both more quantity
and variety on the plate of late; critics cite *"Spartan
decor"* and call it *"tragically hip."*

### Chin Chin/LS                  | 23 | 20 | 21 | $39 |

216 E. 49th St. (bet. 2nd & 3rd Aves.), 888-4555
U – Add up a *"handsome"*, modern (non-Chinese)
setting, *"great, inventive food"*, *"helpful waiters"* and
*"an attractive crowd"*, and the verdict on this Midtown
Cantonese is *"as good as it gets."*

### Chop Suey Looey's Litchi Lounge | – | – | – | M |

1345 Sixth Ave. (55th St.), 262-2020
This unusually good new Cantonese, with lots of original
dishes and drinks, is unfortunately decorated in lurid
red-neon reminiscent of Trader Vic's on a bad day.

### Cho-Sen Garden* (Queens)       | 19 | 16 | 17 | $31 |

64-43 108th St. (bet. 64th Rd. & 65th Ave.), Forest Hills,
718-275-1300
U – This Queens *"discovery"* charges little for the best
Glatt kosher Chinese food in NYC; fans say it's well
worth a trip with the family or a group of friends.

### Choshi/S                      | 20 | 14 | 15 | $26 |

77 Irving Pl. (19th St.), 420-1419
U – *"Great on a spring evening"*, this modestly priced
Gramercy Japanese is pleasing anytime; as its ratings
suggest, decor and service need help.

| F | D | S | C |
|---|---|---|---|

**Christ Cella** | 22 | 13 | 18 | $53 |

160 E. 46th St. (bet. Lexington & 3rd Aves.), 697-2479
*M – To some, this Midtown steakhouse is "good, simple
and old-fashioned", but to others it's "a dinosaur"; for
most of its business customers, any deficiencies in the
"plain" "he-man" decor and "crowded and bustling"
ambiance are just incidentals compared to "consistently
good" steaks, chops, seafood and salads.*

**Christine's**/S | 16 | 7 | 14 | $16 |

462 Second Ave. (26th St.), 779-2220
208 First Ave. (bet. 12th & 13th Sts.), 505-0376
*U – "No prize for atmosphere" will ever be awarded to
these Polish coffee shops with a "homey" if dowdy feel,
but for "hearty ethnic fare", heavy on starch, that's
"cheap and filling", they offer "terrific value."*

**Chumley's**/LS | 12 | 18 | 13 | $20 |

86 Bedford St. (bet. Grove & Barrow Sts.), 675-4449
*U – This "landmark" "old speakeasy" with its "hidden
entrance" is "great for the fireplace in winter"; "stick with
the burgers" and Bass ale.*

**Churchill's**/LS | 12 | 12 | 14 | $25 |

1277 Third Ave. (bet. 73rd & 74th Sts.), 650-1618
*M – Regulars report that this "comfy" "hangout" has
"good" steaks, burgers and brew, plus "outta-this-world
cheesecake" all at affordable prices; nonregulars retort:
"run of the mill", "only if you're desperate."*

**Ciaobella**/LS | 14 | 11 | 10 | $30 |

1311 Third Ave. (75th St.), 288-2555
*M – "If you want to watch models pretending to eat", this
"stylishly overpriced" East Side sidewalk Italian may be
your cup of espresso, but if "not so great" pasta and
preening waiters are unappetizing, say "ciao."*

**Cinquanta**\*/LS | 21 | 21 | 22 | $43 |

50 E. 50th St. (bet. Park & Madison Aves.), 759-5050
*U – A "new and refreshing" Midtown Italian with solid
service and an "interesting" menu featuring unusual
pastas and wild game; high prices deter some.*

**Cite**/LS | 18 | 20 | 17 | $44 |

120 W. 51st St. (bet. 6th & 7th Aves.), 956-7100
*U – A rare successful turnaround, this "handsome"
Midtown "French steakhouse" (with a superb wine list)
has "improved greatly in the past year" in both its food and
decor; it's catching on as a pre-/post-theater destination.*

**Cite Grille**/LS | 18 | 18 | 16 | $37 |

120 W. 51st St. (bet. 6th & 7th Aves.), 956-7262
*U – Good for lunch, after-work drinks or pre-theater, this
Cité sibling is "cost-effective" and "convivial"; its bistro
cooking is uniformly well-liked and "very '90s."*

### City Cafe/S
| 18 | 15 | 17 | $33 |

1481 York Ave. (bet. 78th & 79th Sts.), 570-9810
U – "Always crowded", this great Yorkville joint is
"well-run" and "attractive"; the arrival of "New American"
chef Marc Salonsky puts it on the foodie map.

### Ci Vediamo/LS
| 20 | 16 | 17 | $25 |

1431 Third Ave. (81st St.), 650-0850
85 Ave. A (bet. 5th & 6th Sts.), 995-5300/X
U – "Breezy, hip Italians" that are "instant hits" with a
"young crowd", these "austerely decorated" Eastsiders
offer "better-than-average" "pasta at a perfect price."

### Claire/LS
| 17 | 16 | 16 | $33 |

156 Seventh Ave. (bet. 19th & 20th Sts.), 255-1955
M – Key West in Chelsea with simply prepared seafood,
"great Key lime pie", amusing "tacky green decor" and
"fun people" (guys) who all "seem to know each other."

### Clarke's, P.J./LS
| 13 | 13 | 12 | $23 |

915 Third Ave. (55th St.), 759-1650
M – Popular as ever, this "landmark" saloon sports a
mingling, drinking biz crowd for whom its standard pub
fare and "slightly gruff" service are merely footnotes.

### Cleopatra's Needle/LS
| 13 | 11 | 12 | $22 |

2485 Broadway (92nd St.), 769-6969
M – Some consider this West Side Middle Eastern a
"decent" option at the price, but more regard the food as
"nondescript" and the setting as "weird."

### Cloister Cafe, The/LSX
| 11 | 22 | 11 | $19 |

238 E. 9th St. (bet. 2nd & 3rd Aves.), 777-9128
M – Surveyors love to sip coffee in the lovely courtyard
of this East Village American, but that doesn't justify
"inattentive" service or food that's "a felony."

### Coach House, The/S
| 21 | 19 | 20 | $48 |

110 Waverly Pl. (bet. 5th & 6th Aves.), 777-0303
M – "Venerable" but still handsome, this Village purveyor
of "well-prepared" traditional Southern food at "Uptown
prices" has skeptics who say it "needs a shot of B-12."

### Coastal/S
| 18 | 14 | 16 | $30 |

300 Amsterdam Ave. (74th St.), 769-3988
1359 First Ave. (73rd St.), 472-6200
M – These "crowded", "yupped-out", "very California"
twins serve "good", but "not really memorable" grilled
fish, pasta and the like; if you can deal with noise, you
may be glad to have such neighbors.

|   | F | D | S | C |
|---|---|---|---|---|

**Coconut Grill**/LS     | 15 | 14 | 14 | $26 |
1481 Second Ave. (77th St.), 772-6262
*U – If food and service at this East Side tropical grill leave "not much of an impression", that's because the real focus here is on the "hyperkinetic" scene "full of noise and youth"; P.S. try the "good brunch."*

**Coco Pazzo**/LS     | 22 | 21 | 18 | $51 |
23 E. 74th St. (bet. 5th & Madison Aves.), 794-0205
*M – Even with an "attractive" room, a "robust and hearty" Italian menu and "celebrity-gazing" second to none, diners ask "why doesn't it add up to something better?"; perhaps because this East Side "tough ticket" is "seriously overbooked" and its prices are pazzo.*

**Coffee Shop**/LS     | 14 | 14 | 11 | $25 |
29 Union Sq. W. (16th St.), 243-7969
*M – "Hot, sensual, spicy" – that, sadly, is not the food but the "model wanna-be" crowd at this "still-buzzing", but "uneven" quasi-Brazilian, "noisy, smoky" coffee shop.*

**Collage**/S (92)     | 16 | 16 | 14 | $26 |
314 Bleecker St. (Grove St.), 645-1612
*M – "Pleasant" summer garden dining and "homey friendly" feel are highlights of this West Village French bistro; the downside is an uneven performance.*

**Col Legno**/LS     | 19 | 12 | 16 | $29 |
231 E. 9th St. (bet. 2nd & 3rd Aves.), 777-4650
*U – Diners gladly forgive the "cloying pastels" of this East Villager's "goofy room" in response to "inspiring" Northern Italian food that's the "best in its price range"; it would be better yet if the "waiters would cheer up."*

**Columbia Cottage**\*/S     | 15 | 9 | 13 | $17 |
1034 Amsterdam Ave. (111th St.), 662-1800
*U – Price is key at this "middle-of-the-pack" Upper West Side Chinese, especially since the tab includes free wine; if you can handle the spectacle of "Columbia kids getting drunk", the food is "actually quite good."*

**Coming Or Going**     | – | – | – | M |
38 E. 58th St. (bet. Madison & Park Aves.), 980-5858
*Finding a charming, rustic New England bistro on East 58th Street is like bumping into a cow grazing in Central Park; word has it that this Italo-influenced Americano with a Brazilian chef is worth a try; modest prices to boot.*

**Common Market Cafe**\*/S     | 13 | 8 | 13 | $15 |
709 Lexington Ave. (bet. 57th & 58th Sts.), 308-2070
*U – "Different" but "not compelling", this Midtowner is "a notch above" other area quick-stops for its affordable "cafeteria cuisine with a flair", e.g. pastas, sandwiches, "seasonal choices" and convenience.*

| | F | D | S | C |
|---|---|---|---|---|

### Condon's/LS
<u>13 | 13 | 14 | $30</u>
117 E. 15th St. (bet. Park Ave. S. & Irving Pl.), 254-0960
*U – "Music is the draw" here, so you may want to skip the "just fair" American bistro food and focus on the "fabulous jazz".*

### Conservatory Cafe/LS
<u>13 | 15 | 14 | $32</u>
Mayflower Hotel, 15 Central Park W. (61st St.), 265-0060
*M – The view and crowd at this "glorified coffee shop" are more interesting than the "ordinary food"; it's "Dullsville" and best for breakfast or drinks.*

### Contrapunto/LS
<u>19 | 14 | 16 | $30</u>
200 E. 60th St. (3rd Ave.), 751-8616
*U – "Bright lights, big ziti" could be the motto of this mezzanine "pasta place" across from Bloomie's; despite "tight quarters", its "dependable pastas", "fast service" and "convenience" make it "a real winner."*

### Cooper's Coffee, Ltd./S
<u>– | – | – | I</u>
2151 Broadway (bet. 75th & 76th Sts.), 496-0100
*If this modern West Side newcomer is any indication, coffee houses will be the vogue of the '90s.*

### Copacabana
<u>15 | 16 | 15 | $36</u>
10 E. 60th St. (bet. 5th & Madison Ave.), 755-6010
*M – Once a famed 1950s nightclub, this Continental has risen from its darkest days, but some still "wish they'd figure out what to do with this landmark."*

### Copeland's*/S
<u>19 | 15 | 19 | $24</u>
547 W. 145th St. (bet. B'way & Amsterdam), 234-2357
*M – This Soul Fooder may be "the best in Harlem", but a few soulful surveyors say it's "not what it used to be"; "gracious help" and "moderate prices" are appeals.*

### Cornelia St. CafeLS
<u>16 | 16 | 16 | $25</u>
29 Cornelia St. (bet. Bleecker & W. 4th Sts.), 989-9318
*U – On a Village back street, this "cute" cafe offers "above-average" simple American and coffee-house fare at prices locals like; so what, if "the tables wobble."*

### Corner Bistro/LSX
<u>18 | 10 | 11 | $14</u>
331 W. 4th St. (Jane St.), 242-9502
*U – To try NY's "best burger and fries, hands down", washed down by good brew, head for this "dark, smoky Village dive"; P.S. "wipe your feet on the way out."*

### Corrado/S
<u>20 | 16 | 18 | $37</u>
1373 Sixth Ave. (bet. 55th & 56th Sts.), 333-3133
*M – For a pre–Carnegie Hall "first-rate" risotto or pasta, try this "cheerful, bustling" Midtown Northern Italian; critics call it "another earsplitter."*

**Cottonwood Cafe**/LS (92)          | 16 | 11 | 14 | $20 |
415 Bleecker St. (bet. W. 11th & Bank), 924-6271
*U – Young Villagers line up at his ultrafunky cafe for its
down-home Tex-Mex food; P.S. it can be"loud 'n' rowdy."*

**Country Club**          | 14 | 18 | 15 | $40 |
210 E. 86th St. (bet. 2nd & 3rd Aves.), 879-8400
*M – While the ballroom dancing is "corny but fun" at this
"Waspy" new East Side basement supper club, the
pricey American food is just "ok", so "eat before you go."*

**Courtyard Cafe, The**          | 17 | 21 | 18 | $34 |
Doral Court Hotel, 130 E. 39th St. (bet. Park & Lexington
Aves.), 779-0739
*U – At this Murray Hill Italian grill, it's an "unexpected
pleasure" to sit in the outdoor courtyard; while the
kitchen could be better, it's reliably good.*

**Cowgirl Hall of Fame**/LS          | 14 | 17 | 14 | $21 |
519 Hudson St. (10th St.), 633-1133
*U – The kitschy "memorabilia far surpasses the food"
at this West Village beer-by-the-pitcher Tex-Mex, but
nobody minds – they're having too much fun.*

**Crepes Suzette**/S          | 16 | 15 | 18 | $33 |
363 W. 46th St. (bet. 8th & 9th Aves.), 974-9002
*M – A "standby" on Restaurant Row, this bistro gets
mixed notices: "solid, simple dishes", "quaint" feeling,
"good service" vs. "decent", "needs sprucing up."*

**Crisci's** (Brooklyn)/S          | 19 | 9 | 16 | $31 |
593 Lorimer St. (bet. Metropolitan Ave. & Conselyea St.),
718-384-9204
*U – For most, the "real Southern Italian", "family-style
dining" merits a trip to this "older-than-old" "room with no
view"; to critics it's "a time capsule best left unopened."*

**Cucina**(Brooklyn)/SX          | 23 | 20 | 18 | $30 |
256 Fifth Ave. (bet. Garfield Pl. & Carroll St.), 718-230-0711
*U – This "high-class" Nuovo Italiano yearling "in a
low-class neighborhood" is "racking up raves" for what
some call "the best Italian food in the city, bar none."*

**Cucina & Co.**          | 16 | 14 | 15 | $20 |
Met Life Bldg., 200 Park Ave. (45th St.), 682-2700
*M – Given its unpromising Grand Central location, this
Italian cafe exceeds expectations, with a $20 dinner for
two that's "fast, noisy and solid."*

**Cucina Della Fontana**/LSX          | 16 | 18 | 15 | $20 |
368 Bleecker St. (Charles St.), 242-0636
*M – The most attractive of the Village Cucina clan has
an indoor garden that "adds immensely" to a "bargain"
red-sauce dining experience that's "hit or miss" from
culinary and service standpoints.*

| | F | D | S | C |

### Cucina di Pesce/LSX  | 18 | 13 | 14 | $20 |
87 E. 4th St. (bet. 2nd & 3rd Aves.), 260-6800
*M – "There's always a wait" and free appetizers at this "best bargain", "ultranoisy" and crowded East Village Italian seafooder; "overlook the decor", or lack of it, as well as "service that tends to be brusque."*

### Cucina Stagionale/LSX  | 18 | 12 | 14 | $19 |
275 Bleecker St. (bet. 6th & 7th Aves.), 924-2707
*M – Another Village "Cucina" with long lines, "cramped but convivial" quarters, "haphazard service" and "amazingly inexpensive" tabs for good Italian cookery; there's no getting around its popularity; BYO.*

### Cuisine de Saigon/S  | 17 | 13 | 16 | $27 |
154 W. 13th St. (bet. 6th & 7th Aves.), 255-6003
*M – This Village Vietnamese is showing signs of age; though the "helpful" staff and "delicate, clean-tasting" food remain, the decor has grown "dowdy."*

### Cupcake Cafe/SX  | 19 | 9 | 12 | $12 |
522 Ninth Ave. (39th St.), 465-1530
*M – A "throwback to a Depression-era coffee shop" that offers soups, salads and sandwiches, but it's the "great" baked goods – including "the best doughnuts in town" – that draw hordes to this "scary location."*

### Cupping Room Cafe, The/LS (92)  | 16 | 15 | 14 | $22 |
359 W. Broadway (Broome St.), 925-2898
*M – "SoHo meets Ithaca" at this quaint skylit room, where weekend jazz makes waiting for your brunch a pleasure.*

### Dakota Bar & Grill  | – | – | – | M |
1576 Third Ave. (bet. 88th & 89th Sts.), 427-8889
*The '80s live at this handsome yupscale saloon where the pub food, along with decor, is way above par.*

### Dallas BBQ/LS  | 14 | 9 | 12 | $15 |
1265 Third Ave. (73rd St.), 772-9393
27 W. 72nd St. (bet. CPW & Columbus), 873-2004
21 University Pl. (8th St.), 674-4450
132 Second Ave. (St. Marks Pl.), 777-5574
*U – Not for the effete, this "raucous" chain's ribs and onion loaf "pump up your cholesterol", while margaritas and beer mugs are "big enough to float a boat."*

### Da Noi/LS  | 20 | 18 | 19 | $48 |
1394 York Ave. (74th St.), 628-7733
*M – To most, this East Side Italian is "top notch", with "great food and jazz"; to others it's "overpriced", "schmaltzy" and nicknamed "da noise."*

| F | D | S | C |

### Darbar/S
`| 21 | 19 | 19 | $35 |`
44 W. 56th St. (bet. 5th & 6th Aves.), 432-7227
*U – Fans of this Midtown Indian call it "the best in town",
with tandoori dishes "fit for a prince", "attentive" service
and a "darkly romantic" setting; you can eat until you
drop at the $12.95 lunch buffet.*

### Da Silvano/LS
`| 20 | 16 | 17 | $42 |`
260 Sixth Ave. (bet. Bleecker & W. Houston), 982-0090
*M – This Village Italian standby gets high marks for its
"excellent food", "warm" ambiance and outdoor dining;
still some call it "overpriced" and "inconsistent."*

### Da Tommaso/LS
`| 20 | 15 | 20 | $36 |`
903 Eighth Ave. (bet. 53rd & 54th Sts.), 265-1890
*U – "Molto buono" refers to the "heart-warming",
"dependably good" food and "accommodating" staff, but
not to the west Midtown locale; try it for pre-theater.*

### DA UMBERTO
`| 25 | 18 | 21 | $47 |`
107 W. 17th St. (bet. 6th & 7th Aves.), 989-0303
*U – "Sublime", "fabulous", "a winner", report satisfied
surveyors of this amber-hued Chelsea Italian whose
service is usually "impeccable" and whose ambiance is
"unpretentious" and "laid-back"; expect crowds and
noise at night – it's far more relaxed at lunch.*

### David Keh's Noodle Road
`| – | – | – | E |`
209 E. 49th St. (bet. 2nd & 3rd Aves.), 486-1800
*In the awkward narrow Midtown quarters where Fortune
Garden Pavilion used to be, longtime restaurateur
David Keh has set up a new shop concentrating on
peasant Chinese food at nonpeasant prices.*

### DAWAT/S
`| 23 | 19 | 19 | $36 |`
210 E. 58th St. (bet. 2nd & 3rd Aves.), 355-7555
*U – "Elegant", "upscale" and "authentic" is the consensus
on our city's No. 1 Indian; best known for its "inventive"
dishes, it also has solid comfort and service that's
professionally attentive.*

### Day-O/LSX
`| 14 | 15 | 13 | $20 |`
103 Greenwich Ave. (W. 12th St.), 924-3161
*M – A young crowd enjoys this "funky" West Villager's
Caribbean-Southern grub and "deadly tropical drinks";
to others it's "all gimmick" and "weird."*

### DeGrezia
`| 22 | 21 | 22 | $47 |`
231 E. 50th St. (bet. 2nd & 3rd Aves.), 750-5353
*U – Reviewers "can't say enough" about this Midtown
Northern Italian "wonderful find"; though "pricey", it
"deserves higher visibility."*

|   | F | D | S | C |
|---|---|---|---|---|

**Delmonico's** (92)   | 16 | 19 | 18 | $42 |
56 Beaver St. (William St.), 422-4747
*M – One of the grand old names in American dining, this Wall Street Continental landmark offers "good, but not great" food that really should be great.*

**Demarchelier**/LS   | 16 | 16 | 14 | $38 |
50 E. 86th St. (bet. Madison & Park Aves.), 249-6300
*M – Locals divide on this East Side French newcomer: some call it "a great addition to the area", but to others it's "a great disappointment"; most agree the bistro fare is "authentic", but "surly" service is a turnoff.*

**Denino's Tavern** (S.I.)/LSX   | 23 | 10 | 14 | $16 |
524 Port Richmond Ave. (Hooker Pl.), 718-442-9401
*U – "Simply the best pizza" is the verdict on this Staten Island standby, whose "great" fried calamari and other homemade Italian dishes also come in for praise; most enjoy the "friendly local" tavern" ambiance.*

**Dish of Salt**   | 19 | 20 | 18 | $37 |
133 W. 47th St. (bet. 6th & 7th Aves.), 921-4242
*M – Fans call this Midtown Cantonese "near perfect", while foes find it "Westernized" and " overpriced; the "soaring" space, "magnificent" to some, is "barnlike" to others; our fortune cookie reads "confucius."*

**Divino**/S   | 18 | 14 | 18 | $33 |
1556 Second Ave. (bet. 80th & 81st Sts.), 861-1096
*M – "Always a pleasure" is the majority view of this "good, solid East Side Italian", which has three side-by-side outlets: a formal restaurant, a casual cafe and a takeout; critics call it "ordinary."*

**Dock's Oyster Bar**/S   | 20 | 16 | 16 | $36 |
2427 Broadway (bet. 89th & 90th Sts.), 724-5588
633 Third Ave. (40th St.), 986-8080
*U – "Fresh-fresh" fish draws crowds to these attractive, well-run seafood houses, where the raw bar is "out of this world" and desserts are "sublime"; there's a "buzzing" "high-decibel" happy-hour bar scene at both locations.*

**DoDa's**   | – | – | – | M |
20 W. 20th St. (bet. 5th & 6th Aves.), 727-8840
*"Dancin', eatin' and havin' fun" is how this new Tex-Mex "American country music" saloon–cum–dance hall advertises itself; with live bands after 9 PM on Fridays and Saturdays, it delivers on at least two-thirds of its pledge.*

**Dolce**   | 19 | 20 | 17 | $36 |
60 E. 49th St. (bet. Madison & Park Aves.), 692-9292
*U – This "chic Italian" has kept the best features of its predecessor Aurora while downscaling prices for its good "pasta-plus" menu; "power-lunching" may mean midday crowds, but dinners are low-key and "relaxing."*

| F | D | S | C |
|---|---|---|---|

**Dominick's** (Bronx)/SX    | 22 | 9 | 15 | $27 |
2335 Arthur Ave. (bet. 186th & 187th), 733-2807
*U – For "a veritable feast", try this family-style, no-menu Southern Italian with elbow-to-elbow seating, no reserving and "long lines"; the hearty pastas, salads and great meat at low prices are well "worth the wait."*

**Donald Sacks**/S    | 15 | 12 | 13 | $22 |
220 Vesey St. (West St.), 619-4600
*M – Great for "a picnic at the WFC", this "designer deli"–cum–"mall sandwich shop" gets mixed reviews for its "pricey" but "winning" Contemporary American fare.*

**Dosanko**    | 12 | 6 | 12 | $13 |
10 E. 52nd St. (bet. 5th & Madison Aves.), 759-6361/SX
423 Madison Ave. (bet. 48th & 49th Sts.), 688-8575/SX
123 W. 49th St. (bet. 6th & 7th Aves.), 245-4090/X
329 Fifth Ave. (bet. 32nd & 33rd Sts.), 686-9259/SX
24 W. 56th St. (bet. 5th & 6th Aves.), 757-4339
1500 Broadway (43rd St.), 354-2550/X
217 E. 59th St. (bet. 2nd & 3rd Aves.), 752-3936/SX
*M – "Filling", "fast" and "efficient", these Japanese "McNoodle" shops fill the bill for "cheap eats"; they're good for a "noodle fix", but strictly "geigin."*

**Duane Park Cafe**    | 23 | 18 | 20 | $40 |
157 Duane St. (bet. W. B'way & Hudson), 732-5555
*U – We hear nothing but praise for this TriBeCa New American: the food's "spectacular", the setting "warm" and "intimate", the experience "utterly civilized."*

**Due**/LSX    | 17 | 15 | 16 | $32 |
1396 Third Ave. (bet. 79th & 80th Sts.), 772-3331
*M – For pasta or pizza served in a "chic", "Euro"-setting, this East Side Italian is a local "favorite", but some say it's "long on attitude, short on quality."*

**East**/S    | 18 | 14 | 15 | $25 |
1420 Third Ave. (bet. 80th & 81st Sts.), 472-3975
251 W. 55th St. (bet. B'way & 8th Ave.), 581-2240
210 E. 44th St. (bet. 2nd & 3rd Aves.), 687-5075/L
366 Third Ave. (bet. 26th & 27th Sts.), 889-2326
354 E. 66th St. (bet. 1st & 2nd Aves.), 734-5270
9 E. 38th St. (bet. 5th & Madison Aves.), 685-5205
137 E. 47th St. (bet. 3rd & Lexington), 980-7909
*M – Fans swear the sushi is "so fresh it swims to your table", but many warn this Japanese chain varies from location to location; still most say "take your shoes off and enjoy."*

**E.A.T**/S    | 21 | 11 | 13 | $31 |
1064 Madison Ave. (bet. 80th & 81st Sts.), 772-0022
*U – Perhaps "the most expensive coffee shop in town" ("home of chutzpah"), "bread to die for" and "the best" soups, sandwiches and salads lead Eastsiders to conclude "who cares about prices with food this good."*

| F | D | S | C |

### Ecco
| 20 | 17 | 18 | $38 |

124 Chambers (bet. W. B'way & Church), 227-7074
U – "Casual" yet "competent", this TriBeCa Italian with
its "turn-of-the-century" setting gets "better with age"
and to most, it's "warm and friendly", "bubbly and buzzing."

### Ecco-La/LSX
| 18 | 13 | 14 | $21 |

1660 Third Ave. (bet. 92nd & 93rd Sts.), 860-5609
U – "Fresh" pasta at "unbeatable" prices packs them in
at this simple East Side Italian; some grouse about lines
and warn you "need a shoehorn to get in".

### Ed Debevic's/S
| 11 | 18 | 15 | $18 |

661 Broadway (bet. Bleecker & Bond Sts.), 982-6000
M – At this jukebox-playing "'50s-style" LoBro diner, the
"hi hon" gum-chewing waitresses are "a gas", but the
"theme park food" may cause the same reaction.

### Eden Rock/LS (92)
| 14 | 9 | 14 | $17 |

2325 Broadway (bet. 84th & 85th Sts.), 873-1361
M – Notwithstanding its "luncheonette" ambiance, this
"bargain" Middle Eastern Westsider is popular for a
"quick bite" of "good falafel, hummus" and the like.

### Edison Cafe/SX
| 14 | 10 | 14 | $15 |

Hotel Edison, 228 W. 47th St. (bet. B'way & 8th), 840-5000
U – Don't miss the "homemade" soups, but then "skip to
dessert", at this "hamische", low-budget, no-frills coffee
shop; it's ideal for B'way stargazing on matinee days.

### Edwardian Room/S
| 19 | 26 | 22 | $51 |

The Plaza Hotel, 768 Fifth Ave. (59th St.), 546-5310
U – "Sheer elegance" is the majority verdict on this
"romantic" dining room, where solid service
complements a well-liked pricey New American menu.

### Edward Moran Bar & Grill/S
| 11 | 13 | 11 | $24 |

World Financial Center, 250 Vesey St., 945-2255
M – Hudson sunsets are a big plus at this Downtown
"bar scene"; despite "run-of-the-mill" pub grub and
"zilch" service, after work it's a bustling "meetmarket."

### Eighteenth & Eighth/LS
| 17 | 12 | 16 | $18 |

159 Eighth Ave. (18th St.), 242-5000
M – A real "price-performer", report locals who line up at
this "cozy" Chelsea coffee shop for American "comfort
food"; critics wonder "what's the fuss?"

### EJ's Luncheonette/SX
| 17 | 14 | 15 | $17 |

433 Amsterdam Ave. (bet. 80th & 81st Sts.), 873-3444
1271 Third Ave. (73rd St.), 472-0600/L
M – "Stick-to-your-ribs food" at "best-deal" prices keep
these "perfect-for-the- '90s" twins "mobbed"; breakfast is
a "best bet", as are the blue-plate specials; critics call
them "overhyped" and "terminally cute."

|   | F | D | S | C |
|---|---|---|---|---|

### Elaine's/LS          | 11 | 12 | 12 | $39 |
1703 Second Ave. (bet. 88th & 89th Sts.), 534-8103
*U – "Because Woody's there" isn't much of a recom-*
*mendation these days, and since this "tired" East Side*
*Italian watering hole has little else going for it, you may*
*want to stay home and "save yourself the aggravation."*

### El Charro          | – | – | – | M |
4 Charles St. (bet. 7th & Greenwich Sts.), 243-5413
58 E. 34th St. (bet. Madison & Park Aves.), 689-1019
*You don't last 60 years without doing something right; in*
*this case, it's hearty Spanish food and sangria at low*
*prices (e.g. $12.95 Sunday–Thursday prix fixe dinner)*
*that don't leave much in the budget for decor.*

### Eldorado Petit          | 21 | 24 | 21 | $47 |
47 W. 55th St. (bet. 5th & 6th Aves.), 586-3434
*U – Without fanfare this pricey Midtown "sleeper" has*
*established a reputation as NY's "most elegant" and*
*"best-overall" Spanish restaurant, with an interesting*
*Catalan menu served in an "exquisite" modern space.*

### Elephant & Castle/LS (92)          | 15 | 12 | 14 | $19 |
68 Greenwich Ave. (bet. 7th Ave. & 11th St.), 243-1400
183 Prince St. (bet. Thompson & Sullivan), 260-3600
*U – Every neighborhood needs simple places like these*
*SoHo/West Village twins where a "decent square meal"*
*is always affordable and the staff always pleasant.*

### El Faro/LS          | 19 | 10 | 15 | $28 |
823 Greenwich St. (bet. Horatio & Jane), 929-8210
*M – This "homey" West Village Spanish "continues to*
*impress" with garlic-ladened food and the city's "best*
*paella"; to critics it's just "seedy" and "dark."*

### Elio's/LS          | 21 | 16 | 17 | $42 |
1621 Second Ave. (bet. 84th & 85th Sts.), 772-2242
*U – A "sophisticated", "high-energy" crowd packs this*
*"clubby" Eastsider for "top-flight" Northern Italian food*
*and surefire "celebrity-spotting"; despite "high" prices,*
*diners call it "always reliable", "always delicious."*

### El Parador Cafe/S          | 18 | 15 | 19 | $31 |
325 E. 34th St. (bet. 1st & 2nd Aves.), 679-6812
*M – Opinions were divided on this Mexican standby*
*after a change of owners a few years back: loyalists say*
*it's "still friendly", "reliable" and "authentic", but others*
*call it "a fallen angel" that "needs a face-lift."*

### El Pollo/SX          | 20 | 9 | 14 | $15 |
1746 First Ave. (bet. 90th & 91st Sts.), 996-7810
*M – "Not just another chicken joint", this bargain spot*
*offers "lusty Peruvian chicken" that's the star attraction;*
*with "spare" decor, "Latin-time" service and constant*
*crowds, many opt for takeout.*

|   | F | D | S | C |
|---|---|---|---|---|

**El Rincon de Espana**/S $\quad$ | 18 | 11 | 15 | $30 |
226 Thompson (bet. Bleecker & W. 3rd), 260-4950
*M – "Hefty portions" of "top-notch paella" draw a crowd at this "classic", "small and cozy" Spanish Villager, but most agree the "tacky decor" is due for a redo.*

**El Rio Grande**/LS (92) $\quad$ | 16 | 14 | 14 | $27 |
160 E. 38th St. (bet. Lexington & 3rd Aves.), 867-0922
*M – This sprawling, bustling Murray Hill Tex-Mex is no slouch for food, but is even better as a "pickup" place with "killer margaritas" and an open patio for socializing.*

**El Teddy's**/LS $\quad$ | 16 | 18 | 14 | $30 |
219 W. Broadway (bet. Franklin & White), 941-7070
*U – To "see how the MTV crowd lives" stop by this TriBeCa Mexican, featuring stiff drinks, an "inventive" menu and an "outer-space" inner space and staff.*

**Embers** (Brooklyn)/S $\quad$ | 22 | 13 | 17 | $30 |
9519 Third Ave. (bet. 95th & 96th Sts.), 718-745-3700
*U – "Diner" decor, "tight quarters" and long lines don't deter devotees of "melt-in-your-mouth" steaks; come "early" (before 6 PM) "to beat the crowds."*

**Empire Diner**/LS $\quad$ | 14 | 15 | 13 | $21 |
210 Tenth Ave. (22nd St.), 243-2736
*M – The joint's still "jumping" at 3 AM with "something for everyone" – "good sandwiches", "rich desserts" and a wildly varied late-night crowd; N.B. for some this deco diner "icon" is "wearing thin.*

**Empire Szechuan** $\quad$ | 15 | 8 | 15 | $17 |
381 Third Ave. (bet. 27th & 28th Sts.), 685-6215/LS
193 Columbus Ave. (bet. 68th & 69th Sts.), 496-8778/LS
160 Bleecker St. (Sullivan St.), 260-0206/LS
2574 Broadway (97th St.), 663-6004/S
251 W. 72nd St. (bet. B'way & West End), 496-8460/LS
15 Greenwich Ave. (6th Ave. & W. 10th), 691-1535/LS
1194 First Ave. (bet. 64th & 65th Sts.), 744-9400/LS
173 Seventh Ave. (bet. 11th & Perry), 243-6046/LS
*M – "Consistent if not great" food at "giveaway prices" is the word on this "ubiquitous", always-open Chinese chain; it may be "standard", but it "never lets you down."*

**Ennio and Michael**/S $\quad$ | 19 | 15 | 19 | $37 |
539 La Guardia Pl. (bet. Bleecker & W. 3rd), 677-8577
*U – A "sentimental favorite", this Village Italian keeps 'em "coming back" with "consistently good" food and a warm welcome that makes you "feel like family."*

**Erminia** $\quad$ | 23 | 22 | 22 | $45 |
250 E. 83rd St. (bet. 2nd & 3rd Aves.), 879-4284
*U – This East Side Italian "romantic hideaway" gets raves for its "cozy", "country-inn" setting ("so un-NY") and "lusty" food; reviewers tout it for a "special occasion" or seduction.*

|  F  |  D  |  S  |  C  |

### Ernie's/LS
| 15 | 14 | 14 | $26 |

2150 Broadway (bet. 75th & 76th Sts.), 496-1588
*M – A "bustling" "circus" at "peak" times, but an "oasis of calm at off-hours", this West Side "yuppie pastaria" has a menu and portions to match its stadium size.*

### Est Est Est/S
| 21 | 18 | 21 | $37 |

64 Carmine St. (bet. Bedford & 7th Ave.), 255-6294
*U – A Village "hideaway" that serves "wholesome" Tuscan dishes in a "quaint", if a bit awkward, setting; fans call it "superb", "a sleeper", "a surprise."*

### Eva's Cafe/SX
| 17 | 11 | 15 | $22 |

1589 First Ave. (bet. 82nd & 83rd Sts.), 628-3504
*U – Usually good, this Eastsider features "hearty", "homestyle" Hungarian food in a "comfy" coffee-shop setting; regulars say you "can't beat the prices."*

### Fagiolini
| 15 | 11 | 14 | $23 |

1393B Second Ave. (bet. 72nd & 73rd Sts.), 570-5666/S
334 Lexington Ave. (39th St.), 883-9555/S
*M – This Italian duo offers "good cheap pasta" and "Little Italy"–type food; given minimal decor and so-so service, the best things are its "locations and prices."*

### Fanelli/LSX
| 13 | 16 | 13 | $19 |

94 Prince St. (Mercer St.), 226-9412
*U – There are "no pretensions" at this vintage 1872 SoHo pub; it's "usually crowded" with folks who come for "charbroiled burgers and beer" and old-NY charm.*

### Fannie's Oyster Bar
| – | – | – | M |

765 Washington St. (bet. W. 12th & Bethune), 255-5101
*Defining funk, this tiny Noo Awleens–style dive is about as far off the beaten path as you can get; your best bet is to come with a large group and take over the place.*

### Felidia/L
| 24 | 21 | 21 | $54 |

243 E. 58th St. (bet. 2nd & 3rd Aves.), 758-1479
*U – A "class-act", "first-rate", "an absolute favorite" – this "elegant" East Side brownstone serves "wonderful Northern Italian food"; besides its outstanding menu, patrons praise the "gorgeous bar", "superb wine list" and, most of all, owner Lidia Bastianich.*

### Felix/LSX
| 16 | 20 | 12 | $37 |

340 W. Broadway (Grand St.), 431-0021
*U – A trendy, new "self-aware" SoHo French bistro that's liked for its "airy setting" and "good" food, but not for its "snobby" "French attitude"; "what a scene – everybody must kiss both cheeks and have an accent."*

|   | F | D | S | C |
|---|---|---|---|---|

**Ferrara**/LS (92)    16 | 12 | 12 | $17
195 Grand St. (bet. Mott & Mulberry Sts.), 226-6150
*U – This renowned Little Italy coffee shop is all calories
from its pastries to its cappuccino – the tourists love it,
but locals know better alternatives nearby.*

**Ferrier**/LS    18 | 15 | 13 | $40
29 E. 65th St. (bet. Madison & Park Aves.), 772-9000
*U – Besides its good food, this cramped and noisy East
Side French bistro offers "posturing at its best", with "hot
and cold running blondes and brunettes."*

**Fiesta Mexicana\***/LS    15 | 15 | 16 | $25
2823 Broadway (109th St.), 662-2535
*M – A "decent Mexican in an area that lacks it", this
small restaurant appeals to a "young" "Columbia crowd"
and is "great if you like green hair at 4 AM"; some say
"Taco Bell is better and cheaper."*

**Fine & Schapiro**/S    16 | 6 | 12 | $19
138 W. 72nd St. (bet. B'way & Columbus), 877-2874
*M – A West Side institution since 1923, this recently
renovated Jewish deli still feels as "homey as ever";
regulars say "don't look at the menu, the waiters know
what you want"; critics say its "not so fine."*

**Fino**    20 | 17 | 19 | $40
4 E. 36th St. (bet. 5th & Madison Aves.), 689-8040
*U – A "garment industry favorite", this "pricey" Northern
Italian is "good for business lunch" and "not crowded" at
dinner; "staid" and "comfortable", it has "very good" but
occasionally "overbearing" waiters.*

**Fiorello's Roman Cafe**/LS    16 | 15 | 15 | $32
1900 Broadway (bet. 63rd & 64th Sts.), 595-5330
*U – "Like being on an express to Lincoln Center – easy
in easy out", this "underrated" Italian with its "pleasant"
decor and outdoor cafe is praised for its pastas, pan
pizzas and peerless people-watching.*

**Fiori**    16 | 16 | 16 | $25
4 Park Ave. (33rd St.), 686-0226
*U – Built in Cornelius Vanderbilt's private train station,
this Murray Hill watering hole with a "wonderful"
vaulted-tile ceiling offers "lots of filling for little money";
it's as "comfortable as a pair of old jeans."*

**Firenze**/LS    20 | 16 | 21 | $39
1594 Second Ave. (bet. 82nd & 83rd Sts.), 861-9368
*U – Located in a narrow East Side storefront, this nifty
Northern Italian succeeds in feeling "intimate", thanks to
"very good food" and a staff that "tries to please."*

### 1st Wok/LS                                    | 15 | 8 | 14 | $17 |
1570 Third Ave. (bet. 88th & 89th Sts.), 410-7747
1374 Third Ave. (78th St.), 861-2600
1384 First Ave. (74th St.), 535-8598
585 Second Ave. (32nd St.), 689-6786
*U – "When all else fails", these "good, cheap, Chinese" Eastsiders can be counted on for "very fresh, very fast, very crowded" "family bargains"; they also "deliver in a flash", but what "you eat fast, you forget fast."*

### Fisher & Levy (92)                          | 16 | 8 | 12 | $18 |
875 Third Ave. (bet. 52nd & 53rd Sts.), 832-3880
*U – For "creative" thin-crusted Cal-style pizza that makes a "quick healthy" lunch or a perfect commuter tie-me-over, this is the place.*

### Fishin Eddie/LS                             | 18 | 17 | 16 | $36 |
73 W. 71st St. (east of Columbus Ave.), 874-3474
*M – At this new West Side seafood sibling of Vince and Eddie's, they're "reeling in the crowds with whale-size portions" and "wacky decor"; critics, citing "uneven" quality and service, wonder why.*

### 5 & 10 No Exaggeration/LS                   | 13 | 21 | 16 | $30 |
77 Greene St. (bet. Broome & Spring Sts.), 925-7414
*U – "Conversation never falters with all the kitsch around to talk about" at this one-and-only "restaurant, cabaret, antique shop"; the bland food (e.g. steak and pasta) is incidental at this "adorable cult classic."*

### Flamingo East/LS (92)                       | 16 | 19 | 14 | $34 |
219 Second Ave. (bet. 13th & 14th Sts.), 533-2860
*M – Still semitrendy, this East Village late-night "hangout" is popular with people in black; surprisingly, the Eclectic food is also quite good.*

### Florent/LSX                                 | 18 | 14 | 14 | $27 |
69 Gansevoort St. (bet. Washington & Greenwich), 989-5779
*U – Things only get hot after 10 PM at this "always good" Meat District diner–cum–French bistro – "at 3 AM the place is "jam-packed" with "night creatures" who create "one of the coolest scenes in NYC."*

### Flying Fish                                 | – | – | – | I |
395 West St. (W. 10th St.), 924-5050
*Reggae sets the tone at this crowded hip Caribbean West Villager that offers real cheap Jamaican food in a funky setting ameliorated by Hudson sunsets.*

### Follonico                                   | – | – | – | M |
6 W. 24th St. (bet. 5th & 6th Aves.), 691-6359
*A warm wood-paneled setting and open-brick oven are the backdrop to this "gutsy" Tuscan's "seriously good" cooking; despite NYC's surplus of Italian restaurants, this one is a welcome standout.*

### 44/LS

Royalton Hotel, 44 W. 44th St. (bet. 5th & 6th), 944-8844
*U – For something different, try this "innovative"
American showcased in a "sci-fi setting" near Times
Square; though most enjoy the "hip" scene, some say
"the staff should go back to modeling."*

### 44 Southwest/LS

621 Ninth Ave. (44th St.), 315-4582
*Calling itself a "European bistro" doesn't alter the fact
that this place feels like an American coffee shop, albeit
a nice one; what's key is its good food at a fair price.*

### FOUR SEASONS/L

99 E. 52nd St. (bet. Park & Lexington), 754-9494
*U – "World-class", "a great institution" and a "favorite
any season", this "quintessential NYer" continues to
"delight all the senses" with its "superb", if pricey,
Continental-Eclectic cuisine, "grand architectural
setting" and "impressive service"; the only real debate
is whether the Grill Room (home to NYC's lunchtime
power elite) or the Pool Room is more heavenly.*

### Four Winds*/S

135 E. 63rd St. (bet. Park & Lexington Aves.), 486-1664
*U – "A very nice surprise", this "good", if awkward,
Japanese Eastsider has "character", "decent sushi",
but "slow service"; try the lunch specials.*

### Frank's Restaurant

431 W. 14th St. (bet. 9th & 10th Aves.), 243-1349
*U – "A dive, sawdust and all", this "no-frills" Far West
Village pub/restaurant has "the best steak in the Meat
District", good, "hearty" Italian food and a "charming"
old-NY setting that's "great with a group."*

### Fraunces Tavern

54 Pearl St. (Broad St.), 269-0144
*U – People come to this "warm-and-woodsy" tavern for
its historic qualities (Washington ate here) more than for
its American food which may have "peaked 200 years
ago"; still, it's a Downtown draw with breakfast a best bet.*

### Freddie & Pepper Pizza/LSX

303 Amsterdam Ave. (bet. 74th & 75th Sts.), 799-2378
*M – "Unusual pizza combos" with the freshest and most
varied toppings such as eggplant, soy and spinach on
whole wheat; the low prices are appealing, but not the
"unkempt" quarters.*

### Friend of a Farmer/S

77 Irving Pl. (bet. 17th & 18th Sts.), 477-2188
*U – This rustic Gramercy cafe offers "homey" American
comfort meals including "excellent baked goods" plus a
"great brunch served in skillets"; why go to Vermont?*

|   | F | D | S | C |
|---|---|---|---|---|

### Frutti di Mare/LSX
|19|13|15|$20|

84 E. 4th St. (2nd Ave.), 979-2034
*M – "Plentitude" and "incredibly inexpensive" typify reactions to this East Village Italian that doles out "pastas and seafood in large portions at bargain prices"; critics warn of "deafening noise" and long "lines."*

### Fujiyama Mama/LS
|19|20|16|$31|

467 Columbus Ave. (bet. 82nd & 83rd), 769-1144
*M – Westsiders seeking sushi in a "technopop" "disco-Japanese" setting need to search no farther than this "almost surreal" spot; as far as we know, it's the only sushi bar in the U.S. with its own DJ.*

### FU'S/LS
|21|17|19|$38|

1395 Second Ave. (bet. 72nd & 73rd Sts.), 517-9670
*U – "The Grand Marnier shrimp and Peking duck are still orgasmic" at this "refined" Chinese Eastsider, but so are most other choices on its "thoroughly reliable" menu; P.S. dinner is busy, lunch is quiet; both have good bargain prix fixe menus.*

### Fusillo/LSX
|16|16|15|$32|

1319 Third Ave. (bet. 75th & 76th Sts.), 879-5000
*U – A "neighborhood" Eastsider that's "refreshing" and "breezy"; "good pizza", outdoor dining in fair weather and "value if you stick to entrees" make it "a favorite for those nights you're too lazy to cook."*

### Gabriel/S
|16|13|17|$27|

1370 Lexington Ave. (bet. 90th & 91st), 369-9374
*U – "If you're going to the 92nd Street Y", think of this genial "neighborhood sleeper" for "good value and variety" – "pasta is the best buy."*

### Gabriel's
|21|16|20|$41|

11 W. 60th St. (bet. B'way & 9th Ave.), 956-4600
*U – "Snazzy and sophisticated", this Northern Italian newcomer is "the best thing to happen to the Lincoln Center area in years"; expect a "minimalist modern setting with maximalist taste" of highly "original" homemade pastas, risottos, grills and desserts; get Gabriel's advice and you won't go wrong.*

### Gage & Tollner (Brooklyn)/S
|20|21|20|$38|

372 Fulton St. (bet. Adams & Smith), 718-875-5181
*U – This gaslit Brooklyn landmark has "great old-time atmosphere" that's "awash in nostalgia" and local business men at lunch; Edna Lewis' satisfying Southern cooking is "truly soulful" featuring the likes of clam bellies, crab soup, gumbo and chocolate cake.*

| | | F | D | S | C |
|---|---|---|---|---|---|

**Galil**/S                                          | 17 | 9 | 14 | $23 |

1252 Lexington Ave. (bet. 84th & 85th Sts.), 439-9886
1561 Second Ave. (81st St.), 794-4288
*M – "If you like Israeli food", you'll like this simple
kosher duo's "abundant portions"; its kebabs, falafel
sandwiches and soups all get praise, but not its decor.*

**Gallagher's Steak House**/LS            | 18 | 14 | 16 | $43 |

228 W. 52nd St. (bet. B'way & 8th Ave.), 245-5336
*U – Convenient to Broadway theaters, this "old-NY"
steakhouse serves "possibly the best steak on the West
Side" in what tends to be "a man's world", decorated
with racing memorabilia, red-checked tablecloths and
sawdust on the floor; critics say "past its prime."*

**Garden Cafe*** (Brooklyn)                  | 21 | 15 | 20 | $31 |

620 Vanderbilt Ave. (Prospect Pl.), 718-857-8863
*U – "An oasis in Prospect Heights, this Contemporary
American is "out-of-the-way", but "worth the trip" for its
"charming" ambiance and "diverse, creative" fare.*

**Garibaldi Ristorante**                     | – | – | – | M |

7 Washington Pl. (Mercer St.), 260-3066
*Each year, write-ins point out good restaurants we
missed – this attractive, spacious Village Southern
Italian is a prime example; take the family, it won't strain
the budget.*

**Gascogne**                                      | 21 | 18 | 20 | $40 |

158 Eighth Ave. (bet. 17th & 18th Sts.), 675-6564
*M – A meal at this Chelsea bistro with a "lovely garden"
usually produces pleasant memories, e.g. "a treat", "the
true taste of France", "good hearty fare."*

**Genji***/LS                                      | 18 | 12 | 14 | $25 |

56 Third Ave. (bet. 10th & 11th Sts.), 254-1959
*M – "Die-hard sushi fans with hollow legs cry 'uncle'"
facing the all-you-can-eat deal at this East Villager;
24-hour service, "good value" and "fish so fresh it
jumps" are offset by "too many rules and regulations."*

**Giambelli**/L                                     | 20 | 17 | 18 | $46 |

46 E. 50th St. (bet. Madison & Park Aves.), 688-2760
*U – "A good spot for biz meals", this Midtown Northern
Italian offers pricey, "traditional" food and "decent
decor"; "regulars are taken care of like family."*

**Giando on the Water**                       | 15 | 20 | 16 | $41 |

(Brooklyn)/S (92)
400 Kent Ave. (Broadway), 718-387-7000
*M – You don't get many better locations than that of this
Brooklyn waterfront restaurant with its grand NYC
skyline view, but the Neapolitan meal is no match.*

|  | F | D | S | C |
|---|---|---|---|---|

**Gian Marino on the Park**/S | 21 | 21 | 20 | $45 |

150 Central Park So. (bet. 6th & 7th Aves.), 956-6205
*U – A "welcome addition to Central Park South", this worthy Northern Italian is praised for "understated elegance" and "old-world charm"; except for its '90s prices, "it's like the '50s all over again" – "a treat."*

**Gianni's**/LS | 17 | 18 | 15 | $39 |

15 Fulton St. (South St. Seaport), 608-7300
*U – "Get a table by the window" or "sit outside" to watch "the passing parade" at this "flashy Seaport Italian"; "orgasmic" garlic-gorgonzola bread gets raves and almost anything on the menu will pass muster.*

**Gibbon** | 21 | 20 | 20 | $52 |

24 E. 80th St. (bet. 5th & Madison Aves.), 861-4001
*M – Some feel "a flea would starve here" and that this ethereal East Side townhouse is so "overpriced you'd do better in Tokyo"; however, most say this "classy Japanese-French" is too good not to test for yourself.*

**Gijo's**/S | 20 | 14 | 21 | $34 |

1574 Second Ave. (bet. 81st & 82nd Sts.), 772-0752
*U – Forget the decor, this little East Side Italian is among "NYC's best trattorias"; "huge portions" and "friendly" staff score well, as do the specials.*

**Gino**/SX | 18 | 12 | 17 | $34 |

780 Lexington Ave. (bet. 60th & 61st Sts.), 758-4466
*U – The "wait is worth it" at this Italian standby, which still serves "spaghetti, not pasta"; regulars, who treat it like a club, praise "the secret sauce", "old-world waiters" and even the stained zebra wallpaper.*

**Giordano**/L | 17 | 15 | 17 | $39 |

409 W. 39th St. (bet. 9th & 10th Aves.), 947-3883
*M – Near Madison Square Garden, this Italian is "an oasis", but some claim "time has passed this place by."*

**Girafe** | 22 | 20 | 21 | $49 |

208 E. 58th St. (bet. 2nd & 3rd Aves.), 752-3054
*M – "Consistent good food and service" win by a long neck over complaints about this Northern Italian; "a middle-aged crowd" cites a "wonderfully clubby feel" that's "dimly lit" but "romantic."*

**Girasole**/LS | 20 | 17 | 18 | $43 |

151 E. 82nd St. (bet. Lexington & 3rd Aves.), 772-6690
*U – "A strong player in a tough league", this "bustling" Northern Italian wins applause for "reliable" "good eats", especially the pasta, but some feel service in this townhouse is "perfunctory", "unless you're known."*

| | F | D | S | C |
|---|---|---|---|---|

**Golden Unicorn**/LS          | 21 | 13 | 14 | $24 |

18 E. Broadway (Catherine St.), 941-0911
*U – "Don't go at noon" unless you like waiting; but, this big Chinatown spot's "Kowloon-style" food is sure to be excellent; "all that's missing is the view of Hong Kong harbor"; P.S. ask for Spencer Chan's advice.*

**Gonzalez y Gonzalez**/LS          | 11 | 14 | 12 | $22 |

625 B'way (bet. Bleecker & Houston Sts.), 473-8787
*M – It "doesn't taste as good as it looks", but prices are low here and the "carnival atmosphere" improves after several margaritas.*

**Good Enough to Eat**/S          | 19 | 15 | 15 | $22 |

483 Amsterdam Ave. (bet. 83rd & 84th Sts.), 496-0163
*U – "Like a country restaurant" in New England with "food like Mom's", this Westsider serves meat loaf, mac 'n' cheese", etc.; breakfasts and brunches are standouts, but watch out for weekend waits.*

**GOTHAM BAR & GRILL**/S          | 26 | 24 | 23 | $53 |

12 E. 12th St. (bet. 5th & University Pl.), 620-4020
*U – "One of NYC's best", this "vibrant" Contemporary American cafe has over 2,200 surveyors spewing superlatives: "simply superb", "better and better", "chef Portale's a genius", "what NYC is all about", "a must"; don't miss the $19.93 lunch.*

**Grand Dairy Restaurant**/SX          | 18 | 4 | 10 | $16 |

341 Grand St. (Ludlow St.), 673-1904
*U – "Shlep" down to the Lower East Side for "cheap and good" soups, blintzes, omelettes and gefilte fish, "thrown at you" by waiters out of a Marx Brothers movie" at "possibly the grubbiest eating place in NY."*

**Grand Ticino**          | 17 | 15 | 18 | $33 |

228 Thompson St. (bet. W. 3rd & Bleecker), 777-5922
*M – Featured as a movie location in Moonstruck, this "nice, old Village standby" is decidedly down-to-earth; called "the quintessential Italian cafe", it's good and "reliable", but "unexciting."*

**Grange Hall, The**          | – | – | – | M |

50 Commerce St. (bet. Bedford & Christopher), 924-5246
*Replacing the Blue Mill is now a stylish West Village American spot that has a real easy ambiance and good "farm" food at modest prices; it attracts upscale diners who know a good thing.*

**Grappino***          | 18 | 14 | 15 | $32 |

38 W. 39th St. (bet. 5th & 6th Aves.), 398-0350
*U – "Midtown's lunch secret" offers "innovative" Italian fare (e.g. "terrific risotto") "in a pleasant setting"; it's an ideal choice in an area with few alternatives.*

|   | F | D | S | C |
|---|---|---|---|---|

### Gray's Papaya/LSX
**16 | 4 | 11 | $6**

2090 Broadway (72nd St.), 799-0243
402 Ave. of the Americas (8th St.), 260-3532
*U – "One step up from a streetcart", these "quick"
stand-ups are popular for franks and tropical juices; if
"sleazy", they offer an "honest, tasty value."*

### Great American Health Bar
**12 | 6 | 10 | $14**

35 W. 57th St. (bet. 5th & 6th Aves.), 355-5177/S
2 Park Ave. (bet. 32nd & 33rd Sts.), 685-7117/X
*U – "Neither great, nor healthful", and some say "not too
clean", these yogurt, soup and sandwich joints are "not
bad" for a "quick" bite at "low prices."*

### Great Jones Cafe/LSX
**16 | 13 | 13 | $19**

54 Great Jones (bet. Bowery & Lafayette), 674-9304
*U – "The jukebox is better than the food" – with no
disrespect to the good food – at this "funky" Cajun
"walk-in closet" near NYU; the young crowd calls it
"great fun" – especially after a few "cajun martinis."*

### Great Shanghai/S
**19 | 9 | 12 | $20**

27 Division St. (bet. Bowery & E. B'way), 966-7663
*U – At this "clean, bright", "no-frills" Chinatown spot, the
"huge menu" stars "great" vegetarian dumplings, whole
sea bass and Peking duck; it's "best with a group."*

### Greek Village/SX
**15 | 11 | 14 | $20**

1016 Lexington Ave. (bet. 72nd & 73rd Sts.), 288-7378
*M – Somewhere "between coffee shop and restaurant",
this "friendly" place dishes out "lusty Greek taverna" fare
at "low prices"; it's good, but it's "not Astoria."*

### Grifone
**22 | 19 | 22 | $46**

244 E. 46th St. (bet. 2nd & 3rd Aves.), 490-7275
*U – "If you liked the '50s, you'll like Grifone"; "fine Italian
food" and "sophisticated service and ambiance" are
hallmarks at this Midtowner; it may be "pricey" and a bit
"fussy", but it's "satisfying."*

### Groceries
**– | – | – | I**

Bedford St. (bet. 7th Ave. S. & Barrow St.), no phone
*Tucked away in the West Village, this Eclectic serves
hearty tasty fare at down-to-earth prices in a cozy old
grocery setting that's best on a cold winter night.*

### Grotta Azzurra/SX
**17 | 11 | 15 | $33**

387 Broome St. (Mulberry St.), 925-8775
*M – "Tomato sauce, olive oil and garlic" pour forth at this
"noisy" Little Italy basement favorite; if some call it
"touristy", to most it's "a fun-filled Neapolitan", "worth
waiting for a table" and "forgetting your diet."*

|   | F | D | S | C |
|---|---|---|---|---|

### Grove Street Cafe/LS
| 19 | 15 | 19 | $32 |

53 Grove St. (bet. Bleecker St. & 7th Ave.), 924-8299
*U – BYOW and enjoy the "charm and affordability" of this "best-kept secret in the West Village"; "romantic", "intimate" and "inexpensive", this "sweet little spot" has "good Continental food and obliging service."*

### Gulf Coast/LS
| 14 | 14 | 12 | $23 |

489 West St. (12th St.), 206-8790
*M – You get "Dixie eats at Dixie prices", aka "swamp cuisine", at this "tacky, trashy but tasty", "wild and crazy place"; "if it sinks any lower, it'll be under the bayou."*

### Gus' Place
| – | – | – | M |

149 Waverly Pl. (west of 6th Ave.), 645-8511
*Airy and attractive, this mid-priced Villager has won an early reputation for good Mediterranean food and "gracious service"; dinner only, except for weekend brunch.*

### Halcyon/LS
| 21 | 25 | 21 | $50 |

Rihga Royal Hotel, 151 W. 54th St. (bet. 6th & 7th Aves.), 468-8888
*M – Most diners say this "magnificent" room is the setting for a halcyon Contemporary Continental dining experience that's "impressive from start to finish"; critics are harsh: "like a funeral home", "a bomb."*

### Hamachi
| 22 | 15 | 17 | $29 |

34 E. 20th St. (bet. B'way & Park Ave. S.), 420-8608
*U – A "minimalist" Flatiron District sushi bar, with a "friendly" chef and food that's "different enough", and good enough, to make it a "cut above" the competition.*

### Hamburger Harry's/S (92)
| 14 | 9 | 12 | $17 |

145 W. 45th St. (bet. 6th Ave. & B'way), 840-2756
157 Chambers (bet. W. B'way & Greenwich), 267-4446
*M – These hefty burger specialists at least do one thing right; they also try pasta, chicken and french fries that are good for a "workday lunch" or a meal with the kids.*

### Harbour Lights/LS
| 15 | 21 | 16 | $34 |

South Street Seaport, Pier 17, 3rd fl., 227-2800
*M – "The view is the reason" to come to this Seaport bar and grill with its sweeping harbor vistas; the food is "ok, but not special" with simple grilled items best bets.*

### Hard Rock Cafe/LS
| 12 | 20 | 13 | $22 |

221 W. 57th St. (bet. B'way & 7th Ave.), 459-9320
*U – "An oldie but goodie", this "deafening" rock 'n' roll museum still has "long waits" for its "surprisingly good" sandwiches, burgers and rich desserts, but the hordes of families and teeny tourists are as much interested in seeing the memorabilia and buying T-shirts as in eating.*

### Harlequin/LS
| 20 | 17 | 19 | $40 |

569 Hudson St. (W. 11th St.), 255-4950
*U – This low-key, "haute Spanish" West Villager is little
known despite "superior, authentic cooking" and a solid
Spanish wine list; though "muy especiale", it would be
more special with larger portions and more energy.*

### Harriet's Kitchen*/S
| 16 | 7 | 14 | $14 |

502 Amsterdam Ave. (bet. 84th & 85th Sts.), 721-0045
*U – A NY upgrade of KFC, this takeout turns out "great"
"cheap" chicken dishes including fried, lemon, barbecue,
or pot pie; fowl fans also crow about the mashed
potatoes and cornbread.*

### Harry Cipriani/LS
| 22 | 20 | 21 | $55 |

Sherry Netherland Hotel, 781 Fifth Ave. (bet. 59th & 60th
Sts.), 753-5566
*U – The "glamorous" scene, a mix of Venice, Palm
Beach and Hawaii can be as intoxicating as the Bellinis
at this "mesmerizing" Venetian; but even fans of its
"very good" food are quick to admit it's "overpriced."*

### Harry's at Hanover Square
| 14 | 14 | 16 | $33 |

1 Hanover Sq. (bet. Pearl & Stone Sts.), 425-3412
*M – "Wall Streeters unwind" at this "smoke-filled"
traders' hangout" with "two-fisted macho drinks"; "good"
straightforward American food at "fair prices" keeps this
a Downtown "mainstay."*

### Hasaki/LS
| 24 | 16 | 19 | $30 |

210 E. 9th St. (bet. 2nd & 3rd Aves.), 473-3327
*U – "Fresh, artistic sushi", "amazing" noodle soups,
"excellent" tempura and "guiltily good steamed
dumplings" bring crowds and waits to this East Villager.*

### HATSUHANA
| 24 | 16 | 19 | $38 |

17 E. 48th St. (bet. 5th & Madison Aves.), 355-3345
237 Park Ave. (46th St.), 661-3400
*M – Those with a yen for "top-drawer" sushi head for
these Japanese icons; although other sushi purveyors
are also highly rated, fans feel "one of the first is still
one of the best", with "fish you can trust."*

### Haveli/LS
| 19 | 18 | 17 | $24 |

100 Second Ave. (bet 5th & 6th Sts.), 982-0533
*U – Down in Little India near 6th Street, this affordable
Indian is "a bright spot" with "authentic food", an
attractive, spacious setting, and "excellent service."*

### Health Pub/S
| 17 | 11 | 15 | $22 |

371 Second Ave. (21st St.), 529-9200
*M – "Groovy grub" say sympaticos of this Gramercy
"no-ambiance" haven of politically correct "veg chili" and
other "healthful" cookery; red-meat types say "boring."*

| | F | D | S | C |
|---|---|---|---|---|

**Henry's End** (Brooklyn)/S — | 21 | 13 | 20 | $32 |

44 Henry St. (Cranberry St.), 718-834-1776
*U – "Heights locals praise the fish, game and desserts at this standout French-American; a few cite "cramped" but hey, whaddya want?*

**Hi-Life Bar and Grill**/LS — | 13 | 13 | 13 | $22 |

477 Amsterdam Ave. (83rd St.), 787-7199
*U – A West Side scene with "great-looking" dishes – and good food too; "rather dark" with nonstop music and TV inside, outside tables are welcome.*

**Honeysuckle**/LS — | 14 | 14 | 11 | $26 |

507 Columbus Ave. (bet. 84th & 85th Sts.), 496-8095
*M – A new "bubba hangout", this West Side "fun place" with "down-home cookin' " "ain't Sylvia's", but it sure is "trendy" despite "snail-like" service and live "music too loud to taste the food"; try the jazz brunch.*

**Honmura An**/S — | 21 | 22 | 20 | $35 |

170 Mercer St. (bet. Prince & W. Houston), 334-5253
*U – "Exquisite" buckwheat noodles, known as "soba", are dispensed in a "beautiful" SoHo loft with "sleek Japanese decor"; soba soup fanciers say "better than Tokyo", "strangely wonderful", "hearty and filling."*

**Hosteria Fiorella**/LS — | 17 | 16 | 16 | $32 |

1081 Third Ave. (bet. 63rd & 64th Sts.), 838-7570
*U – Reinventing itself with a "new menu" and "spruced-up" decor, this casual East Side trattoria now emphasizes seafood plus a "terrific antipasti bar."*

**Houlihan's** — | 9 | 10 | 10 | $19 |

50 Broad St. (bet. Beaver & Exchange Sts.), 483-8310
1900 Broadway (63rd St.), 339-8863
380 Lexington Ave. (42nd St.), 922-5660/S
729 Seventh Ave. (49th St.), 626-7312/LS
7 Hanover Sq. (Wall St.), 483-8314
677 Lexington Ave. (56th St.), 339-8858
350 Fifth Ave. (bet. 34th & 35th Sts.), 630-0336/S
767 Fifth Ave. (59th St.), 339-8850/S
196 Broadway (bet. John & Day Sts.), 240-1281
*M – NYers love to hate this chain of fern bars (accused by some of "gastronomic malpractice"), yet over 1,200 critics have dropped in at some point during the last year, since it's so "convenient" and "ok for a quickie."*

**Hourglass Tavern**/SX (92) — | 17 | 16 | 18 | $20 |

373 W. 46th St. (bet. 8th & 9th Aves.), 265-2060
*U – This tiny Restaurant Row tavern is a guaranteed winner for its $11.50 prix fixe pre-theater homespun meal; even going off the menu, it's hard to spend much.*

|   | F | D | S | C |
|---|---|---|---|---|

### Hows Bayou/LS
**13 | 13 | 14 | $22**

355 Greenwich St. (Harrison St.), 925-5405
U – "Cheap", "fun and funky", this TriBeCa dive is as
"Cajun as the Pope"; "quantity doesn't make up for
quality", but the B&T sunset-watchers could care less.

### H.S.F./S
**19 | 12 | 14 | $24**

46 Bowery St. (just south of Canal St.), 374-1319
578 Second Ave. (32nd St.), 689-6969/L
U – "Dim sum without peer" roll by at this Chinese duo
of lunchtimers; Uptown is fancier, but either is "a great
place for groups" to try cheap, but delightful tidbits.

### HUDSON RIVER CLUB/S
**23 | 26 | 22 | $52**

4 World Financial Ctr., 250 Vesey St., 786-1500
U – "Worth the splurge", this handsome Downtowner
showcases chef Waldy Malouf's "outstanding" Hudson
Valley food plus "spectacular" harbor views; brunch
and pre-theater are a "bargain"; while the $19.93 lunch
is a giveaway.

### Hulot's/S
**17 | 16 | 16 | $42**

1007 Lexington Ave. (bet. 72nd & 73rd Sts.), 794-9800
U – A "romantic and cozy" French bistro for "great
chicken" and "delicious" desserts in a "warm, country
setting" that "makes you think you're in Paris."

### Hunan Balcony/LS
**17 | 11 | 15 | $19**

2596 Broadway (98th St.), 865-0400
1417 Second Ave. (74th St.), 517-2088
U – The "view from the balcony" counts in favor of these
"always reliable" "nonglamorous" Chinese; "bring a crowd"
and share the "good food" at good prices.

### Hunan Garden/S
**16 | 11 | 16 | $19**

1 Mott St. (Chatham Sq.), 732-7270
M – Besides basic Hunan dishes, the "engaging
specials", "jumping staff" and Chinatown "street
scenery" improve the nonexistent decor here.

### Hwa Yuan Szechuan Inn/S
**20 | 9 | 13 | $20**

236 E. 53rd St. (bet. 2nd & 3rd Aves.), 355-5096
M – Raves for sesame noodles and Szechuan food
that's called the "best in town", as well as a "best value",
are mixed with negatives: "not attractive", it's "limping."

### Il Cantinori/LS
**23 | 21 | 19 | $48**

32 E. 10th St. (bet. B'way & University Pl.), 673-6044
M – A "charming rustic setting" and "delicious Tuscan
food" (pasta and game "to die for") keep this cozy
celebrity-studded spot a Village favorite; critics say it's
"expensive", "crowded" and has "too much attitude."

|  | F | D | S | C |
|---|---|---|---|---|

### Il–Corallo Trattoria
| – | – | – | I |

176 Prince St. (bet. Thompson & Sullivan Sts.), 941-7119
*Bright and bustling, this new SoHo pastaria is busy at all
hours, thanks to a menu that stays strictly under $10
and yet has plenty of tempting choices.*

### Il Cortile/LS
| 22 | 21 | 18 | $40 |

125 Mulberry St. (bet. Canal & Hester Sts.), 226-6060
*M – "One of the best in Little Italy" with a "wonderful airy
setting", romantic courtyard and "first-class" Northern
Italian fare; on the downside, surveyors dislike the noise
levels, waits and tourist traffic.*

### Il Gabbiano/S
| 22 | 14 | 22 | $39 |

232 E. 58th St. (bet. 2nd & 3rd Aves.), 754-1033
*M – "Solid Italian" with "retro"-food and decor; it's "well
worth the money", but "please redecorate", say critics,
starting with the bathroom.*

### Il Gattopardo/LS
| 18 | 17 | 18 | $41 |

49 W. 56th St. (bet. 5th & 6th Aves.), 586-3978
*M – "Ample portions" of "consistently" "good" Italian
food and "old-world service" keep this attractive
Midtowner "crowded"; detractors say it's just "adequate."*

### Il Giglio
| 24 | 17 | 20 | $49 |

81 Warren St. (bet. W. B'way & Greenwich), 571-5555
*U – "A mini–Il Mulino" in TriBeCa, with the same good
garlicky food, but "less hassle", shorter waits and a
"cozier" feel; only steep prices cause hesitation.*

### Il Menestrello
| 22 | 18 | 21 | $47 |

14 E. 52nd St. (bet. 5th & Madison Aves.), 421-7588
*M – Though "first-class" and "consistently fine", this
Midtown Italian expense accounter strikes some as
"stuffy" and "overpriced."*

### Il Monello/S
| 23 | 20 | 21 | $49 |

1460 Second Ave. (bet. 76th & 77th Sts.), 535-9310
*U – An attractive new open front has dramatically
changed the mood at this East Side standby – once
stuffy, it's now warm and welcoming; happily its
Northern Italian fare is as "delicious" as ever.*

### IL MULINO/L
| 27 | 18 | 22 | $54 |

86 W. 3rd St. (bet. Thompson & Sullivan), 673-3783
*M – "Il Supremo"; once again our surveyors rate this
Villager as NY's Numero Uno Italian; it's "the ultimate"
for "delicious" garlic-ladened dishes, "warm" service and
"superb people-watching"; long waits, "cramped tables"
and high noise levels are the downside of its vast
popularity; at lunch there's less hassle and more light.*

|  | F | D | S | C |
|---|---|---|---|---|

## IL NIDO
| 24 | 19 | 21 | $52 |

251 E. 53rd St. (bet. 2nd & 3rd Aves.), 753-8450
*M – "All those limos know what they're doing" say admirers of this "superb" East Side Italian who call it "divine, delicious and dependable"; naysayers fault the place as "overpriced" and "overcrowded."*

## Il Nonno*
| 21 | 19 | 23 | $39 |

202 W. 14th St. (bet. 7th & 8th Aves.), 255-5042
*M – The word on this recently opened West Village Northern Italian is that it's "like going to the suburbs or the 1950s"; most find the room "quiet" and "relaxing", service "friendly" and call it a "find", if a bit "boring."*

## Il Ponte Vecchio/S
| 19 | 15 | 19 | $35 |

206 Thompson St. (bet. Bleecker & W. 3rd), 228-7701
*U – "Good home cooking " is the draw at this "modest" Village Italian; the "cozy", "friendly neighborhood" feeling keeps customers coming back.*

## Il Tinello
| 22 | 17 | 22 | $47 |

16 W. 56th St. (bet. 5th & 6th Aves.), 245-4388
*M – "Great for business entertaining" because of its "consistently good food", "widely spaced tables", "attentive" service, and "quiet, classy atmosphere", but this Midtown Italian also has expense-account prices.*

## Il Vagabondo/LS
| 15 | 13 | 15 | $30 |

351 E. 62nd St. (bet. 1st & 2nd Aves.), 832-9221
*M – The "attraction is bocce courts" more than food at this "old-fashioned" East Side Southern Italian; in the right mood, it can make "a fun, low-key evening" with family or friends, but it's also "dingy" and "touristy."*

## Inagiku/S
| 21 | 21 | 20 | $44 |

Waldorf-Astoria, 111 E. 49th St. (bet. Lex. & Park), 355-0440
*U – Choices are varied at this "lovely", "traditional" Midtown Japanese that features "sublime" sushi and "flavorful" cooked dishes; high prices and a formal setting draw a business crowd.*

## Indian Cafe/LS
| 16 | 11 | 15 | $19 |

201 W. 95th St. (bet. B'way & Amsterdam), 222-1600
2791 Broadway (bet. 107th & 108th Sts.), 749-9200
*M – Opinions vary about these simple Upper West Side Indians: "fabulous value", "fresh, tasty" tandooris and curries vs. "small portions" and "indifferent service."*

## Indian Oven/S
| 16 | 11 | 15 | $23 |

200 W. 84th St. (bet. B'way & Amsterdam), 874-6900
*M – A nice local spot for "ok" Indian food that's "reasonably priced"; dissenters claim it's a "dive" with "inconsistent" performance both in and out of the oven.*

|  | F | D | S | C |
|---|---|---|---|---|

**India Pavilion**/S ⟨ 18 | 13 | 16 | $21 ⟩
240 W. 56th St. (bet. B'way & 8th Ave.), 489-0035
35 W. 13th St. (bet. 5th & 6th Aves.), 243-8175
*U – Ratings have risen on this understated Indian duo
that provides "6th Street prices Uptown" for "tasty"
cuisine; spice-lovers cheer "go for the burn!"*

**Indochine**/LS ⟨ 17 | 16 | 13 | $36 ⟩
430 Lafayette St. (bet. 4th St. & Astor Pl.), 505-5111
*M – "Intriguing" Vietnamese food keeps a "gorgeous
crowd" coming, despite a "decline" from this restaurant's
trendy heyday; it's most "enjoyable late at night", but the
staff can be "snotty and zombielike."*

**Isabella's**/LS ⟨ 17 | 18 | 15 | $29 ⟩
359 Columbus Ave. (77th St.), 724-2100
*U – This "young-and-hip" West Side "scene" has "great
people-watching" from its streetside tables and solid
Italian food that keep it "crowded and noisy."*

**Island**/LS ⟨ 16 | 16 | 15 | $35 ⟩
1305 Madison Ave. (bet. 92nd & 93rd Sts.), 996-1200
*M – It's a toss-up whether the waiters or customers are
more "preppy" at this Carnegie Hill graze-and-gaze
bistro that specializes in seafood, pasta and salad;
though still popular, say critics it has slipped recently.*

**Island Spice**\*/S ⟨ 21 | 14 | 17 | $23 ⟩
402 W. 44th St. (bet. 9th & 10th Aves.), 765-1737
*It's fun to discover a good new restaurant, and this
"genuinely friendly" Theater District Caribbean is one; it
serves great jerk chicken in a mottled green space that
makes you listen for an island breeze.*

**Isle of Capri** ⟨ 14 | 14 | 16 | $35 ⟩
1028 Third Ave. (61st St.), 223-9430
*"Unsung but excellent" vs. "competent – no more"
states the opposing cases on this quaint old-style Italian
Eastsider; critics call it an "upscale Mamma Leone's";
at least it's "a chance to see Tom Wolfe."*

**Iso**/LS ⟨ 24 | 17 | 19 | $27 ⟩
175 Second Ave. (11th St.), 777-0361
*U – "Not your ordinary fare", this "jumpin' Japanese"
offers "creative" sushi and cooked food at "fair" prices;
Keith Haring art and flowers lend a "fun" "Downtown"
feel to "the cramped quarters."*

**Isola**/LSX ⟨ 18 | 14 | 16 | $27 ⟩
485 Columbus Ave. (bet. 83rd & 84th Sts.), 362-7400
*U – The "lively atmosphere", "nice decor" and "satisfying
Italian" food at this new Upper West Side pasta house
are undercut by a din that makes it a "candidate for
NYC's noisiest restaurant."*

|  F  |  D  |  S  |  C  |

### Itcho*/S
|23|13|22|$31|

402 E. 78th St. (bet. 1st & York Aves.), 517-5340
*U – Why our surveyors say "don't tell anybody" about this and then tell us is a conundrum; here distinctive Japanese dishes and genial service come in a setting which was a secret – until now.*

### I Tre Merli/LS
|15|17|12|$35|

463 W. Broadway (bet. Houston & Prince), 254-8699
*M – An original SoHo "hangout", this "trendy" Italian with its "Euro-crowd" and "sexy staff" is a "place to be if you want to be seen"; others nominate this "so-'80s" scene for "the Posers Hall of Fame."*

### Jackson Hole/LS
|14| 8 |12|$15|

232 E. 64th St. (bet. 2nd & 3rd Aves.), 371-7187/X
517 Columbus Ave. (85th St.), 362-5177
1270 Madison Ave. (91st St.), 427-2820/S
1611 Second Ave. (bet. 83rd & 84th Sts.), 737-8788
521 Third Ave. (35th St.), 679-3264
*M – "Here's the beef" cry fans of this bright neon-lit chain that specializes in bargain-priced "big, juicy" "burgers the size of Wyoming" that "kids love"; others find it "vulgar and noisy", "high on grease, low on decor."*

### Jai Ya Thai (Queens)/LS
|22|11|14|$23|

81-11 Broadway (81st St.), Elmhurst, 718-651-1330
396 Third Ave. (28th St.), 889-1330
*U – The new East Side location of this renowned Thai lives up to the original's legacy of "great gutsy fare" at low prices; both outlets need help on decor and service.*

### Jane Street Seafood Cafe/S
|21|15|18|$32|

31 Eighth Ave. (Jane St.), 242-0003
*U – Simple, "very fresh" seafood, courteous service and a "warm", "rustic" New England setting are the draws at this "unprententious" Villager; the fireplace is cozy in winter, but no reserving may mean a wait outside.*

### Japanese on Hudson/LS
|16|11|15|$23|

551 Hudson St. (bet. Perry & 11th Sts.), 691-5379
*M – The $15.75 "all-you-can-eat" buffet Saturday and Monday nights is the high point at this "funky" Villager; however, it's an example of "quantity over quality."*

### Japonica/S
|23|17|19|$30|

100 University Pl. (12th St.), 243-7752
*U – "Among NYC's great sushi bars", this Villager serves "fresh", "giant-sized" sushi and a wide choice of cooked food in a room notable for its coziness; "very popular", it's well "worth the wait."*

79

| | F | D | S | C |

### Jean Claude/LSX     | 20 | 15 | 15 | $32 |
137 Sullivan St. (bet. Houston & Prince Sts.), 475-9232
*M – "Close your eyes and you're in Paris" is the feeling conveyed by this new SoHo bistro; though service is flawed, the "homey fare" is easy on the wallet.*

### Jean Lafitte/LS     | 17 | 17 | 17 | $40 |
68 W. 58th St. (bet. 5th & 6th Aves.), 751-2323
*U – This "very French"-feeling bistro has stood the test of time, serving "reliable" hearty fare to a "grown-up" crowd at fair prices; it's good for a steak-frites lunch or pre– or post–Carnegie Hall dinner.*

### Jekyll & Hyde/LS     | 12 | 21 | 14 | $21 |
91 7th Ave. So. (bet. Barrow & Grove Sts.), 989-7701
*M – Beer drinking, not eating, is the point at this Village "novelty" pub with a haunted house theme; a "mostly under-25 crowd" find the gimmicks amusing, but their elders don't; as for dining, "the food is Hyde."*

### Jerry's/S     | 18 | 14 | 14 | $27 |
101 Prince St. (bet. Greene & Mercer Sts.), 966-9464
*U – This casual glorified SoHo diner, with its "colorful" "artsy crowd" and "innovative" American fare, is praised as a "hip Downtown hangout" with "consistent value."*

### Jerry's 103/LS     | 18 | 15 | 15 | $28 |
103 Second Ave. (6th St.), 777-4120
*U – "Bring your attitude and earplugs" to this lively late-night East Village grill, with its "minimalist" decor, "large portions" of creative American food, and "narcissistic" waiters in muscle shirts.*

### Jewel of India/S     | 21 | 22 | 19 | $31 |
15 W. 44th St. (bet. 5th & 6th Aves.), 869-5544
*U – "A real gem", this Midtown Northern Indian within walking distance of the Theater District has "decor galore" and a staff that "tries hard to please"; you won't ever do better than the $11.95 lunch buffet.*

### Jezebel/L     | 19 | 25 | 18 | $39 |
630 Ninth Ave. (45th St.), 582-1045
*U – "Blanche DuBois would have loved" "this Southern parlor"; though its food is "very good", it's not up to the super bordello setting, but that's no complaint.*

### Jim McMullen/LS     | 17 | 17 | 17 | $33 |
1341 Third Ave. (bet. 76th & 77th Sts.), 861-4700
*U – Serving everyone from singles to "mature diners", this East Side standby "remains steady", "trustworthy and tasty"; the "uncomplicated American" food, "congenial" "clubby" setting and "good values" keep it cooking at brunch, lunch and dinner.*

**Jockey Club, The**/S    | 19 | 22 | 20 | $49 |
Ritz-Carlton, 112 Central Pk. S. (bet. 6th & 7th), 664-7700
M – At this handsome wood-paneled horse-themed
restaurant, the food has been seen as "overpriced" and
"average" in the past; recent renovations and an
upgrade in the kitchen promise Ritz-Carlton quality.

**Joe Allen**/LS    | 15 | 14 | 15 | $30 |
326 W. 46th St. (bet. 8th & 9th Aves.), 581-6464
U – "Good plain" fare served in "record time" is the
strength of this legendary Theater District pub; best
bets are burgers, salads and "celebrity-gazing."

**John Clancy's**/S **(CLOSED)**    | 23 | 19 | 20 | $47 |
206 E. 63rd St. (bet. 2nd & 3rd Aves.), 752-6666
181 W. 10th St. (7th Ave. So.), 242-7350/L
M – "Fish with grace and taste" is offered at the original
Village and newer East Side locations of this excellent
seafood restaurant that pioneered mesquite grilling in
NYC; all aspects are upscale, even the "fancy" prices.

**John's of 12th Street**/SX    | 21 | 14 | 17 | $24 |
302 E. 12th St. (east of 2nd Ave.), 475-9531
M – Heaping helpings of "lusty" Southern Italian food,
including "very good brick-oven pizza", are served in a
dark, crowded, candlelit East Village room; the menu is
a "great value", but reactions to the decor vary.

**John's Pizzeria**/LSX    | 23 | 8 | 13 | $15 |
408 E. 64th St. (bet. 1st & York Aves.), 935-2895
278 Bleecker St. (bet. 6th & 7th Aves.), 243-1680
U – "NY's most popular pizzeria", because of its thin,
"slightly-charred crust" and myriad toppings; lines are
"long" and the service "crusty", but the general reaction
to this "pizza mecca" is "yum."

**JO JO**    | 24 | 18 | 18 | $47 |
160 E. 64th St. (bet. Lexington & 3rd Aves.), 223-5656
M – Despite star chef Jean-Georges Vongerichten's
"beautifully prepared" bistro fare, this "charming" duplex
Eastsider, with three different seating areas, has critics
who grouse "you're treated with more finesse at Ho-Jo's."

**Josephina**/LS    | 19 | 16 | 17 | $33 |
1900 Broadway (bet. 63rd & 64th Sts.), 799-1000
M – An "imaginative", well-priced New American menu
with lots of fresh fish makes this Lincoln Center
newcomer "a find for dieters", despite a "big, cold" room.

**Jour et Nuit**/LS    | 19 | 18 | 14 | $42 |
337 W. Broadway (Grand St.), 925-5971
M – A young "Euro crowd", "busy kissing cheeks", flocks
to this trendy SoHo bistro with food that's often very
good, but can be "like night and day"; sit upstairs, it's
more "cozy"; query – "does Eileen Ford own this place?"

| | F | D | S | C |
|---|---|---|---|---|

### J. Sung Dynasty/S
`| 20 | 19 | 19 | $32 |`
Hotel Lexington, 511 Lexington Ave. (48th St.), 355-1200
*U – Though this "elegant" Midtown Chinese is mostly described as "superior" and "refreshingly different", we hear hints it's "beginning to slip"; still, its location, lack of crowding and solid service make it a "must try."*

### Juanita's/LS
`| 14 | 11 | 13 | $23 |`
1309 Third Ave. (75th St.), 517-3800
*M – Always jumping, the "twenty-something" crowd considers this "Mexican bar scene" with "memorable margaritas" and piquant salsa to be "great fun"; critics call it "Taco Bell with a liquor license."*

### Kalinka/S
`| 16 | 11 | 14 | $30 |`
1067 Madison Ave. (bet. 80th & 81st Sts.), 472-9656
*M – "Small but charming", this East Side storefront is applauded for its "very filling" stuffed cabbage, borscht, blini and Russian tea served to classical music; the less impressed call it "ersatz Russian."*

### Kan Pai/LS
`| – | – | – | I |`
1482 Second Ave. (bet. 77th & 78th Sts.), 772-9560
245 Park Ave. S. (bet. 19th & 20th Sts.), 529-2888
*Light blue neon is the principal design theme of these attractive Japanese siblings, where the food is both "good" and "real cheap."*

### Karyatis (Queens)/LS
`| 21 | 17 | 17 | $30 |`
35-03 Broadway (bet. 35th & 36th Sts.), 718-204-0666
*U – Evoking "memories of Greece", this "authentic" Astoria spot delivers "great" appetizers and fresh seafood; it's "worth the trip" for an experience that's hard to duplicate in less than ten hours of flight time.*

### Katz's Deli/SX
`| 16 | 7 | 9 | $14 |`
205 E. Houston St. (Ludlow St.), 254-2246
*M – Long "the definition of a NY deli" with "huge sandwiches and "obnoxious" waiters, this sprawling Lower East Side cafeteria has seen better days.*

### Keens Chop House
`| 18 | 19 | 17 | $39 |`
72 W. 36th St. (bet. 5th & 6th Aves.), 947-3636
*U – Steaks and mutton chops in a "cozy", "clubby", 19th-century setting attract Macy's shoppers and Garden-goers; look for "old-world charm" and Americana of museum quality.*

### Keewah Yen/S
`| 19 | 15 | 18 | $30 |`
50 W. 56th St. (bet. 5th & 6th Aves.), 246-0770
*M – Mixed reactions meet this Midtown Cantonese; most see it as "top-drawer" with "excellent", "unusual" fare and "hospitable" service; others find "uninspired" dishes in a "gloomy" setting.*

| | F | D | S | C |
|---|---|---|---|---|

### Khyber Pass/LS
`| 19 | 14 | 14 | $21 |`
34 St. Mark's Pl. (bet. 2nd & 3rd Aves.), 473-0989
*M – Venture into "another time and place" with a visit to this "bargain" "no-frills" East Village Afghan where you sample "exotic flavors" reclining on pillows.*

### Kiev/LSX
`| 17 | 6 | 12 | $14 |`
117 Second Ave. (7th St.), 674-4040
*U – Challah French toast, chicken soup, cheese blintzes and other good "cheap" eats keep this 24-hour East Village "home-cooking" Ukranian filled with students, actors, cabbies and "lots of characters"; at 6 AM, who cares about the "grungy" "coffee-shop" ambiance.*

### Kiiroi Hana/S
`| 20 | 12 | 16 | $29 |`
23 W. 56th St. (bet. 5th & 6th Aves.), 582-7499
*U – "Fresh", "high-quality" sushi and hearty soups at "good prices" keep this Japanese spot packed despite "bland decor" and a Midtown location choked with competitors; sit at the sushi bar and enjoy the specials.*

### King Crab/LS
`| 17 | 13 | 16 | $27 |`
871 Eighth Ave. (52nd St.), 765-4393
*M – This seafood storefront is still a bargain and worth a visit, especially when the "great soft-shell crabs" are in season; seating is "cramped", but gaslights add charm.*

### Kinoko/LS
`| 17 | 10 | 14 | $26 |`
165 W. 72nd St. (bet. Columbus & B'way), 580-5900
*M – "If you're hungry, this all-you-can-eat sushi spot is a "great deal" at $19.95; while "not the best sushi in town", it's a good West Side neighborhood choice.*

### Kitchen Club
`| – | – | – | M |`
30 Prince St. (Mott St.), 274-0025
*Quiet classical music sets the tone at this small Zenlike corner storefront where Dutch-born chef Marja Samson presides from her open kitchen, cooking modestly priced, "Euro cuisine with Japanese accents"; the word we hear is "go!"*

### Kodnoi*/LS
`| 19 | 15 | 16 | $25 |`
208 E. 60th St. (bet. 2nd & 3rd Aves.), 688-9885
*U – Not too well known, but this "affordable", "stylish" Bloomingdale's neighbor deserve more attention for its unusually good and diverse spicy fare.*

### Kom Tang Soot Bul House/LS
`| – | – | – | I |`
32 W. 32nd St. (bet. 5th Ave. & B'way), 947-8482
*The cheap Korean food here is good enough to linger over, but the "drab" decor will make you happy that the service is "fast"; English is definitely a third language here.*

|   | F | D | S | C |
|---|---|---|---|---|

### Koo Koo's Bistro/LS
`| 15 | 15 | 15 | $28 |`
1584 Second Ave. (82nd St.), 737-2322
*M – "Cute" and "kookie" are the selling points of this
East Side bistro, not the "small portions" of "uneven"
fare that runs from French to peanut butter sandwiches.*

### Kulu/S
`| – | – | – | E |`
1770 Second Ave. (bet. 92nd & 93rd Sts.), 996-4550
*Large video screens over the bar are usually sure signs
of second-rate food and a young scene; surprisingly,
neither applies at this new Eastsider; in the back a
sedate upscale crowd on handsome green banquettes
is clearly enjoying the French-American cuisine.*

### Kurumazushi
`| 22 | 13 | 19 | $43 |`
18 W. 56th St. (bet. 5th & 6th Aves.), 541-9030
*M – An old favorite for its "excellent, very fresh" sushi
and quiet, efficient service, but not for its "steep" prices
or dreary decor – they ought to "fix this place up."*

### La Barca
`| 20 | 17 | 17 | $41 |`
40 Fletcher St. (bet. Front & South Sts.), 514-9704
*U – You can rely on this "quiet" Northern Italian for
"excellent" seafood, antipasto" and "good service";
though "expensive", Wall Streeters aren't complaining.*

### La Boheme/LS
`| 18 | 16 | 16 | $33 |`
24 Minetta Ln. (bet. W. 3rd & Bleecker), 473-6447
*U – "Cute" and "cozy", this Village bistro is popular for
its thin-crust pizzas, pastas and other Provençal fare
served in a "rustic" setting with high-tech touches; "slow"
service and noise are drawbacks.*

### La Boite en Bois/SX
`| 20 | 16 | 19 | $40 |`
75 W. 68th St. (bet. CPW & Columbus), 874-2705
*U – This "teeny-weeny" bistro stands tall in the Lincoln
Center area, thanks to "good" country French cooking,
"charming" ambiance, and "lovely, personal" service.*

### La Bonne Soupe/LS
`| 14 | 11 | 12 | $19 |`
48 W. 55th St. (bet. 5th & 6th Aves.), 586-7650
*M – Usually "bonne", this "no-frills" low-budget
Midtowner is ok for "fast, hearty" soups, salads and
other bistro basics; critics rate it "comme ci, comme ça.*

### La Boulangere/SX
`| 17 | 11 | 13 | $19 |`
49 E. 21st St. (bet. Park Ave. & B'way), 475-8582
*U – "A flour-filled menu of breads, pastries, sandwiches
and pizzas make this Gramercy bakery/cafe a "nice
change from NY coffee shops for a French breakfast" or
a "quick" midday pick-me-up.*

**L'Acajou**/LS | 20 | 13 | 18 | $37 |

53 W. 19th St. (bet. 5th & 6th Aves.), 645-1706
*U – Picture an "Alsatian bistro by Edward Hopper" and you get the feel of this offbeat Chelsea French, which fans call "a great find" for its "hearty", "consistently good" food that "doesn't bust one's bank account."*

**LA CARAVELLE** | 25 | 24 | 25 | $62 |

33 W. 55th St. (bet. 5th & 6th Aves.), 586-4252
*U – Enjoying a "renaissance", this French Classic is once again "superb in every regard", from "exquisite" haute cuisine and "gracious" service to its flower-filled setting; try it again for yourself.*

**La Caridad**/LSX | 18 | 5 | 12 | $13 |

2199 Broadway (78th St.), 874-2780
*M – Everyone from lawyers to cabbies likes a "big" bargain, which is why they can be found at this "basic-as-they-come" West Side Cubano-Chino, "impatient" service and lines notwithstanding.*

**La Chandelle**\*/S | 16 | 15 | 19 | $24 |

2231 Broadway (bet. 79th & 80th Sts.), 787-8466
*U – "Quality with a casual touch" distinguishes this West Side French bistro; those who've tried it praise it as a "lovely little brunch find" with affordable prices.*

**La Collina**\*/S | 17 | 16 | 17 | $26 |

1402 Lexington Ave. (92nd St.), 860-1218
*U – "Once the word gets out, this place will fly", say those who've discovered this East Side Italian newcomer's home cooking", "pleasant, nonpretentious" atmosphere and "doting" service.*

**La Colombe d'Or**/S | 22 | 20 | 20 | $45 |

134 E. 26th St. (bet. Lexington & 3rd Aves.), 689-0666
*U – Exuding "true French country charm", this Murray Hill brownstone bistro further beguiles with its "robust", "well-done" provincial fare ("outstanding cassoulet" is a winter favorite); it's "like a quick trip to France."*

**LA COTE BASQUE** | 27 | 27 | 25 | $63 |

5 E. 55th St. (bet. 5th & Madison Aves.), 688-6525
*M – A "timeless classic", this French standby's fervent fans find it a "favorite forever" for its "exceptional" haute cuisine ("give up on your cholesterol for tonight"), "superb" service and "ever-so-beautiful" setting, highlighted by murals of the Basque coast; critics call it "heavy", "stuffy" and "old."*

|   | F | D | S | C |
|---|---|---|---|---|

### Lafayette
| 24 | 24 | 24 | $63 |

Drake Hotel, 65 E. 56th St. (bet. Madison & Park), 832-1565
*M – As always, this expensive and elegant haute French gets high praise for its "polished and sophisticated" performance; but in the wake of chef turnovers, some say "the magic has gone."*

### La Focaccia/LSX
| 18 | 15 | 15 | $28 |

51 Bank St. (W. 4th St.), 675-3754
*M – "Romantic and cozy in winter, open and airy in summer", this West Village Northern Italian cafe would be a real winner if it were more consistent.*

### La Fondue/LS
| 15 | 11 | 13 | $21 |

43 W. 55th St. (bet. 5th & 6th Aves.), 581-0820
*M – Fondue fanciers consider this "a dipper's delight" thanks to its "decent, cheap" fare; however, as ratings show, the dated decor and service need help.*

### La Fusta* (Queens)/SX
| 19 | 12 | 18 | $27 |

80-32 Baxter Ave. (Broadway), 718-429-8222
*M – The setting is "homely", but grilled meats and other "good gaucho food" compensate at this Argentine-Italian in Elmhurst; it's as close to the pampas as you get in NY.*

### La Goulue/S
| 17 | 20 | 16 | $45 |

28 E. 70th St. (bet. Madison & Park Aves.), 988-8169
*M – "So elegant, so European, and so mediocre" is the prevailing view of this "stylish" East Side bistro, but a rise in food ratings makes another taste in order.*

### LA GRENOUILLE/L
| 27 | 27 | 25 | $66 |

3 E. 52nd St. (bet. 5th & Madison Aves.), 752-1495
*U – "Exquisite in every way", this Classic French beauty is one of those rare "grand dames" that keeps improving with age; the "superb" cuisine is "better than ever", service exudes "charm and finesse", and the setting is forever a "flower-filled paradise"; most of its celebrated clientele consider it "one of NYC's treasures"; N.B. there's a charming studio upstairs for private parties.*

### Laguna/S
| 17 | 13 | 14 | $26 |

148 E. 91st St. (2nd Ave.), 427-3106
*U – "Good food at good prices" is a '90s formula for success; this East Side Italian's simple fare is overcoming minimal decor and spotty service.*

### Lai Lai West/S
| 16 | 13 | 15 | $19 |

859 Ninth Ave. (56th St.), 586-5083
*M – Though "nothing special", this Mandarin-Szechuan offers "better-than-average" Chinese food in a "pleasant", if simple, setting at "wok-bottom" prices.*

### La Jumelle/LS
| 16 | 14 | 12 | $27 |

55 Grand St. (bet. Wooster & W. B'way), 941-9651
*U – With "surprisingly good" food at low prices, this SoHo bistro is "a scene" with "young bodies in black"; "flaky service" is the price you pay to be in on the action.*

### La Luncheonette/L
| 20 | 16 | 18 | $32 |

130 Tenth Ave. (18th St.), 675-0342
*U – "It doesn't look like much from the outside", but this "offbeat" Chelsea bistro has "wonderful" French country cooking and "cozy", "stylishly funky" quarters.*

### La Maison Japonaise
| 19 | 18 | 18 | $32 |

125 E. 39th St. (bet. Park & Lexington Aves.), 682-7375
*M – Despite an attractive townhouse setting, this Murray Hill Franco-Japanese mixes cuisines and in turn gets mixed reactions: e.g. "delightful marriage of East and West" vs. "this marriage could use counseling."*

### La Mangeoire/S (92)
| 17 | 17 | 17 | $40 |

1008 Second Ave. (bet. 53rd & 54th Sts.), 759-7086
*U – This rustic Midtown French bistro is a solid performer across the board with "heavy but good" food, "charming" decor and "attentive" service.*

### Lamarca
| 20 | 8 | 13 | $17 |

161 E. 22nd St. (3rd Ave.), 674-6363
*U – Pasta and BYO lovers say "you can't go wrong" with the "fresh, made-to-order pastas" at this "no-frills" Eastsider; it's "strictly a Formica place", but "cheap."*

### La Mediterranee/S (92)
| 17 | 14 | 16 | $37 |

947 Second Ave. (bet. 50th & 51st Sts.), 755-4155
*U – A "good old-fashioned" Midtown French bistros that's always "pleasurable" for a "reliable", fairly priced meal.*

### La Metairie/LS
| 23 | 20 | 20 | $43 |

189 W. 10th St. (corner of W. 4th St.), 989-0343
*U – "More charming than ever" since it expanded, this West Village bistro inspires effusive praise for both its French country cooking (four points up from last year).*

### La Mirabelle/S
| 19 | 14 | 19 | $36 |

Cambridge Hotel, 333 W. 86th (bet. West End & Riverside), 496-0458
*U – "Modest" by most standards, this "low-key" bistro is called the "miracle on 86th Street" by Westsiders who say it's "homey, comfy, and easygoing" – "quel plaisir."*

### Landmark Tavern/LS
| 16 | 19 | 17 | $28 |

626 11th Ave. (46th St.), 757-8595
*U – Still open and going strong after 124 years, this tavern with good Irish pub food exudes charm.*

| | F | D | S | C |
|---|---|---|---|---|

### La Petite Auberge/S
| | 19 | 16 | 19 | $35 |

116 Lexington Ave. (28th St.), 689-5003
*U – "A real bistro that's been around since long before bistros were in", this Country French satisfies with "hearty", affordable food, "caring service" and a "cozy" (if "timeworn") setting; don't miss the soufflés!*

### La Petite Ferme
| | 19 | 19 | 19 | $45 |

973 Lexington Ave. (bet. 70th & 71st Sts.), 249-3272
*U – Take "a trip to Provence" via this "rustic" East Side French; though "very good", the bistro food takes a back seat to the "beguiling" setting and rear garden.*

### La Primavera
| | 19 | 19 | 19 | $44 |

234 W. 48th St. (bet. B'way & 8th Ave.), 586-2797
*M – A "spacious" setting and "above-average" food make this a "top Italian choice" in the Theater District; since the "polite and caring" service may become "erratic" in the pre-curtain rush, go at off-hours.*

### LA RESERVE
| | 25 | 25 | 24 | $55 |

4 W. 49th St. (bet. 5th & 6th Aves.), 247-2993
*U – NYers are unreserved in praising this "gracious and relaxing" Midtown French; what fuels their enthusiasm is the "outstanding" Classic cuisine, "impeccable" service, presided over by owner Jean-Louis Missud, and a lovely flower-filled setting that's "very impressive" for business or romance.*

### La Ripaille/L
| | 21 | 19 | 19 | $41 |

605 Hudson St. (bet. W. 12th & Bethune Sts.), 255-4406
*U – "French to its core", this "small but cozy" and "rustic" West Village "hideaway" has "excellent" bistro food; it's "like going to Paris without the jet lag."*

### La Rivista
| | 17 | 14 | 16 | $41 |

313 W. 46th St. (bet. 8th & 9th Aves.), 245-1707
*M – To some this is "one of the better Restaurant Row spots", but to others it's "just average" with "rushed, erratic" service; timing may be key: "try it after curtain time when it simmers down."*

### La Sarten/S
| | 16 | 11 | 14 | $21 |

564 Amsterdam Ave. (bet. 87th & 88th Sts.), 787-6448
*U – "Well-seasoned" Dominican dishes, and a "fun, friendly" ambiance make this West Side "hole in the wall" a lifesaver "when funds are low."*

### Las Marcias*/LS
| | 14 | 8 | 13 | $16 |

588 Amsterdam Ave. (bet. 88th & 89th Sts.), 595-8121
*U – Enjoy an "authentic taste" of Dominican; service and decor are strictly no-frills, but so are the prices; after their hearty breakfast, "you won't need dinner."*

|   |   | F | D | S | C |
|---|---|---|---|---|---|

**La Strada** (S.I.)/LS | 19 | 15 | 17 | $33 |
78-80 E. 4th St. (bet. 2nd & 3rd Aves.), 353-8026
M – "Tasty" Southern Italian food makes this
"comfortable, folksy" place a "pleasant surprise" with
"the feeling of Sicily", critics call it "underwhelming."

**La Taza De Oro**/LS | – | – | – | I |
96 Eighth Ave. (bet. 14th & 15th Sts.), 243-9946
The taxis lined up in front of this "very basic" Cuban
coffee shop are a sure sign that the food inside is both
good and cheap ($6.50 and under); the soup alone
makes a meal.

**La Topiaire** | 18 | 17 | 18 | $36 |
120 W. 45th St. (bet. 6th & B'way), 819-1405
M – Times Square needs more French restaurants like
this newcomer; though the food can be "wonderful" and
the staff tries hard, oddly it's often "deserted."

**Lattanzi Ristorante** | 20 | 16 | 18 | $41 |
361 W. 46th St. (bet. 8th & 9th Aves.), 315-0980
M – "Very good" Northern Italian food along with "unique"
Roman-Jewish specials make this a Restaurant Row
"winner"; "a hassle pre-theater", it's best after 8 PM,
especially in the garden.

**L'Auberge du Midi***/LS | 22 | 21 | 19 | $38 |
310 W. 4th St. (bet. Bank & 12th Sts.), 242-4705
U – "Very French", this "underrated" West Village bistro
provides "really outstanding" food in a "very nice"
setting; critics say it's "too expensive".

**Laura Belle**/L | 16 | 24 | 17 | $49 |
120 W. 43rd St. (bet. 6th Ave. & B'way), 819-1000
M – The "setting is the main attraction" at this "elegant"
'90s version of a '40s supper club; it's ideal for dancing
and dallying, though sadly not for dining, since the
Eclectic food "could be better" and service is "aloof".

**La Vieille Auberge** | 18 | 15 | 19 | $35 |
347 W. 46th St. (bet. 8th & 9th Aves.), 247-4284
U – This "cramped but cozy" "time warp" Theater
District bistro is a "favorite" of many, thanks to its well
prepared, well-priced food and "welcoming" staff.

**Le Bar Bat**/LS | 12 | 21 | 13 | $33 |
311 W. 57th St. (bet. 8th & 9th Aves.), 307-7228
M – "You have to be batty" to eat at this cavernous multi-
level French-Vietnamese club/restaurant, but the real
point is to flit about, dance, drink "wacky" cocktails and
admire the "Addams Family"–meets–"Miss Saigon" decor.

|  | F | D | S | C |
|---|---|---|---|---|

## LE BERNARDIN
| 27 | 26 | 25 | $69 |
|---|---|---|---|

155 W. 51st St. (bet. 6th & 7th Aves.), 489-1515
*U – "Neptune himself couldn't do better" than this "phenomenal" but "pricey" French fish specialist; it draws oceans of praise for its "simply smashing" seafood, "comfortable" and "serene" setting and "perfect" service; the gates of this "seafood heaven" open most affordably at its $42 prix fixe lunch.*

### Le Bilboquet/S
| 18 | 16 | 13 | $40 |
|---|---|---|---|

25 E. 63rd St. (bet. Madison & Park Aves.), 751-3036
*U – "A French accent" or fashion model's looks get you a "warm reception" at this stylish East Side bistro, where a "Euro-chic" crowd nibbles between cheek kisses.*

### Le Boeuf a la Mode
| 19 | 18 | 19 | $41 |
|---|---|---|---|

539 E. 81st St. (bet. York & East End), 249-1473
*U – Locals rely on this "warm", "neighborly" Yorkville bistro for "reasonably priced", "solid" French food enhanced by a "pretty" setting.*

### Le Chantilly/S
| 22 | 23 | 22 | $55 |
|---|---|---|---|

106 E. 57th St. (bet. Park & Lexington Aves.), 751-2931
*M – "Lovely" and "very civilized", this Classic French standby may not be a trailblazer, but it covers familiar ground well, providing "excellent" haute cuisine, a "plush" setting and good service; critics find it "staid", but many feel it "never gets the recognition it deserves."*

## LE CIRQUE
| 27 | 25 | 25 | $69 |
|---|---|---|---|

The Mayfair Hotel, 58 E. 65th St. (bet. Madison & Park Aves.), 794-9292
*U – "One of the best shows in town", this "charged-up" electric circus is not only "the ultimate NY society restaurant", but a culinary "powerhouse" as well; fans of its "flawless" French cuisine report that chef Daniel Boulud's departure hasn't dimmed the luster of the food, and they know nothing can dim the luster of NY's No.1 host, Sirio Maccioni; yes, it's "too damn crowded", but who cares when the people at your elbow are named Kissinger, Lauder or Jagger.*

### L'Ecole
| 21 | 18 | 19 | $40 |
|---|---|---|---|

462 Broadway (Grand St.), 219-3300
*U – Catch a rising culinary star at this airy SoHo postmodern, where students from the French Culinary Institute run the kitchen; "they do their homework" and it shows, with most of their efforts getting "high marks"; even the rare failure is at a low prix fixe tab.*

### Le Comptoir/LS
| 15 | 19 | 14 | $45 |
|---|---|---|---|

227 E. 67th St. (bet. 2nd & 3rd Aves.), 794-4950
*U – Ever wonder how models stay so thin? they hang out at places like this "chic" East Side hot spot; P.S. the word is the food has improved of late.*

### Lello Ristorante
| 20 | 18 | 19 | $49 |

65 E. 54th St. (bet. Madison & Park Aves.), 751-1555
*M – This Midtown Northern Italian's "staying power" is easy to explain: it caters to an "executive crowd" with "always good", if "pricey", food, a "smart, subdued" (if rather "dark") setting, and staff who "know their business"; still some find it "boring" and depressing.*

### Le Madeleine/S
| 17 | 17 | 16 | $33 |

403 W. 43rd St. (bet. 9th & 10th Aves.), 246-2993
*M – A "charming" enclosed garden room and convenience to off-Broadway theaters are the main assets of this "unpretentious" West Midtown French bistro; the food may be "modest" but so are the prices; brunch is "a winner."*

### Le Madri/LS
| 22 | 22 | 19 | $50 |

168 W. 18th St. (7th Ave.), 727-8022
*U – You "can't get more stylish" than this "handsome" Chelsea Tuscan; nearly everyone praises its "creative" Classic Italian cuisine, calling the results "excellent" and "always interesting"; only prices and attitude get knocks.*

### Le Max/LS
| 18 | 17 | 18 | $34 |

147 W. 43rd St. (bet. 6th Ave. & B'way), 764-3705
*U – "Up and coming" new Theater District bistro with a "large, well-prepared menu", "spacious" setting, and fair prices; "if trying harder counts, these people should make it"; the $19.95 prix fixe dinner is a good intro.*

### Lenge/S (92)
| 17 | 12 | 15 | $25 |

1465 Third Ave. (bet. 82nd & 83rd Sts.), 535-9661
200 Columbus Ave. (69th St.), 799-9188
*U – No big deal, with "ho-hum" decor, these crosstown siblings retain local followings with "above-average" Japanese food at below-average prices.*

### L'Entrecote
| 18 | 16 | 19 | $35 |

1057 First Ave. (bet. 57th & 58th Sts.), 755-0080
*U – A "local favorite" for 20 years, this "cozy", "friendly" bistro provides good steaks, pommes frites and other "sturdy French fare" at a fair price.*

### Leopard, The
| 22 | 22 | 23 | $52 |

253 E. 50th St. (bet. 2nd & 3rd Aves.), 759-3735
*U – Perfect for parties, this East Midtown townhouse with its "romantic" dining rooms offers first-rate French-Continental food and unlimited wine as part of its prix fixe menus ($36 at lunch, $46 at dinner).*

### Le Pactole/S
| 19 | 23 | 18 | $49 |

2 World Fin. Ctr., 225 Liberty St. (West St.), 945-9444
*U – "One of the prettiest" and "perfect at sunset", thanks to its Hudson views, this WFC French's food "can't match the magnificent setting", but by any other standard, it's "very good", with Sunday brunch tops.*

| F | D | S | C |
|---|---|---|---|

### LE PERIGORD
| 25 | 22 | 24 | $59 |

405 E. 52nd St. (east of 1st Ave.), 755-6244
*U – "Always wonderful", this "timeless" Classic French
is regarded as "one of the best" for its "superb" food,
"plush, quiet" setting, and "impeccable service with a
smile"; "you're made to feel like an old friend here", and
the prix fixe meals are a "best value among top gourmet
places"; all in all, "you can't ask for more."*

### Le Pescadou/S
| 20 | 16 | 18 | $42 |

18 King St. (6th Ave.), 924-3434
*M – To admirers, this SoHo seafood bistro is a "poor
man's Le Bernardin", serving "fab" fresh fish in a
"charming", "very French" setting, but not everyone's
reeled in by high prices and "cramped" quarters.*

### Le Pistou
| 21 | 18 | 20 | $42 |

134 E. 61st St. (bet. Park & Lexington Aves.), 838-7987
*U – The "limos outside" this Eastsider prove that even
the wealthy love a "bargain"; "a spin-off of La Cote
Basque", LP offers "haute" bistro food at non-haute
prices ($20 lunch, $30 dinner) – no wonder it's "jammed."*

### Le Quercy
| 19 | 15 | 19 | $36 |

52 W. 55th St. (bet. 5th & 6th Aves.), 265-8141
*U – Like "dropping into France without dropping the
airfare", this "easygoing" Midtown bistro has "reliable"
food, a "low-key" ambiance and genial service.*

### Le Refuge/LSX
| 22 | 20 | 20 | $46 |

166 E. 82nd St. (bet. Lexington & 3rd Aves.), 861-4505
*U – "True to its name", this Eastsider resembles a
"French country inn" with "good, solid" bourgeois
cooking, "personal" service and a "lovely", "rustic"
setting; it would be totally "idyllic", but for its prices.*

### Le Regence/S
| 25 | 27 | 26 | $65 |

Hotel Plaza Athenee, 37 E. 64th St. (bet. Madison & Park
Aves.), 606-4647
*M – "Versailles in NY"; this "luxurious" French Classic
is rated "magnifique" by most diners for its "fine" food,
"impeccable" service and sky-blue "baroque fantasy"
decor plus a Sunday brunch fit for royalty; despite the
above, it has never been adopted by NYers.*

### Le Relais/LS
| 17 | 17 | 15 | $43 |

712 Madison Ave. (bet. 63rd & 64th Sts.), 751-5108
*M – At this "imitation of Paris", the pricey bistro fare is
good, but watching the Chanel crowd parade from a
sidewalk seat is the main game; "service leans toward
surly" and some say "you're at a disadvantage if not French."*

### Le Rivage                                         | 18 | 15 | 18 | $36 |
340 W. 46th St. (bet. 8th & 9th Aves.), 765-7374
*U – "Priced right", this "old-fashioned but nice" Theater District bistro leaves diners with a "full stomach" and a happy disposition; the $22.75 prix fixe dinner is "almost too much of a good thing."*

### L'Escale                                          | 19 | 16 | 18 | $36 |
43 E. 20th St. (bet. B'way & Park Ave.), 477-1180
*M – Fans call this "comfortable" Flatiron District bistro "a sleeper that deserves to be better known" for its "above-average food", "friendly" service and reasonable prices; critics call it "run-of-the-mill" and "a little tired."*

### LES CELEBRITES                                    | 26 | 28 | 25 | $74 |
Essex House, 160 Central Park So. (59th St.), 247-0300
*U – "The Newcomer of the Year", this French Classic draws rave reviews that correspond to its high ratings (No. 1 for decor and No. 4 overall); star chef Christian Delouvrier's "spectacular" creations are beautifully served in a small but "stunning" room dotted with paintings by Hollywood stars (i.e. the celebrities); some say the prices are hard to swallow, but most consider this "one of the very best", especially for that "special occasion."*

### Les Friandises*/X                                 | 24 | 17 | 20 | $18 |
972 Lexington Ave. (bet. 70th & 71st Sts.), 988-1616
*U – Divine desserts – including "heavenly" tarte tatin and chocolate mousse cake – make this "tiny" Eastsider a paradise for pastry partisans; it's the "perfect afternoon stop-off" and a "sweet treat" anytime.*

### Les Halles/LS                                     | 20 | 15 | 16 | $36 |
411 Park Ave. So. (bet. 28th & 29th Sts.), 679-4111
*M – "Wonderful, but not for your arteries or your ears, this "noisy, bustling" bistro–cum–butcher shop provides "dynamite" meats and frites and other "hearty" French fare in a very "Left Bank", often "frenzied", setting.*

### LESPINASSE/S                                      | 25 | 27 | 25 | $66 |
St. Regis Hotel, 2 East 55th St. (5th Ave.), 339-6719
*M – This "ultra-elegant" Louis XV room is a "plush" showcase for the "original" flavorsome cooking of chef Gray Kunz; to the majority, his Asian-accented French creations are backed up by "gorgeous" decor and "attentive" service; but a minority say "the pieces don't quite fit" and the place feels like 1950 redux.*

### Les Pyrenees/LS                                   | 18 | 16 | 18 | $37 |
251 W. 51st St. (bet. B'way & 8th Ave.), 246-0044
*U – It's "been around forever", but this Theater District "war-horse" now looks and tastes "better than ever", thanks to a renovation that happily included the kitchen.*

| | F | D | S | C |
|---|---|---|---|---|

### Les Routiers/S

| 19 | 17 | 19 | $35 |

568 Amsterdam Ave. (bet. 87th & 88th Sts.), 874-2742
*M* – "Like France" only "friendlier", this West Side bistro
provides "satisfying" food in "cozy", "unassuming" digs;
it's "very basic and very needed" in the area.

### Les Sans Culottes/LS

| 15 | 13 | 16 | $30 |

1085 Second Ave. (bet. 57th & 58th Sts.), 838-6660
*M* – Regulars love to stuff themselves on the "amazing"
choucroute at this homey (or is it "dingy") Eastsider;
most report it's "fun" and "friendly", too.

### Le Steak/S

| 17 | 12 | 16 | $33 |

1089 Second Ave. (bet. 57th & 58th Sts.), 421-9072
*U* – Add "le fish" to the name and you've got the whole
menu at this East Side bistro that offers only steak or
swordfish plus salad or fries; they do both well, which is
why it's "crowded and noisy"; critics yawn "how boring."

### Letizia/LS

| 19 | 17 | 18 | $40 |

1352 First Ave. (bet. 72nd & 73rd Sts.), 517-2244
*U* – Not flashy, but this Eastsider is "most enjoyable" for
its "consistently good" Northern Italian food and
"comfortable" setting; "they try hard" and it shows.

### Le Train Bleu

| 16 | 21 | 17 | $30 |

Bloomingdale's, 6th fl., 1000 Third Ave., 705-2100
*M* – A pleasant place to "drop after you shop", this
"oasis of calm" amid the bustle of Bloomie's provides
"surprisingly good" food in an "Orient Express"–style
setting; critics say it would be "derailed" anywhere else.

### Levana/S

| 20 | 18 | 18 | $45 |

141 W. 69th St. (bet. B'way & Columbus Ave.), 877-8457
*U* – "You can't tell it's kosher", which, ironically, is why
many consider this pricey Westsider to be "the best
kosher in town"; besides "imaginative" Continental fare,
it has a "classy" interior and good service.

### Le Veau d'Or

| 17 | 13 | 16 | $42 |

129 E. 60th St. (bet. Park & Lexington Aves.), 838-8133
*M* – The "granddaddy of bistros" has fans who shout
"vive Le Veau", praising its "simple, good" food; critics
say it's "old and tired", "near retirement."

### Levee, The

| – | – | – | I |

1 First Ave. (1st St.), 505-9263
"It's all 'Bs'" here – bargains, BBQ, brunch, burgers and
brew in a bustling bohemian barroom that's either "a
beaut" or "blah" depending on whom who ask.

| | F | D | S | C |
|---|---|---|---|---|

**Lexington Avenue Grill**/LS                       | 15 | 14 | 14 | $28 |

Loews NY Hotel, 569 Lexington Ave. (51st St.), 753-1515
*M – "Not bad for what it is", this East Side hotel bar
provides "decent", "straightforward" American food, a
"comfortable" setting, and "friendly" (if "spotty") service;
it's "nothing fancy", but neither are the prices.*

**Lido's\*** (S.I.)/S                       | 18 | 8 | 16 | $27 |

37 Victory Blvd. (Bay St.), Tompkinsville, 718-447-1137
*M – The kind of "old-fashioned, family restaurant" they
just don't make anymore, this "landmark" Italian's
"wholesome" food tastes like it came from "Grandma's
kitchen"; ditto the decor and prices.*

**Lion's Head**/LS                       | 14 | 15 | 16 | $26 |

59 Christopher St. (7th Ave. S.), 929-0670
*U – One of the "last bastions of Village bohemianism",
this casual pub remains "a writer's hangout", where
drinking and debating take precedence over dining.*

**Lion's Rock**/S                       | 17 | 21 | 17 | $35 |

316 E. 77th St. (bet. 1st & 2nd Aves.), 988-3610
*M – Though hardly a king of the culinary jungle, word is
that, under new management, "food and service have
improved" at this "casual" Continental, making it worth
another look, perhaps over brunch in the garden.*

**Lipstick Cafe**                       | – | – | – | M |

885 Third Ave. (bet. 53rd & 54th Sts.), 486-8664
*Imaginative fresh breakfasts, sandwiches and salads
produced under the tutelage of star-chef Jean-Georges
Vongerichten in the spacious, airy lobby of the "Lipstick
Building"; no dinner.*

**Little Mushroom Cafe**/S                       | 16 | 11 | 14 | $21 |

183 W. 10th St. (W. 4th St.), 242-1058
*M – Whoever dreamed up this "surprise combo" of
cuisines – Thai, Italian and Indonesian – must have
been eating funny mushrooms, but most say the concept
"works", yielding "light, interesting" and "cheap" results.*

**Little Poland**/S                       | – | – | – | I |

200 Second Ave. (bet. 12th & 13th Sts.), 777-9728
*For "authentic Polish home cooking" at Warsaw prices,
you can't beat this Lower East Side coffee shop where
$10 will leave you stuffed for days.*

**Little Shanghai**/SX (92)                       | 17 | 5 | 11 | $16 |

26 E. Broadway (near Division St.), 925-4238
*U – Only at a "dumpy" Chinatown "hole-in-the-wall" like
this would you expect such "low, low" prices for such
good food – "best dumplings in the world", "amazing
pan fried noodles" – it's almost like being in Shanghai.*

| | F | D | S | C |
|---|---|---|---|---|

**Live Bait**/LS     | 12 | 12 | 11 | $21 |

14 E. 23rd St. (bet. B'way & Madison Ave.), 353-2400
*M – This Dixie dive reels in a rowdy "frat house" crowd
hoping to "hook a model" or at least cast her a line; if you
get past the bar you'll find decent down-home cooking.*

**Lobster Box**(Bronx)/S     | 15 | 13 | 14 | $35 |

34 City Island Ave. (Rochelle St.), 885-1952
*M – For a "pleasant outing", head up to this simple City
Island "landmark", where you can "watch the boats go
by" while enjoying lobster and other seafood.*

**Lofland's N.Y. Grill\***/LS     | 14 | 12 | 15 | $24 |

29 W. 21st St. (bet. 5th & 6th Aves.), 924-3264
*M – "Still a secret", this "friendly" Flatiron pub is "great
for ribs", burgers, beer and other "decent" cheap bar
basics, served in a "casual", neighborhoody setting;
"local flavor" isn't on the menu, but it's the main asset.*

**Lola**/LS     | 20 | 20 | 18 | $38 |

30 W. 22nd St. (bet. 5th & 6th Aves.), 675-6700
*U – "The party continues" at this "festive" Caribbean
with its "sassy, spicy food", "luscious" libations, "swanky"
decor and crowd to match; it's a "supercharged" scene,
with Sunday's "Gospel Brunch" hopping and "bopping."*

**Lora**     | 20 | 19 | 17 | $47 |

104 W. 13th St. (bet. 6th & 7th Aves.), 675-5655
*U – This "romantic, low-key" Village townhouse (ex La
Tulipe) serves always "creative", often "sublime" Eclectic
cuisine; high prices and "spotty" service are its only
drawbacks.*

**Lou G. Siegel**/S     | 13 | 10 | 12 | $32 |

209 W. 38th St. (west of 7th Ave.), 921-4433
*M – "Results vary" at this Garment District kosher:
partisans claim it serves "solid" Jewish food "like
Grandma's"; critics counter "kosher at its expensive
worst"; one writes, "I got married here, but it didn't take."*

**Louie's Westside Cafe**/S     | 17 | 14 | 16 | $29 |

441 Amsterdam Ave. (81st St.), 877-1900
*U – This recently enlarged Westsider has "yummy",
"unpretentious" American food and moderate prices;
despite "off nights", it's said to be "getting better all the
time" and is popular for brunch.*

**Lucky Strike**/LS     | 15 | 15 | 12 | $26 |

59 Grand St. (bet. Wooster & W. B'way), 941-0479
*M – SoHo scene-makers still like to strike poses at this
"truly hip" and "funky" French bistro; the food's good, but
that's not what concerns the late-night "dressed-in-black",
"hoping-to-see-Madonna" crowd.*

|   | F | D | S | C |
|---|---|---|---|---|

**Lucy's Retired Surfers**  | 11 | 13 | 12 | $21 |
503 Columbus Ave. (bet. 84th & 85th Sts.), 787-3009
*U – Jello shots are the culinary high watermark of this
West Side Cal-Mex theme bar, but hey, "who needs
food?" certainly not the young wanna-be "surfer dudes
and babes" who "drink blue whales, shoot the worm",
and admire the wacky Day-Glo decor.*

**Ludlow Street Cafe/LS**  | 16 | 14 | 17 | $18 |
165 Ludlow (bet. E. Houston & Stanton Sts.), 353-0536
*M – Like finding "Vermont on the Lower East Side", this
dark-paneled cafe/bar's Eclectic menu and late-night
live music can be "very good", and it's a "great deal" for
brunch or shopping breaks.*

**Luke's Bar and Grill/LSX**  | 14 | 13 | 14 | $21 |
1394 Third Ave. (bet. 79th & 80th Sts.), 249-7070
*U – "Popular because it's priced right", this "casual"
East Side bar and grill provides "simple", "all-American"
fare in a "warm and friendly" setting that attracts
everyone from "baby-bankers" to "bikers."*

**Luma/S**  | 20 | 15 | 18 | $35 |
200 Ninth Ave. (bet. 22nd & 23rd Sts.), 633-8033
*M – "Not only good for you, but good", this "inventive"
Chelsea seafood-vegetarian serves "haute macro" food;
"polished" service and a "serene" (if small) setting add
appeal; critics say "pass the salt and lower the price."*

**Lum Chin/LS**  | 17 | 16 | 16 | $24 |
91-10 Fourth Ave. (bet. 91st & 92nd Sts.), Brooklyn,
718-238-1822
1640 Forest Ave. (Willowbrook), S.I., 718-442-1707
1771 Highland Blvd. (Liberty St.), S.I., 718-979-6100
4326 Amboy Rd. (bet. Richmond & Armstrong Aves.),
S.I., 718-984-8044
*U – "Not just another Chinese", this minichain is
distinguished by "better-than-average" food, "very nice
(by Chinese standards) decor" and service to match.*

**Lupe's East L.A. Kitchen/SX**  | 17 | 11 | 14 | $17 |
110 Sixth Ave. (Watts St.), 966-1326
*U – A taste of "authentic East LA" in West SoHo, this
"funky" hole-in-the-wall serves "cheap, filling and zesty"
burritos and other Mexican fare at "Mexican prices"; it's
"always a riot" (but not the LA kind).*

**Lusardi's/LS**  | 21 | 17 | 19 | $46 |
1494 Second Ave. (bet. 77th & 78th Sts.), 249-2020
*M – "Fine Northern Italian food", "solid service" and a
comfortable setting have helped this once-trendy
Eastsider mature into a "favorite" neighbor; a few call
it "expensive for nothing special."*

| F | D | S | C |

## LUTECE
### 27 | 24 | 26 | $71
249 E. 50th St. (bet. 2nd & 3rd Aves.), 752-2225
*U – Like a long-time lover, Lutece can still arouse
NYers' culinary passions even though it no longer holds
exclusive reign over their affections; Andre Soltner "still
has the touch", and his "pluperfect" French haute bistro
food remains the "gold standard" against which all
others are judged; yes, it has faults – service can be
"less than superb" and the decor, though elegant, is
"showing its age" – but to most it's still seductive.*

## Luxe
### – | – | – | E
24 E. 21st St. (bet. Park Ave. So. & B'way), 674-7900
*As in "deluxe", this elegant, new Gramercy American
has a most handsome setting divided into an entryway
bar and four separate dining areas; the limited American
regional menu with a French accent and well-chosen,
well-priced wine list puts it on our "must-try" list.*

## Mackinac Bar & Grill/LS
### 17 | 18 | 16 | $30
384 Columbus Ave. (bet. 78th & 79th Sts.), 799-1750
*M – Though the hunting-lodge decor resembles "a
Ralph Lauren ad", the usually "good", "basic" American
food can be "inconsistent" and the staff "look like they'd
rather be someplace else."*

## Malaga/LS
### 18 | 9 | 15 | $28
406 E. 73rd St. (bet. 1st & York Aves.), 737-7659
*M – "A touch of Spain on the East Side", this casual
Spanish standby is known for its "cheap" prices,
"magnificent paella" and "killer white sangria" that helps
one to ignore the "drab", "tacky" surroundings.*

## Mambo Grill/LS
### 18 | 16 | 17 | $34
174 E. 82nd St. (bet. Lexington & 3rd Aves.), 879-5516
*U – "Leave NYC for a few hours" and try this "bouncy"
"fun" East Side Venezuelan for "wonderful creative
dishes", especially the "excellent" grilled fish; its "good
value" "earthy" Latino menu is helped by "super sangria."*

## Mamma Leone's/LS
### 9 | 11 | 12 | $32
Milford Plaza, 261 W. 44th St. (bet. B'way & 8th Ave.),
391-8270
*M – A perennial bomba; the overwhelming majority
report that no one should visit this "campy" Italian
"bastion of tourism" "unless you deeply miss Cleveland."*

## Mandarin Court/LS
### 19 | 10 | 13 | $21
61 Mott St. (bet. Canal & Bayard Sts.), 608-3838
*U – Said to "serve the best dim sum in Chinatown", this
"lively" Cantonese offers "great variety" and a "true
Chinatown experience" with minimal decor and prices.*

| | F | D | S | C |
|---|---|---|---|---|

**Manganaro's Hero-Boy**/S    | 18 | 5 | 11 | $13 |

492 Ninth Ave. (bet. 37th & 38th Sts.), 947-7325
*U – "The home of the six-foot hero", this is a sandwich
lover's paradise; hearty, filling and cheap, it's "like
having your mama make you lunch."*

**Manhattan Cafe**/S    | 20 | 18 | 19 | $43 |

1161 First Ave. (bet. 63rd & 64th Sts.), 888-6556
*M – For "reliably good" steaks, chops and seafood and
lots of it, this relaxed, "clubby" East Side steakhouse
can't be beat; it's ideal for a group of big eaters.*

**Manhattan Chili Co.**/LS    | 15 | 11 | 13 | $19 |

302 Bleecker St. (7th Ave. S.), 206-7163
*M – "Good, fast and cheap", this Villager is known for its
choice of chili dishes but for little else on its menu, nor
for its "tacky" interior; "the garden is a delight."*

**MANHATTAN OCEAN
CLUB**/LS    | 25 | 22 | 22 | $53 |

57 W. 58th St. (bet. 5th & 6th Aves.), 371-7777
*U – Popularly acclaimed for "the best seafood in the
city" with fish "so fresh it's almost swimming", a "great
wine list" and polished service, this "stylish" seafood
house is "what dining in Manhattan should be."*

**Manhattan Plaza Cafe**    | 21 | 22 | 21 | $22 |

482 W. 43rd St. (bet. 9th & 10th Aves.), 695-5808
*U – "A heavenly oasis from the hustle and bustle of
the city", this superb newcomer offers great bargains,
wonderful American fare and "terrific views."*

**Man Ray**/S    | 16 | 16 | 15 | $30 |

169 Eighth Ave. (bet. 18th & 19th Sts.), 627-4220
*M – This Chelsea bistro next to the Joyce Theater has
an "interesting" menu and "trendy feel"; others say it's
"hit or miss", "austere" and "dull."*

**Mappamondo**/LSX    | – | – | – | I |

11 Abington Sq. (8th Ave.), 675-3100
581 Hudson St. (Bank St.), 675-7474
*Unusually interesting and cheap, zesty Northern Italian
food keeps these lively Villagers full of smart 20-year-
olds who, by their presence, add to the appeal.*

**March**    | 25 | 24 | 24 | $60 |

405 E. 58th St. (bet. 1st Ave. & Sutton Pl.), 838-9393
*U – For a "romantic", "intimate" dinner in a "delightful
townhouse", nearly everyone admires this "innovative"
American that presents the "creations" of chef Wayne
Nish; only a few complain: "steep prices", "too staid."*

|   | F | D | S | C |
|---|---|---|---|---|

**Mario's** (Bronx)/S | 20 | 14 | 19 | $31 |
2342 Arthur Ave. (south of 187th St.), 584-1188
*U – Worth "trekking to", this "reliable", "old" Italian
pleases its patrons, with "awesome" pizza, "excellent
service" and vital valet parking.*

**Marion's Continental** | 15 | 19 | 16 | $27 |
**Restaurant & Lounge**/SX
354 Bowery (bet. Great Jones & 4th Sts.), 475-7621
*M – This "fun, funky" '40s-style East Village spot is "for
the young at heart" and folks who don't mind the
Bowery locale and odd "ersatz Nouvelle" cuisine.*

**Mark's**/S | 23 | 25 | 23 | $57 |
Mark Hotel, 25 E. 77th St. (Madison Ave.), 879-1864
*U – Now entering its third year, this "elegant" East Side
Contemporary Continental gets high marks across the
board, but especially for its wood-paneled "sedate
English grill" ambiance; the brunch is "outstanding", but
any meal here is likely to be a winner.*

**Marnie's Noodle Shop**/X | 15 | 7 | 13 | $15 |
466 Hudson (bet. Barrow & Christopher Sts.), 741-3214
*M – The "wonderful", "fresh" Asian-style noodles at this
West Village Chinese "shoebox" "can't be beat"; our
reviewers recommend "the sampler plate".*

**Marti Kebab**/LS | 17 | 6 | 15 | $18 |
238 E. 24th St. (bet. 2nd & 3rd Aves.), 545-0602
*U – Year after year, this "tiny" Gramercy Park BYOB
Middle Eastern "hole-in-the-wall" delivers "tasty Turkish
delights" that are "a great buy."*

**Mary Ann's**/LSX | 18 | 11 | 13 | $20 |
116 Eighth Ave. (16th St.), 633-0877
1503 Second Ave. (78th St.), 249-6165
300 E. 5th St. (2nd Ave.), 475-5939
*M – These Mexican siblings may "look like Taco Bell",
but if "you're willing to wait and squeeze", some of the
"best" and cheapest Mexican food in town awaits you;
N.B. "don't stay long or you'll go deaf."*

**Maryland Crab House**/S | 15 | 10 | 13 | $28 |
237 Third Ave. (bet. 19th & 20th Sts.), 598-4890
*U – "Not to sound crabby", but "go for the crab cakes,
not the decor or service" at this Gramercy "shack"
serving "pretty authentic" Chesapeake Bay fare; try the
hard-shells only if you don't mind making a mess.*

**Marylou's**/LS | 18 | 18 | 17 | $37 |
21 W. 9th St. (bet. 5th & 6th Aves.), 533-0012
*M – Earning continued acclaim for its "excellent fresh
fish", Sunday brunch and lovely garden room, this
"beautiful" Village "standby" still satisfies; some say it
has "lost its luster" and needs "sprucing up."*

|   | F | D | S | C |
|---|---|---|---|---|

### Mary's Restaurant/LS  | 18 | 16 | 17 | $34 |
42 Bedford St. (bet. Carmine & Leroy Sts.), 243-9755
*M – An "intimate and homey" feel keeps locals coming back to this Village Italian old-timer; however, critics feel it has "faded into decline."*

### Masada Cafe\*/S  | 17 | 8 | 14 | $21 |
1239 First Ave. (bet. 66th & 67th Sts.), 988-0950
*M – Offering kosher Middle Eastern food, "not fancy" but good and easily affordable, this Eastsider holds a loyal local following, but is almost unknown elsewhere.*

### Maurya/S  | 17 | 13 | 16 | $23 |
129 E. 27th St. (bet. Park & Lexington Aves.), 689-7925
*U – "Quality tandoori and Mughlai fare served with care" is what you find at this lower Lexington Indian; low prices, especially at the "marvelous buffet lunch" make it a "great value" for a "hearty, tasty, no-frills meal."*

### Mayfair/LS  | 16 | 12 | 18 | $28 |
964 First Ave. (53rd St.), 421-6216
*U – For "good, wholesome home cooking" at "a small-town fee", this East Side "meat-and-potato mainstay" is like a warm quilt, "dependable and comforting"; it's aka "the Truman Capote memorial."*

### May We/S  | 18 | 16 | 18 | $44 |
1022 Lexington Ave. (73rd St.), 249-0200
*M – The jury's still out on this new Eastsider; despite "friendly staff" and "excellent" Mediterranean Nouvelle cuisine, some find the cooking "terribly complex" and getting around the duplex layout awkward.*

### Maz Mescal/S  | – | – | – | M |
316 E. 86th St. (bet.1st & 2nd Aves.), 472-1599
*A soft rosy hue makes this East Side Mexican inviting, as is its "real Mexican", not Tex-Mex, menu; but reports on performance and prices are mixed.*

### Mazzei/S  | 22 | 18 | 20 | $42 |
1564 Second Ave. (bet. 81st & 82nd Sts.), 628-3131
*U – This "almost magical" Italian" may transport your "heart and stomach" to Italy, with "spectacular" dishes prepared in its wood-burning brick oven; it's a local favorite worthy of the attention of nonlocals.*

### McDonald's/S  | 10 | 17 | 16 | $8 |
160 Broadway (bet. Maiden Ln. & Liberty St.), 385-2063
*U – "A must for McD lovers", this Wall Street version boasts a doorman, pianist, stock quotes, hostesses, table service, cappuccino and even takes reservations; it's debatable whether "the burgers taste better with piano music", but its ranking as No. 1 on our Bang-for-the-Buck Index explains why McDonald's are so popular.*

|  | F | D | S | C |
|---|---|---|---|---|

### McFeely's American
**Bistro** (Brooklyn)                               | – | – | – | M |

847 Union St. (bet. 6th & 7th Aves.), 718-638-0099
*This new American bistro flirts with a variety of foreign
cuisines, including Moroccan and Catalan and whatever
appeals to chef Robin Geller that day; prices are
reasonable and the publike setting is light and airy.*

### Mediterraneo                                    | – | – | – | I |
1260 Second Ave. (66th St.), 734-7407
*Cheap pasta ($10 is tops) comes to the elegant East
60s in the form of this sprightly well-designed Florentine
newcomer – now cheap pasta joints are everywhere!*

### Melon, J.G./LS                                  | 14 | 11 | 13 | $21 |
340 Amsterdam Ave. (76th St.), 874-8291
1291 Third Ave. (74th St.), 650-1310/X
*U – Standouts for brew and burgers, these "preppy"
pubs also offer "cheap", "dependable" bar food; they're
"one of the few bars where a lady can walk in alone."*

### Memphis/S                                       | 20 | 18 | 17 | $36 |
329 Columbus Ave. (bet. 75th & 76th Sts.), 496-1840
*U – " Best known as an incredible bar scene", this West
Sider boasts "good imaginative" Cajun-Southern food.*

### Menchanko-tei/LS                                | 19 | 11 | 15 | $19 |
39 W. 55th St. (bet. 5th & 6th Aves.), 247-1585
*U – For "comfortable tummy food", this bargain Midtown
Japanese "noodle emporium" is "a must", especially in
winter, when its steaming broths make a meal.*

### Merchants                                       | – | – | – | M |
112 Seventh Ave. (17th St.), 366-7267
*It's been a few years since a wine bar opened in NY;
this most attractive wood-paneled newcomer has a
simple menu seemingly designed to prevent one from
drinking on an empty stomach.*

### Meridiana/S                                     | – | – | – | M |
2756 Broadway (bet. 105th & 106th Sts.), 222-4453
*With theatrical trompe l'oeil Roman ruin decor, and
reasonably priced Italian food, this Upper West Side
newcomer is setting in for what locals hope will be a
long run.*

### Meriken/LS                                      | 19 | 16 | 18 | $28 |
189 Seventh Ave. (21st St.), 620-9684
*M – This art deco Chelsea "sushi pad" is "still cool after
all these years"; its "stark minimalist" setting and
"excellent sushi" at fair prices please more than ever.*

|  F | D | S | C |

**Mesa de Espana**/S · 19 | 13 | 18 | \$31
45 E. 28th St. (bet. Park & Madison Aves.), 679-2263
M – For the truly famished, this "old-world Spanish spot complete with guitar player" may be just the ticket; its "massive portions" of paella and seafood offer "great value"; dumpy decor is a negative.

**Mesa Grill**/S · 23 | 20 | 18 | \$40
102 Fifth Ave. (bet. 15th & 16th Sts.), 807-7400
U – "Originality abounds" at this "hip", upscale SW grill that draws rave reviews and "packs 'em in"; customers report that chef Bobby Flay "creates magic" daily; bright colors and a soaring ceiling help you endure the "incredible noise" at this "David Hockney" of restaurants.

**Meson Botin**/S (92) · 15 | 14 | 16 | \$34
145 W. 58th St. (bet. 6th & 7th Aves.), 265-4567
M – "Decent food at a fair price", especially good tapas, keeps this Midtown Spanish standby going, despite "a less-than-up-to-date feel."

**Metro C.C.**/L · 16 | 18 | 13 | \$39
21 W. 17th St. (bet. 5th & 6th Aves.), 727-3500
M – Recently reopened to a steady stream of "the tall, the young and the gorgeous", this stylish Chelsean also has a rooftop garden; however, tables are cramped and the bland California-grill food "comes with too much attitude."

**Metropolis Cafe**/LS · 18 | 21 | 17 | \$35
31 Union Sq. W. (16th St.), 675-2300
M – This 1902 Union Square bank is now a grill/cafe with "marble everywhere" and a live pianist at brunch; its outdoor tables afford great people-watching.

**Metropolitan Cafe**/LS (92) · 15 | 15 | 14 | \$30
959 First Ave. (bet. 52nd & 53rd Sts.), 759-5600
U – In good weather, eating in the garden at this East Side Continental cafe is a pleasure; otherwise this is merely a place for an "easy" local meal.

**Mezzaluna**/LSX · 18 | 14 | 13 | \$32
1295 Third Ave. (bet. 74th & 75th Sts.), 535-9600
M – "If you don't mind sitting on top of people", you'll find some of the "best pasta in NY" at this tiny East Side Italian; drawbacks are "rude waiters" and noise.

**Mezzanine Restaurant**/LS · 19 | 23 | 16 | \$30
Paramount Hotel, 235 W. 46th St. (bet. 8th Ave. & B'way), 764-5500
U – The menu of sandwiches, salads and sweets may be simple, but the "movie set" design affords fine people-watching and is also perfect for "quiet chats."

| | F | D | S | C |
|---|---|---|---|---|

**Mezzogiorno**/LSX  | 19 | 16 | 15 | $34 |
195 Spring St. (Sullivan St.), 334-2112
*M – This SoHo Italian's specialities include authentic
pasta, brick-oven pizza, grilled vegetables and a
"seafood platter to die for"; only the "pretentious" staff
and no-plastic policy are causes for complaint.*

**Michael's**/S  | 21 | 21 | 19 | $47 |
24 W. 55th St. (bet. 5th & 6th Aves.), 767-0555
*U – California comes to NYC at this "very chic", "very
LA" dining room–cum–art gallery; the "fresh",
"consistently good" food is "light" American Nouvelle.*

**Mickey Mantle's**/S  | 12 | 17 | 14 | $29 |
42 Central Park S. (bet. 5th & 6th Aves.), 688-7777
*U – "It's the best sports bar around" and a "great value"
for "decent" bar food and memorabilia that "will excite
any baseball fan"; it's great for families with kids.*

**Mi Cocina**/S  | 21 | 13 | 16 | $27 |
57 Jane St. (Hudson St.), 627-8273
*U – A West Village "hidden treasure" that serves "light,
nongreasy", "authentic" Mexican food; the "appetizers
are better than the entrees" and the setting, a simple
brick-walled storefront, also "feels Mexican."*

**Mimosa**/S  | 20 | 17 | 18 | $43 |
1354 First Ave. (72nd St.), 988-0002
*M – A year old now, this East Side Mediterranean gets
discordant reactions: "best new one in a long time",
"wonderful", "interesting combo of flavors" vs. "erratic",
"unprofessional", "declining already."*

**Minetta Tavern**/LS  | 16 | 15 | 17 | $31 |
113 MacDougal St. (bet. W. 3rd & Bleecker), 475-3850
*M – A "cozy Village hangout that has stood the test of
time", this 1927 vintage Italian is "ok if you stick to the
usual dishes" – otherwise, don't expect much.*

**Mingala Burmese**/S  | 16 | 9 | 14 | $18 |
21 E. 7th St. (bet. 2nd & 3rd Aves.), 529-3656
325 Amsterdam Ave. (bet. 75th & 76th Sts.), 873-0787
*U – India and China unite in these bargain Burmese
kitchens; for a "delicious mix" of tastes, try the
thousand-layer pancakes, Rangoon beef or night
market noodles and try to ignore the "schizo decor."*

**Miracle Grill**/LS  | 21 | 16 | 16 | $27 |
112 First Ave. (bet. 6th & 7th Sts.), 254-2353
*U – The "miracle is getting a seat" at this East Village
Southwestern that "packs them in" with "interesting
taste combos", a "beautiful garden" in back, low prices
and a "great brunch."*

| | F | D | S | C |
|---|---|---|---|---|

**Mitali East/West**/LS     | 20 | 14 | 17 | $23 |
334 E. 6th St. (bet. 1st & 2nd Aves.), 533-2508
296 Bleecker St. (7th Ave. So.), 989-1367
*U – "There's a reason there's always a line to get into"
this pair of Village Indians: good food at low prices; "go
with a crowd and enjoy."*

**Mi Tierra\***/LS     | 15 | 9 | 16 | $22 |
668 Amsterdam Ave. (bet. 92nd & 93rd Sts.), 874-9514
*M – Hearty portions and a "friendly" staff make this
elemental Mexican-Venezuelan storefront a real find;
"tacky decor" is outweighed by "warm" service and bargains.*

**Mitsukoshi**     | 22 | 18 | 20 | $44 |
461 Park Ave. (57th St.), 935-6444
*M – Arguably the "best and most expensive sushi
spot in NYC", this "formal", "serene" Japanese has
"top-notch" food and fine service; it's a favorite for
business lunches.*

**Mme. Romaine de Lyon**/S     | 17 | 15 | 15 | $28 |
29 E. 61st St. (bet. Madison & Park Aves.), 758-2422
*U – An East Side institution, this French "queen of
omelettes" offers over 500 choices, which is rather
"egg-cessive" and not "for the cholesterol-conscious."*

**Mocca Hungarian**/SX     | 17 | 8 | 15 | $22 |
1588 Second Ave. (bet. 82nd & 83rd Sts.), 734-6470
*U – The "closest thing to Budapest in NY", this "good,
old-fashioned Hungarian corners the market on "stick-
to-the-ribs" home cooking; for the price, you won't find
better schnitzel or goulash anywhere.*

**Monreale**/LS     | 17 | 17 | 18 | $34 |
1803 Second Ave. (bet. 93rd & 94th Sts.), 360-5500
*M – Diners debate over this attractive, pastel East Side
Italian: "healthy, diet-conscious", "quiet" and "spacious"
vs. "overpriced" and "ordinary."*

**Montebello**     | 21 | 18 | 20 | $43 |
120 E. 56th St. (bet. Park & Lexington Aves.), 753-1447
*M – You be the judge of this Midtown Italian newcomer:
"high-class", "reasonably priced", "excellent for business
lunch", or "a bit stuffy" and "run-of-the-mill?"*

**MONTRACHET**     | 25 | 19 | 23 | $56 |
239 W. Broadway (bet. Walker & White Sts.), 219-2777
*U – Hard to get to but worth it, this TriBeCa Nouvelle
French rates "among the very best", thanks to chef
Deborah Ponzek's "remarkable cooking"; most proclaim
it a "gourmet's delight" with an "excellent wine list" too;
the prix fixe menus are a real bargain.*

|   | F | D | S | C |
|---|---|---|---|---|

**Moran's**/S     | 14 | 15 | 15 | $30 |
146 Tenth Ave. (19th St.), 627-3030
*M – The '60s live again at this West Chelsea pub, a converted church with "delightful Irish staff" and old-fashioned NYC charm.*

**Moreno**/S     | 20 | 19 | 20 | $41 |
65 Irving Place (18th St.), 673-3939
*U – "Closely supervised by Moreno himself", this "stylish" Gramercy Park Northern Italian with outdoor seating is "always a pleasure", and draws diners from all over.*

**Mortimer's**/LS     | 12 | 13 | 12 | $39 |
1057 Lexington Ave. (75th St.), 517-6400
*U – "Still a favorite of the NY-social crowd", "go for the people-watching, not the food", at this East Side "Americana" club; if you've ever wondered why the jet set is so thin, here's why.*

**Mr. Chow**/LS     | 21 | 22 | 19 | $49 |
324 E. 57th St. (bet. 1st & 2nd Aves.), 751-9030
*U – Though past its heyday, this "high-class gourmet" Chinese is still praised for its art deco interior and a host of specialities; critics call it "expensive", "ostentatious."*

**Mr. Fuji's Tropicana**     | – | – | – | M |
61 Fifth Ave. (13th St.), 243-7900
*This large deco tropical Villager with an Asian-Caribbean–influenced American grill menu has to be seen to be believed; staff and patrons compete to see who has longer legs and shorter skirts.*

**Mr. Tang's** (Brooklyn)/LS     | 18 | 16 | 16 | $24 |
1884 86th St. (19th Ave.), 718-256-2100
7523 Third Ave. (76th St.), 718-748-3131
3344 Nostrand Ave. (Ave. T), 718-769-6633
2650 Coney Island Ave. (Ave. X), 718-769-9444
*M – A "once-great" chain of Chinese has reportedly "deteriorated"; however, many still love the "flavorful dishes" and "pleasant surroundings."*

**Mueng Thai**\*/S     | 17 | 6 | 14 | $18 |
23 Pell St. (bet. Mott & Bowery Sts.), 406-4259
*M – Comments on this elemental Chinatown Thai range from "good and tasty" to "terrible"; two things are for sure – it's "nothing to look at" and "very cheap."*

**Mughlai**/LS     | 15 | 12 | 14 | $27 |
320 Columbus Ave. (75th St.), 724-6363
*U – The best thing about this West Side Indian may be its address; with no local competition, it survives with only "decent" food and minimal service.*

|  | F | D | S | C |
|--|---|---|---|---|

**Mulholland Drive Cafe**/LS  | 15 | 14 | 14 | $31 |

1059 Third Ave. (bet. 62nd & 63rd Sts.), 319-7740
*U – Being owned – though seldom frequented – by
Patrick Swayze helps pack the "gold chain" and "big
hair" crowd into this noisy, pastel retro-LA bar/cafe; if
you're "into projecting 'me' ", belly up to the bar.*

**Museum Cafe**/LS  | 15 | 14 | 15 | $24 |

366 Columbus Ave. (77th St.), 799-0150
*M – Convenient to the Natural History Museum, this
"casual" American cafe is a "pleasant spot for relaxing
and people-watching"; critics say it's "a dime a dozen."*

**Nadine's**/LS  | 16 | 17 | 16 | $26 |

99 Bank St. (Greenwich St.), 824-3165
*U – A "cozy", "quirkily appealing" West Villager that's "a
local focal point" with good basic American food "like
Mom's", along with play and poetry readings and the
"perfect" brunch.*

**Nanni Il Valletto**  | 21 | 18 | 20 | $52 |

133 E. 61st St. (bet. Park & Lexington Aves.), 838-3939
*M – At this "fine", formal East Side Italian, you'll find
some of the "best bruschetta and angel hair" anywhere,
but pay dearly for it; while "very good", some consider
this "old-timer" "a generation behind."*

**Nanni's**  | 22 | 15 | 20 | $46 |

146 E. 46th St. (bet. Lexington & 3rd Aves.), 697-4161
*U – This Grand Central–area "Classic" Northern Italian
has been making people happy since 1968; overlook
the atmosphere, it has "exquisite angel hair" and is "part
of an old NY scene that's hard to find these days."*

**Natalino**  | 19 | 11 | 18 | $31 |

243 E. 78th St. (bet. 2nd & 3rd Aves.), 737-3771
*U – "Tiny but tasty", this Italian with only 10 tables is
also "friendly and cheap" and makes you feel as though
you're eating in someone's home.*

**National** (Brooklyn)/S  | 13 | 13 | 13 | $38 |

273 Brighton Beach Ave. (2nd St.), 718-646-1225
*M – "The party goes on all night" at this "wild" old-style
Russian where pitchers of vodka help you forget the
mundane food; "bring a fun-loving crowd" and plenty
of cabfare.*

**Nawab**  | – | – | – | M |

246 E. 49th St. (west of 2nd Ave.), 755-9100
*Pungent spices greet you at this modest North Indian
that recently replaced Akbar, but largely duplicates its
repertoire of mid-priced tandoori dishes and curries.*

| | F | D | S | C |
|---|---|---|---|---|

**Nazareth Restaurant**/S · · · · 16 | 13 | 15 | $27
1590 Second Ave. (bet. 82nd & 83rd Sts.), 650-1009
*U – "Skip the belly dancers" and entrees, and focus
on the "excellent appetizers" at this affordable and
"spotlessly clean" East Side Middle Eastern.*

**Neary's**/LS · · · · 17 | 13 | 19 | $32
358 E. 57th St. (bet. 1st & 2nd Aves.), 751-1434
*U – The luck of the Irish finds a home at this "warm,
endearing" pub presided over by Jimmy Neary, a
"real-life leprechaun", with the "friendliest staff in town"
and "always good" reasonably priced food.*

**Nello** · · · · – | – | – | E
696 Madison Ave. (bet. 62nd & 63rd Sts.), 980-9099
*Just when you'd think the East Side had reached the
saturation point for Italian restaurants, this attractive,
all-white Tuscan opened to a full house; besides good, if
pricey, food it has super sidewalk seating and viewing.*

**New Deal**/S · · · · 19 | 16 | 17 | $33
133 W. 13th St. (bet. 6th & 7th Aves.), 741-3663
*M – In a new location, this "comfortable eatery" has fans
who "love the exotic game", Sunday jazz brunch and
prix fixe dinner; foes seeing beaver, hippo, snake and
even lion served, say "get a conscience."*

**New Prospect Cafe** (Bklyn.)/S · · · · 18 | 12 | 16 | $25
393 Flatbush Ave. (8th Ave.), 718-638-2148
*U – "Groovy" is the word for this Park Slope "nice little
gourmet Californian cafe" serving healthy light fare;
though it can get a little "hippie-ish" and looks "like a
diner", you can't beat it for the price.*

**Nice Restaurant, The**/S · · · · 19 | 11 | 14 | $24
35 E. Broadway (bet. Catherine & Market Sts.), 406-9510
64 Fulton St. (bet. Gold & Cliff Sts.), 732-8788
*M – Hailed for the "best dim sum in the city – by day",
this Chinatown Cantonese is a real treat, especially the
banquet for 10; once again, decor and service lag.*

**Nick & Eddie**/LS · · · · 20 | 17 | 16 | $33
203 Spring St. (Sullivan St.), 219-9090
*U – "Great home-cooked food" at modest prices has
"made it hard to get into" this "busy SoHo hangout"; its
'40s ambiance, outdoor garden and "interesting culinary
twists" are praised, but waits and noise are not.*

**Nicola Paone** · · · · 19 | 17 | 19 | $48
207 E. 34th St. (bet 2nd & 3rd Aves.), 889-3239
*M – Many feel this "old-fashioned" Murray Hill "time
warp" Italian is "heavy-handed" and "mucho overpriced",
but regulars like the "outdoor feeling" Roman garden
setting and extensive wine cellar.*

|  F  |  D  |  S  |  C  |

### Nicola's/LS
| 19 | 15 | 17 | $42 |

146 E. 84th St. (bet. Lexington & 3rd Aves.), 249-9850
M – A "good basic" Italian, this wood-paneled East Side
"club for locals" ("regulars get preference") wins kudos
for "delicious preparation" and "gracious service."

### Nicole Brasserie de Paris*/LS
| 18 | 16 | 19 | $35 |

Omni Park Central, 870 Seventh Ave. (56th St.), 765-5108
M – Despite a convenient Midtown location, "good, light
food" and not bad prices, few surveyors go here and
some who do call it an "imitation" French bistro.

### Nippon
| 23 | 17 | 21 | $43 |

155 E. 52nd St. (bet. Lexington & 3rd Aves.), 355-9020
U – Arguably "the best Japanese in the city", this Midtown
"old faithful" delivers "excellent fresh sushi" in a "formal
setting", with "tatami rooms for business meetings."

### Nirvana/LS (92)
| 14 | 24 | 16 | $39 |

30 Central Park So. (bet. 5th & 6th Aves.), 486-5700
U – Wasting one of the nicest rooftop locations in NY,
this Indian out of The Arabian Nights produces
"pedestrian" food that's "expensive" for what it is.

### NoHo Star/LS
| 17 | 15 | 15 | $23 |

330 Lafayette St. (Bleecker St.), 925-0070
M – At this NoHo "art diner", they serve "everything from
Chinese to American" – all easily affordable; locals like
the open kitchen and "nice and airy" seating.

### Nosmo King/S
| 21 | 19 | 19 | $35 |

54 Varick St. (south of Canal St.), 966-1239
U – "Food as healthy as this was never as creatively
prepared", say fans of this odd TriBeCa organic
American; if "hard to find", it's worth searching out.

### Nusantara
| 18 | 21 | 19 | $35 |

219 E. 44th St. (bet. 2nd & 3rd Aves.), 983-1919
M – "One of the only places to get real Indonesian in the
city" – try the rijsttafel – this "elegant" Midtowner may be
"NY's best-kept secret"; critics call it "beautiful, but cold."

### N.Y. Delicatessen, The/S
| 13 | 12 | 12 | $20 |

104 W. 57th St. (bet. 6th & 7th Aves.), 541-8320
M – Calling yourself a NY deli doesn't make you one;
despite serving soup and sandwiches at not bad prices,
this art deco former Horn & Hardart is basically "for the
tourist crowd" who don't know better.

|   | F | D | S | C |
|---|---|---|---|---|

**Oak Room and Bar, The**/LS        | 19 | 25 | 21 | $49 |

The Plaza Hotel, 768 Fifth Ave. (59th St.), 546-5330
*U – Although The Plaza should be able to do better with
steaks and chops, people keep coming to this "great old
NY" room for its "lion-in-winter feeling" of "warm",
wood-paneled decor, steady service and "timeless"
"elegance", and for the adjoining old-world bar.*

**Oceana**        | 24 | 23 | 24 | $54 |

55 E. 54th St. (bet. Madison & Park Aves.) 759-5941
*U – This East Side newcomer impresses with its
"consistently good fish", "excellent prix fixe" meals
($26 lunch, $36 dinner), "striking" decor (inherited from
Le Cygne), and "very helpful", if "overeager", staff; put
it on your list.*

**Odeon**/LS        | 18 | 17 | 16 | $36 |

145 W. Broadway (Thompson St.), 233-0507
*M – Some say this busy TriBeCa "Euro-diner" is "passé"
but most agree the "granddaddy of trendy restaurants"
is "still good and stylish after all these years."*

**Odessa**/SX (92)        | 14 | 7 | 12 | $21 |

117 Ave. A (bet. 7th & 8th Sts.), 473-8916
*M – No-frills is an understatement at this Lower East
Side Ukranian, but you can eat yourself silly on its home-
cooked pierogies, blintzes and always-good soups.*

**Old Bermuda Inn\*** (S.I.)/S        | 19 | 24 | 17 | $36 |

2512 Arthur Kill Rd. (Hervery St.), 718-948-7600
*U – Though reviewers like the "fine" traditional American
food, the prime attraction of this "elegant" Richmonder
is its setting in a charming old Victorian mansion.*

**Old Homestead**/S        | 18 | 13 | 16 | $43 |

56 Ninth Ave. (bet. 14th & 15th Sts.), 242-9040
*M – Diners either swear by, or at, this century-old "pre-
cholesterol–conscious" steakhouse; some drool over
the "giant-sized steaks", lobster and kobe beef, but
many say, "fading", "past its prime", "needs a face-lift."*

**Old Town Bar**/LS        | 14 | 18 | 14 | $17 |

45 E. 18th St. (bet. B'way & Park Ave. So.), 529-6732
*U – Nearing its centennial, David Letterman's favorite
tavern earns kudos for its burgers, fries, wings, draft
beers and wonderful old wooden bar and booths.*

**Olio**/SX (92)        | 16 | 13 | 14 | $27 |

788 Lexington Ave. (bet. 61st & 62nd), 308-3552
*M – When shopping in Bloomie's, consider this Italian
pastaria and grill for "better-than-average" food at below
average prices.*

|   | F | D | S | C |
|---|---|---|---|---|

**Ollie's**/LS  `| 17 | 8 | 13 |$17 |`
2957 Broadway (116th St.), 932-3300
2315 Broadway (84th St.), 362-3712
200 W. 44th St. (bet. B'way & 8th Ave.), 921-5988
U – "Always crowded", these West Side noodle joints
have moved the Chinatown dining formula Uptown, i.e.
they look like coffee shops but are "good, cheap and fast."

**Omen**/S  `| 23 | 18 | 19 |$35 |`
113 Thompson St. (bet. Prince & Spring Sts.), 925-8923
U – "Not your average sushi joint", this "Zen-like" SoHo
spot offers "authentic Kyoto flavors and flair", especially
soups and noodles.

**One Hudson Cafe**  `| 19 | 20 | 19 |$39 |`
1 Hudson St. (Chambers St.), 608-5835
U – Most love the "charming", "flower-and-brick" setting
of this TriBeCa Continental; the food gets less praise,
but fans cite "excellent seafood" and "sinful desserts."

**ONE IF BY LAND, TIBS**/LS  `| 23 | 27 | 23 |$52 |`
17 Barrow St. (bet. 7th Ave. & W. 4th St.), 228-0822
U – "The perfect place to pop the question", this Village
Continental in Aaron Burr's old house is a "romantic
ideal" thanks to its fireplace, candlelight, fresh flowers,
piano music and "three-star service"; try it on a "snowy
night" or in the "lovely garden" in summer.

**101** (Brooklyn)/LS  `| 19 | 17 | 17 |$26 |`
10018 Fourth Ave. (101st St.), 718-833-1313
**101 Seafood** (Brooklyn)/S
8203 Third Ave. (82nd St.), 718-833-6666
U – Locals calls this Bay Ridge Northern Italian "home"
as much for its "value, variety and tasty pasta" as for its
"bar scene in the evening"; its nearby seafood sibling is
improving after an uneven start.

**107 West**/S  `| 17 | 13 | 15 |$25 |`
2787 Broadway (bet. l07th & l08th Sts.), 864-1555
M – A favorite with the Columbia crowd, this "friendly"
Cajun can "pack 'em in" for jambalaya, smoky pork
chops, mashed potatoes with gravy and "great
cornbread"; critics say it's "tired" and "going downhill."

**Oriental Pearl**/S  `| 19 | 8 | 11 |$22 |`
103 Mott St. (bet. Hester & Canal Sts.), 219-8388
M – "Yum, yum dim sum" draws crowds (up to 500) to
this Chinatown "vast warehouse", despite "Formica
decor", "rough service" and "Asian gang types outside";
"come with a group" – lazy Susans make sharing easy.

| F | D | S | C |
|---|---|---|---|

### Oriental Town Seafood/LS
`20 | 6 | 10 | $22`
14 Elizabeth St. (bet. Canal & Bayard Sts.), 619-0085
U – Surveyors advise each other to "keep your eyes closed", "cover your ears" and "brace yourself for 'who-cares' service" when dining at this all-time favorite Chinatown Cantonese seafood specialist.

### Original California
### Taqueria* (Brooklyn)/SX
`18 | 5 | 12 | $9`
8 Bergen St. (Court St.), 718-624-7498
72 Seventh Ave. (bet. Lincoln & Berkeley), 718-398-4300
341 Seventh Ave. (bet. 9th & 10th Sts.), 718-965-0006
U – "Finally a real California taqueria", Brooklyn's "version of Benny's Burritos" does a lot for little money; but $9 doesn't buy much in the way of decor or service.

### Orso/LS
`21 | 18 | 18 | $40`
322 W. 46th St. (bet. 8th & 9th Aves.), 489-7212
U – "Best on Restaurant Row", this Northern Italian tops the bill for "creative" thin-crust pizza, pasta and post-theater stargazing; "book in advance."

### Orson's*/LS
`23 | 21 | 23 | $24`
175 Second Ave. (bet. 11th & 12th Sts.), 475-1530
U – "Funky" and crowded, this hip, year-old American is a well-kept East Village secret; "seek it out" for its well-priced, "innovative" dinner-only menu.

### Ossie's Table* (Brooklyn)/S
`18 | 13 | 16 | $28`
1314 50th St. (bet. 13th & 14th Aves.), 718-435-0635
M – A "good kosher" fish place in Borough Park; while some call it "top-notch", others say its "age is showing."

### Osso Buco/S
`17 | 16 | 17 | $27`
88 University Pl. (bet. 11th & 12th Sts.), 645-4525
M – This family-style Italian in the Village scores "some hits and some misses", but most say the "huge portions" are a "value", service is "warm" and setting "attractive".

### Ottomanelli's Cafe/S
`11 | 8 | 12 | $17`
1404 Madison Ave. (bet. 97th & 98th Sts.), 996-7700
1626 York Ave. (bet. 85th & 86th Sts.), 772-7722
439 E. 82nd St. (York Ave.), 737-1888
1518 First Ave. (79th St.), 734-5544
1370 York Ave. (73rd St.), 794-9696/X
50 W. 72nd St. (Columbus Ave.), 787-9493
1315 Second Ave (69th St.), 249-5656
1199 First Ave. (65th St.), 249-7878
951 First Ave. (bet. 52nd & 53rd Sts.), 758-3725
538 Third Ave. (bet. 35th & 36th Sts.), 686-6660
337 Third Ave. (25th St.), 532-2929
119 E. 18th St. (bet. Irving Pl. & Park), 979-1200
62 Reade St. (bet. B'way & Church), 349-3430
96-24 Queens Blvd., Rego Park, 718-459-7427

## Ottomanelli's Cafe (Cont.)
*M – Popular for its convenience and low prices, this ubiquitous neon-lit, green-and-white chain serves burgers, pastas, pizza and chicken for when you want a break from the Greek coffee shop.*

## Our Place/S
| 20 | 16 | 18 | $31 |
1444 Third Ave. (82nd St.), 288-4888
*U – Despite its "stiff, cold decor", this all-white East Side Chinese gets good grades for its "imaginative" menu and "friendly" service; check out the prix fixe menus.*

## OYSTER BAR
| 22 | 15 | 15 | $38 |
Grand Central Station, Lower Level (bet. Vanderbilt & Lexington Aves.), 490-6650
*U – This huge animated seafood classic is called "the quintessential NY restaurant"; it's an international destination for its raw bar, pan roasts, "fresh fish of all types", "amazing" desserts and American white wine list; if noise gets to you, try the "much quieter" adjacent Saloon Room.*

## Palio
| 22 | 26 | 21 | $58 |
Equitable Ctr. Arcade, 151 W. 51st St. (bet. 6th & 7th Aves.), 245-4850
*M – "Classy" but "cocky", this Midtown Italian is an "art-director's dream": quietly "elegant" upstairs, "dramatic" and "dazzling" at the downstairs bar, with its Sandro Chia mural, but despite "excellent" food, many dub this one "not worth the pomp or the price."*

## Palm Court, The/LS
| 18 | 24 | 19 | $42 |
The Plaza Hotel, 768 Fifth Ave. (58th St.), 546-5350
*M – "Out of another era", "exquisite", "enchanting", rave "refined" reviewers, who come for tea, dessert or the brunch buffet under "real palms"; the less genteel say it "borders on a cliché" and find the violins "too much."*

## PALM/L
| 24 | 13 | 17 | $50 |
837 Second Ave. (bet. 44th & 45th Sts.), 687-2953
### Palm Too
840 Second Ave. (bet. 44th & 45th Sts.), 697-5198
*U – "Brassy" and "abrasive", this NY "legend", with caricatures of its famous patrons on its walls, is for many "the city's best steakhouse", with "brontosaurus-sized portions"; for cost-control, try sharing or the $19.93 lunch.*

## Pamir/S
| 20 | 15 | 17 | $29 |
1437 Second Ave. (bet. 74th & 75th Sts.), 734-3791
1065 First Ave. (58th St.), 644-9258
*U – These East Side Afghans manage to be both "homey" and "exotic"; their "consistently good" food and value add up to a winning ticket.*

| F | D | S | C |
|---|---|---|---|

**Panarella**    | – | – | – | M |

513 Columbus Ave. (bet. 84th & 85th Sts.), 799-5784
*Featuring regional Italian cuisine with rustic leanings,
this Westsider is best for outdoor dining since the
cramped interior leaves a lot to be desired; there's
excellent takeout next door at Cucina Rustica which
shares the same kitchen.*

**Pandit\*/S**    | 20 | 13 | 21 | $22 |

566 Amsterdam Ave. (bet. 87th & 88th Sts.), 724-1217
U – Locals hail this Westsider as the area's "best
Indian" with "good and spicy" food, "tranquil" ambiance
and "warm and personal" service; no one praises the
storefront setting.

**Paola's/S**    | 23 | 19 | 22 | $43 |

347 E. 85th St. (bet. 1st & 2nd Aves.), 794-1890
U – "Like being in Paola's home", confide contented
customers who say this "intimate" East Side Italian is
"worth a detour"; long on "charm", it's short on space.

**Paolucci's/S**    | 17 | 12 | 16 | $30 |

149 Mulberry St. (Grand St.), 226-9653
M – "Solid" and "friendly", this Little Italy enclave gets
high marks for "authentic", "hearty" fare at "good" prices;
but some say it's "dilapidated" and "past its time."

**Papaya King/LSX**    | 17 | 4 | 10 | $7 |

179 E. 86th St. (3rd Ave.), 369-0648
983 Third Ave. (bet. 58th & 59th Sts.), 753-2014
U – For the "quintessential stand-up" "nosh", these
"bargain" franks-and-fruit-juice joints are "top dog"; they
make "the best 90-second lunch in town."

**Paper Moon Milano**    | 18 | 17 | 15 | $38 |

39 E. 58th St. (bet. Madison & Park), 758-8600
U – To some, this East Side Milanese import is a "slick,
chic hot spot" with high "people-watching" potential;
pizzas and antipasto are "delicioso" if "overpriced."

**Pappardella/LS**    | 16 | 15 | 14 | $29 |

316 Columbus Ave. (75th St.), 595-7996
M – "Cute and cozy" inside, "see-and-be-seen" outside,
this Westsider runs "on Italian time", the better to
"savor" its pastas and people-watching; many find the
food "ordinary" and "acting-school" service "flaky."

**Paradis Barcelona**    | 17 | 20 | 17 | $42 |

145 E. 50th St. (bet. Lexington & 3rd), 754-3333
M – Amigos of this Midtown Catalan report "superior"
food and "smooth service"; to an equal number, the food
is "unremarkable" and "disappointing."

| | F | D | S | C |
|---|---|---|---|---|

**Parioli Romanissimo**/L        | 24 | 24 | 21 | $68 |

24 E. 81st St. (bet. 5th & Madison Aves.), 288-2391
*M – "High-class" and "haughty", this East Side
townhouse Italian draws praise for "splendid" Italian
fare, but also virulent criticism as "pompous",
"overblown" and "expensive" – "bring the gold card."*

**Paris Commune**/LS        | 17 | 17 | 16 | $27 |

411 Bleecker St. (bet. W. 11th & Bank), 929-0509
*U – This "cozy" and "romantic" West Village bistro offers
a taste of the "French countryside in NYC" with its
"good, steady" home cooking, a "welcoming" staff,
fireplace and "awesome value"; sure, it's "crowded."*

**PARK AVENUE CAFE**/S        | 22 | 22 | 21 | $49 |

100 E. 63rd St. (Park Ave.), 644-1900
*U – "Audaciously good" is the verdict on this American
newcomer, whose chef, David Burke, is hailed as "a
genius"; befitting its "new hot spot" status, the place is
"jumping" (read "noisy and crowded"), but satisfied
surveyors hail it as "slick, efficient and smart"; a few call
it "creative but contrived", wishing that every dish had at
least one less ingredient.*

**Park Avenue Country Club**        | – | – | – | M |

381 Park Ave. S. (27th St.), 685-3636
*Modeled on the renowned Rockaway Hunt Club, this
soon-to-open super-upscale sports-themed spot feels
like an elite country club, including "must-see" state-of-
the-art 36-hole golf simulators; of course, we can't
predict its yet-to-be-tasted American country club food.*

**Park Bistro**/S        | 22 | 16 | 18 | $42 |

414 Park Ave. So. (bet. 28th & 29th Sts.), 689-1360
*U – To many, this is NY's "best French bistro" with "fine"
food and a "European feel"; most react with a Gallic
shrug to "high noise levels" and "cramped quarters."*

**Parker's Lighthouse** (Bklyn)/S        | 13 | 20 | 15 | $30 |

1 Main St. (bet. Water & Plymouth), 718-237-1555
*M – The waterfront spot, dubbed "a poor man's River
Cafe", rates high on its "breathtaking" Manhattan views
but low on its "bland", "mediocre" food.*

**Park Side** (Queens)/LS        | 23 | 18 | 19 | $37 |

107-01 Corona Ave. (108th St. & 51st Ave.), 718-271-9274
*U – "They don't come any better than this" "festive"
Corona-area "family" Italian; "big portions" of "fantastic
pasta" and other "wholesome", "home-cooked" dishes
keep the place packed and often mean a wait.*

|   | F | D | S | C |
|---|---|---|---|---|

### Parma/LS — | 18 | 12 | 17 | $40 |

1404 Third Ave. (bet. 79th & 80th Sts.), 535-3520
*M – "A great neighborhood restaurant", "cozy and
old-fashioned", "slow and steady", say regulars of this
East Side Italian; others find it "basking in its former
glory" – in a word, "boring."*

### Passage To India/LS — | 18 | 14 | 16 | $19 |

308 E. 6th St. (bet. 1st & 2nd Aves.), 529-5770
*U – "The best" of Little India, say spice-searchers who
come for the "excellent" tandoori dishes, breads and
"great prices"; it's a "tight squeeze", but "worth it."*

### Passports*/LS — | 18 | 19 | 14 | $21 |

79 St. Marks Pl. (bet. 1st & 2nd Aves.), 979-2680
*U – "Go for it", say customers of this crowd-pleasing
East Village Tex-Mex whose "excellent eats", "wonderful
value" and multilevel room have definite potential.*

## PASTARIAS

### Pasta Lovers/S — | 15 | 12 | 15 | $23 |

158 W. 58th St. (bet. 6th & 7th Aves.), 582-1355

### Pasta Place, A* (S.I.)/SX — | 22 | 16 | 22 | $23 |

1612 Forest Ave. (Pontiac St.), 718-876-7427

### Pasta Presto/L — | 13 | 9 | 13 | $19 |

959 Second Ave. (51st St.), 754-4880/S
613 Second Ave. (bet. 33rd & 34th Sts.), 889-4131/S
37 Barrow St. (bet. Bleecker & 7th Sts.), 691-0480/S
93 MacDougal St. (bet. Bleecker & W. 3rd), 260-5679/LS

### Pasta Roma/S — | 16 | 13 | 16 | $25 |

315 W. 57th St. (bet. 8th & 9th Aves.), 265-5050

### Pasta Vicci/S — | 13 | 9 | 13 | $19 |

294 Third Ave. (bet. 22nd & 23rd Sts.), 260-4216
1423 Second Ave. (bet. 74th & 75th Sts.), 535-1100

### Pasticcio — | 18 | 13 | 17 | $30 |

447 Third Ave. (bet. 30th & 31st Sts.), 679-2551
*U – Though independently owned and operated, these
cookie-cutter pastarias feature similar pasta-based
menus and affordable prices; Staten Island's A Pasta
Place is the standout.*

### Pastis/LS — | 17 | 16 | 16 | $34 |

1387 Third Ave. (bet. 78th & 79th Sts.), 734-7942
*U – A "creative newcomer" with "hot spot" potential, this
Eastsider draws early praise for its "great-for-grazing"
International menu and warm ambiance.*

| F | D | S | C |

**Patisserie J. Lanciani**/S　　　| 22 | 12 | 12 | $14 |
271 W. 4th St. (bet. Perry & W. 11th Sts.), 929-0739
*M – For a surefire "sugar fix", this West Villager's
"sumptuous" pastries have some calling it a "midsummer
night's dream"; it's also called "user-unfriendly" with
"crowded" quarters and a "hostile" staff.*

**Patric**　　　| 17 | 16 | 17 | $44 |
150 Varick St. (Vandam St.), 691-5550
*M – Early reports on this Downtown Contemporary
American newcomer range from "inventive" to "pre-fab",
from "cool and chic" to "dated" and "disappointing."*

**Patriccio's\*** (S.I.)/S　　　| 20 | 17 | 17 | $35 |
695 Bay St. (Broad St.), 718-720-1861
*U – "Great" "homemade" dishes, a casual brick-walled
setting and "marvelous" view are the consensus on this
Italian yearling.*

**Patrissy's**/S　　　| 21 | 13 | 20 | $35 |
98 Kenmare St. (bet. Mulberry & Centre Sts.), 226-2888
*M – Loyalists like this Little Italy enclave for being "solid
and basic", i.e. "down-to-earth"; only the decor – "dated"
and "gloomy" – turns some people off.*

**Patsy's Pizza**/LSX　　　| 22 | 6 | 12 | $16 |
2287-91 First Ave. (bet. 117th & 118th Sts.), 534-9783
*U – Despite its location, pizza addicts keep coming to
this East Harlem brick-oven pizzeria for its "great"
extra-thin-crust pizzas.*

**PATSY'S PIZZA** (Bklyn)/LX　　　| 25 | 10 | 14 | $16 |
19 Fulton St. (Water & Front Sts.), 718-858-4300
*U – At this new Brooklyn pizzeria, brick-oven-baking
and "the freshest ingredients" spell success; "Numero
Uno" with our pizza partisans.*

**Patzo**/LS　　　| 14 | 15 | 14 | $23 |
2330 Broadway (85th St.), 496-9240
*U – "Adequate" if unexciting food, high-ceilinged,
"split-level" space and "reasonable" prices make this
West Side Italian a "pleasant" pre- or post-Loews option.*

**Paul & Jimmy's**/S　　　| 18 | 15 | 18 | $38 |
123 E. 18th St. (bet. Irving Pl. & Park Ave.), 475-9540
*U – A Gramercy standby known for its "lusty,
no-nonsense" Southern Italian food, "terrific service"
and warm ambiance; ex-fans recall "better times."*

| | F | D | S | C |
|---|---|---|---|---|

**Peacock Alley**/S     | 17 | 22 | 19 | $45 |

Waldorf-Astoria Hotel, 301 Park Ave. (bet. 49th & 50th Sts.), 872-4895
*M – A renovation "makes it shine" for "power breakfasts" and Sunday brunch, but despite "refined service" and "Cole Porter music", most opt to "leave it to the tourists"; N.B. they've hired a new chef, so maybe there's hope.*

**Pedro Paramo**/S     | 19 | 14 | 19 | $21 |

430 E. 14th St. (bet. 1st Ave. & Ave. A), 475-4581
*U – "Outstanding" and "authentic", this East Village Mexican "find" has "peso prices" that add to its "unprent.entious" and "cozy" appeal.*

**Pellegrino***/LS     | 22 | 17 | 18 | $29 |

138 Mulberry St. (bet. Hester & Grand Sts.), 226-3177
*U – "Pleasant and pretty", this Little Italy newcomer gets high marks for its pasta and "service"; an all-around "good Italian", it's worth recalling when on jury.*

**Pembroke Room***/S     | 19 | 26 | 22 | $36 |

Lowell Hotel, 28 E. 63rd St. (bet. Madison & Park), 838-1400
*U – With the charm of a gracious private home, this second-floor room is "enchanting for high tea" or for weekend brunch, the only times it's open.*

**Pen & Pencil Restaurant**/S     | 19 | 17 | 19 | $43 |

205 E. 45th St. (bet. 2nd & 3rd Aves.), 682-8660
*M – "A longtime favorite" for business dining due to its "old-NY feeling", "great" steaks and chops, and "friendly waiters"; yet a few dub it "dated" and "out of gas."*

**Periyali**     | 24 | 20 | 21 | $43 |

35 W. 20th St. (bet. 5th & 6th Aves.), 463-7890
*M – Many hail this "warm, inviting" Chelsea taverna as NY's "best Greek", with confirming high ratings; however, those in the know look to Astoria for their Greek restaurants.*

**Perk's Fine Cuisine***/S     | – | – | – | M |

553 Manhattan Ave. (123rd St.), 666-8500
*Black is beautiful at this "stylish", "gracious", mod upscale Harlem "oasis" that serves Nouvelle Soul Food that diners "like a whole lot"; if it were in Midtown, there'd be lines twice around the block.*

**Perretti Italian Cafe**/LS     | 15 | 9 | 14 | $20 |

270 Columbus Ave. (bet. 72nd & 73rd Sts.), 362-3939
*U – A West Side staple, this busy Italian gets the nod for "solid", "cheap", "crowd-pleasing" food for when you "don't wanna cook"; still, it's "uninspired."*

| | **F** | **D** | **S** | **C** |

**Peruvian Restaurant**/SX     | 17 | 8 | 14 | $22 |
688 Tenth Ave. (bet. 48th & 49th Sts.), 581-5814
M – "Great ethnic food" at a modest price is the draw at
this Far West Side joint, whose fans overlook its "Lima
luncheonette" setting.

**Petaluma**/LS     | 18 | 17 | 17 | $35 |
1356 First Ave. (73rd St.), 772-8800
U – This "popular" Eastsider has survived its "trendy"
stage and become "a comfy", "kid-friendly" local
favorite; for most the pastas, mini-pizzas and grills
"never disappoint" and the "price is right."

**PETER LUGER**     | 27 | 15 | 19 | $49 |
**STEAK HOUSE** (Brooklyn)/SX
178 Broadway (Driggs Ave.), 718-387-7400
U – "The gold standard" of steakhouses is "head and
shoulders above the rest"; "mammoth", "melt-in-your-
mouth" steaks, creamed spinach, fried potatoes and
pecan pie ("love the schlag") make it "fabulous from
start to finish"; despite the "earthy", "beer-hall" ambiance
and service ("the waiters are aged to perfection"), it's
"worth the trip."

**Pete's Place**/LS     | 13 | 13 | 15 | $19 |
256 Third Ave. (bet. 20th & 21st Sts.), 260-2900
U – "Just a diner", but most call it "above-average", with
"fresh", "surprisingly good" food; "warm, cozy, reliable."

**Pete's Tavern**/LS     | 12 | 15 | 14 | $25 |
129 E. 18th St. (Irving Pl.), 473-7676
M – "History" and "charm" make this Gramercy pub a
"great hangout"; the mood is "casual" and "low-key", but
aside from "ok burgers", the food is "blah."

**Petrossian**/LS     | 23 | 24 | 21 | $60 |
182 W. 58th St. (7th Ave.), 245-2214
U – Part "Czarist Russia", part "Gatsby", part Paris, this
"candlelit, crystal and caviar" emporium excels on all
counts; "sleek" art deco decor, and truly "decadent"
dining (Beluga, foie gras, smoked salmon) add up to a
"magnificent" experience; try the $29 prix fixe lunch.

**Phoebe's**/S     | 16 | 17 | 16 | $24 |
380 Columbus Ave. (78th St.), 724-5145
U – Locals call this "casual" West Side newcomer "a
breath of fresh air", citing its affordable American
"comfort food" menu and simple brick-walled setting.

**Piccola Venezia** (Queens)/S     | 23 | 14 | 19 | $40 |
42-01 28th Ave. (42nd St.), 718-721-8470
U – "Hearty" "home-cooked" food and "wonderful" service
make this Northern Italian "a place of pilgrimage" and "well
worth the trip"; only the "gaudy" "rococo" decor detracts.

119

|   | F | D | S | C |
|---|---|---|---|---|

**Piccolino**/S `| 18 | 11 | 17 | $23 |`
448 Amsterdam Ave. (bet. 81st & 82nd Sts.), 873-8004
*U – Regulars of this "cozy" West Side Italian happily
recall "lotsa pasta for not alotta dough"; a few fastidious
fault-finders find it "overpraised" and overcrowded.*

**Piccolo Mondo**/L `| 18 | 14 | 17 | $41 |`
1269 First Ave. (bet. 68th & 69th Sts.), 249-3141
*M – This East Side Italian standby remains a "good"
local choice, though former fans say it "lacks warmth."*

**Piccolo Pomodoro**/S `| 18 | 10 | 16 | $24 |`
1742 Second Ave. (bet. 90th & 91st Sts.), 831-8167
*U – "Affordable fresh pasta" draws crowds to this "tiny"
yellow Upper East Side storefront; its admirers say it's
"the tops", but even they admit it's "cramped."*

**Pie, The**/S `| 19 | 13 | 18 | $23 |`
340 E. 86th St. (bet. 1st & 2nd Aves.), 517-8717
*U – Requiring "suspension of your usual standards", this
"offbeat" Eastsider serves "super" Slavic dishes at low
prices; the "postage-stamp–size" room makes for "tight
seating", but the "zany" hostess "couldn't be nicer."*

**Pierre au Tunnel**/L `| 18 | 15 | 19 | $36 |`
250 W. 47th St. (bet. B'way & 8th Ave.), 582-2166
*U – "Safe" and "steady", this Theater District French
bistro "from the old school" is "well-run" with good food,
prix fixe value and "knowing service."*

**Pierre's**/LSX `| 17 | 17 | 16 | $34 |`
170 Waverly Pl. (bet. Christopher & Grove), 929-7194
*M – The waiters' "antics" keep this "cozy" West Village
French bistro jumping; though some say it has good
"solid" food, others find it "silly."*

**Pier 25A** (Queens)/S `| 18 | 16 | 17 | $29 |`
215-16 Northern Blvd. (bet. 215th & 216th Sts.), Bayside,
718-423-6395
*M – "Huge portions" of "fresh" "Greek-style" seafood
draw crowds, especially on weekends", but for many
this is "glorified diner cuisine."*

**Pietro & Vanessa**/S `| 20 | 12 | 17 | $26 |`
23 Cleveland Pl. (bet. Lafayette & Spring), 941-0286
*U – Most praise this SoHo Italian for its "good" "unfussy"
food, "comfy" "unrushed" feel, "magical" garden and
staff that "treats you like family"; critics cite "long waits."*

**Pietro's** `| 21 | 14 | 20 | $50 |`
232 E. 43rd St. (bet. 2nd & 3rd Aves.), 682-9760
*M – Loyalists of this Italian steakhouse keep coming for
its "consistently great" steaks and Caesar salad;
however, memories of the warmer old location have
some saying "I'll never forgive them for moving."*

**Pigalle**/LS | 20 | 18 | 19 | $38 |

111 E. 29th St. (bet. Lexington & Park Aves.), 779-7830
*M – Early reports on this newcomer are mixed: "terrific",
"fresh and friendly", "a new favorite", "very, very French"
vs. "too small", "too precious", "only average"; in
between, there's "promising" and "work in progress."*

**Pig Heaven**/LS | 17 | 13 | 15 | $26 |

1540 Second Ave. (bet. 80th & 81st Sts.), 744-4333
*M – Popular with East Side families, but "less than
heavenly", this East Side Chinese with its pig theme,
"barnyard setting" and "terrific pork dishes" is usually
bustling; still, some say it's "gimmicky" and getting "tired."*

**Pinocchio** | 18 | 17 | 18 | $41 |

170 E. 81st St. (bet. Lexington & 3rd), 650-1513
*M – For some, this candlelit Eastsider is a "small
treasure", "charming", "quiet" and "very relaxed", with
"authentic" "Italian hilltown" cooking; others say
"someone's nose is getting longer."*

**Pizzapiazza**/LS | 14 | 12 | 14 | $18 |

785 Broadway (10th St.), 505-0977
*M – Some praise this Villager's deep-dish pizzas,
pastas and salads as "a terrific bargain"; but for many,
the place is "ebbing" and is "borderline fast food" (but
with "slow" service).*

**Pizzeria Uno**/LS | 14 | 11 | 12 | $16 |

432 Columbus Ave. (81st St.), 595-4700
55 Third Ave. (bet. 10th & 11th Sts.), 995-9668
391 Sixth Ave. (bet. 8th & Waverly), 242-5230
*M – "Cheap, predictable" and "convenient", this Chicago
deep-dish chain's fans say it "can't be beat" to "feed
your face"; critics call it "mass-produced", "mall pizza"
that's like a "lead sleeping pill."*

**Planet Hollywood**/LS | 14 | 23 | 15 | $24 |

140 W. 57th St. (bet. 6th & 7th Aves.), 333-7827
*U – "A real treat" for any movie buff, this newcomer lives
up to its hype with a "great set" filled with "wonderful
movie memorabilia", "loud music" and a sufficiently
good burger-pizza-fajita menu not to spoil the "fun";
within a few years, Planet Hollywoods will be around the
world and every kid on the planet will own a PH
sweatshirt; see, "PT Barnum was right."*

**Plaza Oyster Bar, The**/LS | 19 | 19 | 17 | $40 |

The Plaza Hotel, 768 Fifth Ave. (58th St.), 546-5340
*U – This "classic" seafood bar jumped in its ratings over
last year, with surveyors reporting it has noticeably
improved and is "worth trying again."*

| | F | D | S | C |

### Poiret/S
**20 | 16 | 18 | $38**

474 Columbus Ave. (bet. 82nd & 83rd), 724-6880
*U – A "great plus" for the West Side, this "class-act"
French bistro packs in a "noisy" crowd (get there before
6 PM "if you want to talk"); though most find it "dependably
good", to some it's getting "a little tacky of late."*

### Polo, The/S
**21 | 23 | 22 | $55**

Westbury Hotel, 840 Madison Ave. (bet. 69th & 70th Sts.),
439-4835
*U – "Superb ambiance and service" have long been the
watchwords at this "comfy", "clubby", "low-key" East
Side dining room; now, our surveyors report a "new chef
and a new menu" mean a "big improvement."*

### Pongsri Thai Restaurant/LS
**19 | 12 | 16 | $22**

244 W. 48th St. (bet. B'way & 8th Ave.), 582-3392
*M – A "friendly" Downtown Thai that gets high marks for
its "delicate" "dependable" dishes that are "not
overpriced"; only fire-eaters say it "needs more spice."*

### Ponte's
**16 | 13 | 17 | $44**

39 Desbrosses St. (West St.), 226-4621
*M – "A slice of old NY" down by the Holland Tunnel, this
Italian standby serves up "food you can't refuse" in
quarters that some compare to an "Italian funeral
parlor"; it's a "special treat" if you "go with a wise guy."*

### Ponticello* (Queens)/S
**23 | 15 | 21 | $33**

46-11 Broadway (bet. 46th & 47th Sts.), 718-278-4514
*U – Locals call this "friendly, casual" Astoria Italian "a
real winner" for "well-prepared", "home-cooked fare" at
"good value", including NYC's "best roast chicken."*

### Popover Cafe/S
**18 | 15 | 15 | $21**

551 Amsterdam Ave. (bet. 86th & 87th Sts.), 595-8555
*M – "Scrumptious homemade popovers" are big draws
at this "casual", "cozy" West Side "favorite"; it's "worth
the wait" on weekends since "nobody beats their brunch."*

### Portico
**– | – | – | M**

1431 SecondAve. (bet. 74th & 75th Sts.), 794-1032
*With the appeal of an outdoor portico, this new mid-priced
East Side Genovese offers a menu with a bit more
originality and variety than the rest of the pasta pack.*

### Positano/L
**20 | 19 | 18 | $40**

250 Park Ave. So. (20th St.), 777-6211
*U – "Exceptional" Italian food and "wonderful" ambiance
have turned this "sleek" white-decored former "hot spot"
into a "satisfying" "old reliable" that's "stood the test of
time"; P.S. the bar scene is still "active."*

122

| | F | D | S | C |
|---|---|---|---|---|

**POST HOUSE**/S      | 22 | 19 | 20 | $53 |

28 E. 63rd St. (bet. Madison & Park Aves.), 935-2888
*U – "Excellent in every way" is the consensus on
this "classy" steakhouse where the "steaks are as
soft as butter"; "handsome" surroundings, a "wonderful
wine list" and "knowledgeable" service make this a
"perennial favorite."*

**Presto's**/LS      | 14 | 12 | 14 | $21 |

2770 Broadway (bet. 106th & 107th Sts.), 222-1760
434 Amsterdam Ave. (81st St.), 721-9141
*M – These "cost-efficient", "low-key" Italians provide
"big portions" of "functional" food, principally pastas,
but diners say "don't go out of your way."*

**PRIMAVERA**/LS      | 25 | 21 | 22 | $58 |

1578 First Ave. (82nd St.), 861-8608
*U – A "classy crowd" gives this Upper East Side Tuscan
"four stars" for "ingenious", "consistently excellent" food,
for its "sophisticated", "clubby" wood-paneled setting,
and service that makes you feel like "royalty"; N.B. if
owner-host Nicola Civetta recommends it, order it!*

**Primola**/LS      | 20 | 15 | 18 | $44 |

1226 Second Ave. (bet. 64th & 65th Sts.), 758-1775
*U – "Always jammed", this "popular" East Side Italian
gets high praise from a "clique-y crowd" for "just about
flawless food"; for most this is "a true star."*

**Prix Fixe**/LS      | 21 | 18 | 17 | $36 |

18 W. 18th St. (bet. 5th & 6th Aves.), 675-6777
*U – "Everything works" at this bustling Flatiron District
American: the bargain prix fixe concept ($18.50 lunch,
$24 dinner) and "grand", "dramatic" space combine
with an "inspired" if "limited" menu to make this a
"best value."*

**Provence**/S      | 22 | 21 | 18 | $42 |

38 MacDougal St. (Prince St.), 475-7500
*U – "Like its namesake", this SoHo bistro is "sunny" and
"friendly", with "excellent Country French" cuisine
served by a "congenial" staff; the "cheerful bustle" is
"casual", "comfortable" and "never feels rushed."*

**Puket**/LS      | 20 | 16 | 18 | $29 |

945 E. 50th St. (2nd Ave.), 759-6339
*U – Regulars swear by this "hot" and "very tasty Thai",
calling it "a cut above" the competition; the $8.95 prix
fixe lunch is a cut below.*

**Quartiere** (Queens)/LS      | 17 | 17 | 15 | $31 |

107-02 Queens Blvd. (70th Ave.), 718-520-8037
*U – "A find in Forest Hills" for "great brick-oven pizza"
and "Euro-cafe ambiance"; fans call it their "favorite
Manhattan restaurant outside Manhattan."*

|  | F | D | S | C |
|---|---|---|---|---|

**Quatorze**/LS · | 21 | 17 | 19 | $39 |
240 W. 14th St. (bet. 7th & 8th Aves.), 206-7006
*U – This "charming" bistro has become "a classic",
thanks to its "authentic" hearty fare ("best cassoulet this
side of Provence", "formidable pommes frites" and an
"exceptional" apple tart); $11.50 lunch, whew!*

**Quatorze Bis**/LS · | 20 | 18 | 18 | $42 |
323 E. 79th St. (bet. 1st & 2nd Aves.), 535-1414
*M – Eastsiders report this "lively" Uptown Quatorze has
fine bistro food that's "worth the price", especially the
prix fixe lunch; a few say it's "hectic" and "overpriced."*

**QUILTED GIRAFFE, THE** · | 25 | 24 | 24 | $73 |
Sony Plaza, 550 Madison Ave. (bet. 55th & 56th), 593-1221
*U – Despite its reputation as NY's "most extravagant"
restaurant, this Nouvelle American that some say is
"turning Japanese" wins praise for chef Barry Wine's
"exquisite" "creative" cooking; the extraordinary
"21st-century" stainless-steel decor softened by flowers
and artwork adds the right touch for dining that is truly
"postmodern"; at $45, the prix fixe lunch is a bargain.*

**RAINBOW ROOM**/LS · | 19 | 28 | 22 | $63 |
GE Bldg., 30 Rockefeller Plaza, 65th Floor (bet. 49th &
50th Sts.), 632-5100
*U – For a "dinner and dancing extravaganza" or "for
drinks and admiring the view", there's "nothing like it";
RR "lives up to all its notices" as "the perfect NY dream
evening", "unequaled for glamour", with "the most
romantic" art deco atmosphere; if the Continental menu
falls a bit short, the "fab '40s" "Fred and Ginger fantasy"
is sufficient compensation.*

**Rao's**/X · | 23 | 13 | 19 | $48 |
455 E. 114th St. (Pleasant Ave.), 722-6709
*U – Like a set from The Godfather, this East Harlem
Southern Italian is the toughest ticket in town; "Frankie
runs the show", "the aunts do the delicious home
cooking" and, though "frustrating", most say it's "worth
the wait – up to two months – for a reservation to sit at
one of the few tables next-to-a who's who of NYC.*

**Raoul's**/LS · | 20 | 18 | 17 | $43 |
180 Prince St. (bet. Sullivan & Thompson Sts.), 966-3518
*U – "It's got character" enough for several restaurants –
at this "always crowded", "always tempting" old SoHo
bistro that draws a "great late crowd" with "good vibes."*

**Raoul's Brasserie & Grill\*** · | 18 | 18 | 16 | $39 |
231 Varick St. (bet. Houston & Clarkson), 929-1630
*M – Having slipped a notch or two, this spacious SoHo
brasserie still attracts a "semi-Euro, semi-yuppie" "party
crowd" that calls it a "great getaway."*

## Raphael

| 22 | 22 | 22 | $54 |

33 W. 54th St. (bet. 5th & 6th Aves.), 582-8993
U – The arrival of chef Jean-Michel Bergounoux (ex Le
Cygne) has been met by a chorus of raves for this
"intimate", "low-key" Midtown French "hideaway"; if you
care about French food, hustle on over.

## Rascals/L

| 11 | 11 | 11 | $21 |

12 E. 22nd St. (bet. B'way & Park Ave. So.), 420-1777
M – A "young" crowd favors this Gramercy "drink and
dance" "hangout", but ex-diners say this "makes
Houlihan's and Charlie O's look highbrow."

## Ratner's/LS

| 17 | 8 | 12 | $21 |

138 Delancey St. (bet. Norfolk & Suffolk), 677-5588
M – "For nostalgia" at least, this Formica Lower East
Side kosher dairy gets high marks; "a Jewish landmark",
"never copied, never equaled", it's been "the same for
the last 50 years" with the best onion rolls, gefilte fish,
blintzes, matzo brei and soup "better than Grandma's";
even the "heartburn is pleasant" here.

## Raymond's Cafe*/S

| 18 | 16 | 19 | $29 |

88 Seventh Ave. (bet. 15th & 16th Sts.), 929-1778
U – "Warm and welcoming", this Chelsea French
newcomer gets praise for "wonderful", fairly priced food,
"friendly staff" and "relaxed" atmosphere; some say it's
"serviceable but hardly remarkable."

## Red Tulip/S

| 18 | 18 | 17 | $35 |

439 E. 75th St. (bet. 1st & York Aves.), 734-4893
U – An East Side Hungarian with "stick-to-your-ribs",
"Pepto-Bismol, please" food and "old-world atmosphere"
right out of a "Hedy Lamarr movie"; gypsy violins add
to the effect.

## Regency/S
(aka 540 Park)

| 20 | 22 | 21 | $48 |

The Regency Hotel, 540 Park Ave. (61st St.), 759-4100
U – "Home of the power breakfast" with top execs at
almost every table, this American Eastsider is also a
"great lunch and dinner secret"; a new "improved" menu
and renovation have given it "a shot in the arm."

## Regional Thai Taste/S

| 19 | 15 | 16 | $28 |

208 Seventh Ave. (22nd St.), 807-9872
M – Opinions are divided on this Chelsea newcomer:
most praise the "generous portions" of "savory" and
"visually interesting" food, calling it "innovative" and
"unique"; critics say it's "wimpy" and "nothing special."

### Remi/LS
145 W. 53rd St. (bet. 6th & 7th Aves.), 581-4242
U – Adam Tihamy's "hip", "high energy" Midtown Italian
is "a keeper" that's "destined to become a classic"; the
"handsome", "airy" space with a huge mural of Venice is
"drop-dead gorgeous", and the Venetian-style food is
"the best this side of the Grand Canal."

### Rendez-vous/S (92)
Omni Berkshire Hotel, 21 E. 52nd St. (bet. 5th &
Madison Aves.), 753-5970
U – "Pleasant French food and good value" are the keys
to this "pretty" place's success as a bar, brunch and
business lunch venue; it's a cut above a coffee shop,
but not so fancy as to intimidate.

### Rene Pujol
321 W. 51st St. (bet. 8th & 9th Aves.), 246-3023
U – "Solid" and "reliable", this Theater District standby is
enjoying a revival; its hearty "French country cooking" at
"reasonable prices" "never fails to please."

### R.H. Tugs (S.I.)/LSX
1115 Richmond Terrace (bet. Bard & Snug Harbor Rds.),
718-447-6369
U – Locals like the Carib-Mex-BBQ and brew menu at this
"casual" Staten Islander with "waterfront views" of "Joisey";
"try the shrimp Louie and order Tugg pie for dessert."

### Rio Mar/LSX
7 Ninth Ave. (Little W. 12th St.), 243-9015
U – It doesn't take a keen sense of smell to sniff out this
"garlicky", "smoky" West Village Spanish "dive" where
paella, sangria and French fries "to die for" at "cheap
prices" keep them coming.

### RIVER CAFE (Brooklyn)/LS
1 Water St. (East River), 718-522-5200
U – "One of NY's treasures", this "beautiful" barge cafe
is "everything it's cracked up to be" – matching a
"brilliant" New American menu with "breathtaking views"
of Downtown Manhattan; regulars report "the tasting
menu is a must" and suggest brunch, late lunch or drinks
on the outdoor deck; for a "romantic" or "celebratory"
evening, it's "magical."

### Road to Mandalay/S
380 Broome St. (bet. Mott & Mulberry Sts.), 226-4218
U – "A real find" that's "fun with a group", this Burmese
may be "out-of-the-way" but it's "worth the trip"; despite
"sterile" decor, "inspired" "exotic" food at modest prices
may produce crowds.

| F | D | S | C |

**Rocking Horse Mexican Cafe**/S  | 17 | 14 | 15 | $22 |
182 Eighth Ave. (bet. 19th & 20th Sts.), 463-9511
*M – Though this "exuberant" Chelsea Tex-Mexican is very "popular", unimpressed diners say it's "one step from frozen" and "doesn't cut it."*

**Roebling's**/S  | 13 | 14 | 13 | $28 |
South St. Seaport, 11 Fulton (South St.), 608-3980
*M – Fans call this "lively" "watering hole" "one of the better Seaport choices", for "after work" when it's "suit city"; critics say it's "touristy" and "pedestrian."*

**Roettelle A.G.**  | 18 | 17 | 17 | $32 |
126 E. 7th St. (bet. 1st Ave. & Ave. A), 674-4140
*U – It's "like dining in a European village" at this artsy German-Swiss East Villager tucked into a brownstone; good food and a nice garden get high grades.*

**Rogers & Barbero**/LS  | 18 | 18 | 18 | $33 |
149 Eighth Ave. (bet. 17th & 18th Sts.), 243-2020
*U – Locals call this straightforward American their "Chelsea favorite": "reliable", "comfortable", "friendly" and "affordable"; its prix fixe is a "best buy."*

**Rolf's**/S  | 19 | 18 | 16 | $30 |
281 Third Ave. (22nd St.), 473-8718
*U – For "a real fun fest" this "Xmas fantasy" Gramercy German is "the only game in town"; besides a "quaint" Black Forest setting, it offers "filling" food at fair prices.*

**Romeo Salta**  | 19 | 17 | 19 | $47 |
30 W. 56th St. (bet. 5th & 6th Aves.), 246-5772
*M – A loyal majority praise this handsome Midtown Italian old-timer as "steady and solid" and "still good"; dissenters say it's "aging", "frayed around the edges", and no longer worth its high tab.*

**Ronasi Ristorante**/S  | 18 | 15 | 18 | $38 |
1160 First Ave. (64th St.), 751-0360
*M – Locals say this East Side Sicilian has cooking "like your grandmother's best"; an equal number find it "ho-hum" and "a little pricey."*

**Rosa Mexicano**/LS  | 20 | 17 | 18 | $36 |
1063 First Ave. (58th St.), 753-7407
*U – For the "real stuff" that's "creative", "classy" and "consistently good", try this East Side Mexican, where the chunky guacamole made tableside is "to die for"; the menu is taco-free – real "upscale" Mexicano.*

**Rose Cafe**/LS  | 18 | 16 | 16 | $32 |
24 Fifth Ave. (9th St.), 260-4118
*U – Most diners like this New American's "inventive" "Cal menu", "good prices", and "relaxing, plush setting"; a few say "the bloom is off the rose."*

| | F | D | S | C |

### Rosemarie's   | 23 | 20 | 21 | $42 |
145 Duane St. (bet. W. B'way & Church), 285-2610
*U – A "hidden treasure" in TriBeCa, this "gracious" and
"warm" Northern Italian has just about everyone raving
over its "magnificent" food, "attention to detail",
"intimate" "romantic" setting and "excellent value";
diners have only one regret – they "wish it was closer."*

### Rosolio/S   | 19 | 15 | 17 | $38 |
11 Barrow St. (bet. 7th Ave. & W. 4th St.), 645-9224
*U – Locals mostly love this amber-toned West Village
Italian; though they concede that it can be "hit or miss",
they emphasize that "when it's good, it's terrific."*

### Roumeli Taverna (Queens)/LS   | 20 | 12 | 16 | $25 |
33-04 Broadway (bet. 33rd & 34th Sts.), 718-278-7533
*U – "Honest to goodness" "Greek soul food" at low
prices is the draw at this simple, but wonderful, Astoria
taverna; "real food, real people" make it "worth the trip."*

### Royal Canadian Pancake/LSX   | 16 | 8 | 11 | $16 |
145 Hudson St. (bet. Hubert & Beach Sts.), 219-3038
1004 Second Ave. (53rd St.), 980-4131/LS
*U – For "pancakes the size of hubcaps" ("flying
saucers", "pizzas", "sewer caps"), big eaters, who don't
mind long lines, advise "come hungry" and "bring a
forklift"; others say it's "too much of a good thing."*

### Rumpelmayer's/LS   | 13 | 16 | 14 | $25 |
St. Moritz Hotel, 50 Central Pk. So. (6th Ave.), 755-5800
*M – Though a "good place to take the grandchildren",
this old ice cream parlor, famed for its sandwiches, rich
desserts and stuffed animals, has "slipped" – it "needs a
major face-lift" if it's to live up to its once great name.*

### Ruppert's/LS   | 13 | 12 | 14 | $21 |
269 Columbus Ave. (bet. 72nd & 73rd Sts.), 873-9400
1662 Third Ave. (93rd St.), 831-1900
*M – These "casual" pub "hangouts" get praise for their
"'70s prices", but diners divide after that: "at these
prices, why complain?" vs. "you get what you pay for."*

### Russell's American Grill*/S   | 18 | 19 | 19 | $37 |
Sheraton Park Avenue Hotel, 100 E. 37th St. (Park Ave.),
685-7676, x6122
*U – A "Murray Hill sleeper", this "comfortable" room with
"good" simple American food at modest prices reminds
one of dining well in Omaha.*

### Russian Samovar/LS   | 19 | 16 | 18 | $33 |
256 W. 52nd St. (bet. B'way & 8th Ave.), 757-0168
*U – At this affordable Theater District Russian, "real
Russian" ambiance and live music in the evening are "a
pleasant surprise"; Americans may go to the Russian
Tea Room, but Russians come here.*

|   | F | D | S | C |
|---|---|---|---|---|

**RUSSIAN TEA ROOM**/LS     | 17 | 23 | 17 |$49|

150 W. 57th St. (bet. 6th & 7th Aves.), 265-0947
*U – "Incomparable", this "glitzy" and "grand" Midtown
landmark over the years has won the hearts of diners
by offering "a Russian gala" of blinis, caviar, chilled
vodka and other Romanov dishes; most love its "always
festive" green, red and gold Christmas feeling, but a few
say its food "needs perestroyka."*

**Sabor**/LS     | 18 | 11 | 16 |$30|

20 Cornelia St. (bet. Bleecker & W. 4th Sts.), 243-9579
*U – Once the Cuban champ, this "tiny", "no ambiance"
Village storefront has lost some of its punch in recent
years, but most still like its odds for "tasty, affordable" fare.*

**Sabra Kitchen\***     | 16 | 7 | 13 |$17|

285 Columbus Ave. (bet. 73rd & 74th Sts.), 721-5333
*M – "For that Tel Aviv feeling", head to this Westsider
and "enjoy" good couscous, falafel, hummus and other
Middle Eastern treats; it could use a decorator and
service may act like they're "doing you a favor."*

**Saigon**/S     | 16 | 8 | 13 |$23|

60 Mulberry St. (bet. Bayard & Mosco Sts.), 227-8825
*M – Declining food ratings suggest that this Chinatown
Vietnamese has "lost its touch", but many argue it still
turns out flavorful, fairly priced Far East fare; all agree
that both decor and service are elemental.*

**Sakura of Japan**/LS (92)     | 15 | 13 | 16 |$25|

2298 Broadway (83rd St.), 769-1003
581 Third Ave. (38th St.), 972-8540
*M – "Nothing really special", these low-key Japanese
twins are at least "reliable" in producing "fast and decent"
sushi and other Japanese basics at fair prices.*

**Sal Anthony's**     | 18 | 17 | 18 |$36|

55 Irving Pl. (bet. 17th & 18th Sts.), 982-9030
*U – "Still around for good reason", this Gramercy Italian
has "perenially good (not great)" food, "agreeable"
service and a "comfortable" setting (including sidewalk
seating); the early-bird dinner is an "amazing value."*

**Sala Thai**/LS     | 20 | 14 | 17 |$26|

1718 Second Ave. (bet 89th & 90th Sts.), 410-5557
*U – Thai lovers sala-vate over the fiery, flavorful fare
served at this simple Eastsider; along with "top-notch"
food, it has "friendly service" and reasonable prices.*

**Saloon, The**/LS     | 13 | 12 | 12 |$26|

1920 Broadway (64th St.), 874-1500
*M – The sidewalk seats are a prime people-watching
spot at this "sprawling", "lively and loud" Lincoln Center
standby; the menu offers "everything including the
kitchen sink", for best results stick to basics.*

| F | D | S | C |
| --- | --- | --- | --- |

### Sambuca/S
| 18 | 13 | 16 | $24 |

20 W. 72nd St. (bet. CPW & Columbus Ave.), 787-5656
*U – "Easier to get into than Carmine's", this Westsider
provides "lotsa pasta" and other Southern Italian food
family-style at "terrific" prices; service is friendly to boot.*

### Sammy's Roumanian/S
| 17 | 9 | 14 | $41 |

157 Chrystie St. (Delancey St.), 673-0330
*M – "Great fun till you wake up the next day", this Lower
Eastsider serves huge portions of "vampire-scaring",
heartbeat-inducing Jewish-Romanian food, along with
rivers of schmaltz and vodka, loud "bar mitzvah music",
and insults from theatrically "obnoxious" waiters; "you
can't help but have a good time"; but "once a year may
be too often" for this "Yiddish mugging."*

### Sam's Cafe/S
| 15 | 15 | 14 | $33 |

1406 Third Ave. (80th St.), 988-5300
*M – Despite "very average" American grill food, this
casual Eastsider remains popular thanks to a "too cool
to be true" bar scene that attracts "pretty people" nightly.*

### Sam's Restaurant
| 16 | 17 | 15 | $35 |

Equitable Ctr., 152 W. 52nd St. (bet. 6th & 7th), 582-8700
*U – The grill food may be "nothing spectacular", but this
"comfortable" Midtown grand cafe has a "handsome",
high-ceilinged setting and a "lively" ambiance that make
it popular for lunch, afterwork and pre-theater.*

### San Domenico/S
| 23 | 22 | 21 | $62 |

240 Central Park S. (bet. B'way & 7th Ave. ), 265-5959
*U – "Not the Italian most people think of", this "stylish"
Bolognese has "light, delicious" food that's the Italian
equivalent of French haute cuisine; the prix fixe $19.93
lunch and $24.93 dinner are among NYC's best buys.*

### Sandro's
| 20 | 17 | 18 | $47 |

420 E. 59th St. (bet. 1st Ave. & Sutton Pl.), 355-5150
*U – We hear mostly good things about this "spacious"
East Side Italian: "always excellent"; "eager to please";
"a nice surprise"; a "very pleasant place to be."*

### San Giusto
| 19 | 19 | 20 | $44 |

935 Second Ave. (bet. 49th & 50th Sts.), 319-0900
*U – "Relaxed" and "reliable", this Midtown Northern
Italian has "good, solid" food, skilled service and a
"pretty" setting; if "pricey" and not that distinctive, it's a
"good environment for business" or pleasure dining.*

### San Pietro*/L
| 18 | 18 | 18 | $48 |

18 E. 54th St. (bet. 5th & Madison Aves.), 753-9015
*U – In the space that once housed Prunelle, this Sistina
sibling is serving fresh Amalfi-style riffs on Italian
cuisine; it's almost a relief to discover an Italian putting
quality and originality above low prices.*

|  F  |  D  |  S  |  C  |

### Santa Fe/S
| 18 | 19 | 17 | $35 |

72 W. 69th St. (bet. CPW & Columbus Ave.), 724-0822
*M – "Several cuts above the usual", the West Side's best "Tex-Mex has a "pretty" pastel townhouse setting that captures both the look and taste of Santa Fe; small portions and not so small prices are its negatives.*

### Sant Ambroeus/S
| 18 | 16 | 16 | $38 |

1000 Madison Ave. (bet. 77th & 78th Sts.), 570-2211
*M – "As European as you can get", this Madison Milanese gets high marks for "great gelati e sorbetti" and "desserts made in heaven", but mixed reviews for its other "precious" offerings.*

### Santerello/LS
| 18 | 17 | 19 | $33 |

239 W. 105th St. (bet. B'way & Amsterdam), 749-7044
*U – "Everyone should have a perfect little local restaurant" like this "cozy hideaway"; besides "good" Italian food, it's got "super service."*

### Sarabeth's/S
| 20 | 17 | 16 | $28 |

1295 Madison Ave. (bet. 92nd & 93rd Sts.), 410-7335
423 Amsterdam Ave. (bet. 80th & 81st Sts.), 496-6280
Whitney Museum, 945 Madison Ave. (75th St.), 570-3670
*M – Wonderful baked goods, jams and jellies and other "wholesome" American basics have made these country-style siblings a "Sunday brunch institution" that also keeps a following throughout the week.*

### Saranac/LS
| 15 | 17 | 15 | $27 |

1350 Madison Ave. (bet. 94th & 95th Sts.), 289-9600
*M – With its Adirondack hunting-lodge decor, this casual Carnegie Hill spot conjures up "memories of summer camp"; the basic American food may do the same.*

### Sardi's/L
| 11 | 17 | 15 | $40 |

234 W. 44th St. (bet. B'way & 8th Ave.), 221-8444
*M – Optimists insist that since Vincent Sardi's return, this Theater District landmark's Italian food is "a bit better"; however, as its ratings show, it still has a long way to go to return to its glory days; try the prix fixe.*

### Savoy/X
| 23 | 19 | 20 | $38 |

70 Prince St. (Crosby St.), 219-8570
*U – This SoHo bistro gets raves for its "vivacious", American-Mediterranean food, "intimate", "warm-toned" setting and "friendly" service; lunch is "a steal."*

### Sawadee Thai Cuisine/LS
| 15 | 10 | 14 | $20 |

888 Eighth Ave. (52nd St.), 977-3002
225 Columbus Ave. (bet. 70th & 71st Sts.), 787-3002
*M – There may be "many better Thais", but this West Side duo is "ok in a pinch" with "decent" food, fast service and low prices plus "Woolworth decor."*

| | F | D | S | C |

### Sazerac House/S

| 15 | 13 | 15 | $26 |

533 Hudson St. (Charles St.), 989-0313
*M – The Cajun-Creole food's pretty good, but regulars
don't much care what this "old Village standby" serves –
they go for its "homey" "unpressured" atmosphere.*

### Scaletta/S

| 20 | 18 | 19 | $38 |

50 W. 77th St. (east of Columbus Ave.), 769-9191
*U – Those who happen upon this West Side "sleeper"
find it has "very good" Northern Italian food ("nothing
inventive, but well-done") and a "spacious" setting.*

### Scalinatella

| – | – | – | E |

201 E. 61st St. (3rd Ave.), 207-8280
*Down a short flight of stairs ("scalinatella" in Italian), a
talented designer and even more talented chef have
created the feel and taste of Capri; though too new to
rate, it's clearly a serious newcomer.*

### Scarlatti/S

| 21 | 20 | 20 | $48 |

34 E. 52nd St. (bet. Madison & Park Aves.), 753-2444
*M – "Few treat regulars better" than this "elegant"
Midtown Northern Italian with "fine" food and "impeccable"
service; to critics, it's a "typical high-rent" spot.*

### Scoop

| 18 | 14 | 18 | $40 |

210 E. 43rd St. (bet. 2nd & 3rd Aves.), 682-0483
*M – "Old-fashioned" describes everything about this
veteran wood-paneled Midtown Italian, and that's why
most people like it; it's a "solid performer" at a fair price.*

### Seafood Palace*/LS

| 18 | 14 | 16 | $28 |

50 Mott St. (Bayard St.), 233-8898
*M – Though hardly a palace in looks, most say this
modest spot provides "surprisingly good Thai and
seafood" dishes at fair prices.*

### Sea Grill, The

| 22 | 23 | 20 | $48 |

19 W. 49th St. (Rockefeller Skating Rink), 246-9201
*U – This "cool, calm and comfortable" seafood specialist
serves "fine fresh fish" while affording "sensational
views" of the Rockefeller Center ice rink in winter or
"lovely" patio in summer.*

### 2nd Ave. Brasserie

| – | – | – | M |

1043 Second Ave. (55th St.), 980-8686
*Call it a brasserie, but note that this Midtowner is little
more than a good upscale coffee shop with soups,
salads, "pizzettes", pastas, burgers, etc.*

| F | D | S | C |
|---|---|---|---|

**Second Avenue Deli**/LS        | 21 | 8 | 13 | $19 |

156 Second Ave. (10th St.), 677-0606
*U – Beating out the Carnegie as NYC's No. 1 deli, but
"you can't beat the chopped liver", matzo ball soup,
pastrami or pickles, and you can barely eat the "six-inch-
high" sandwiches at this kosher East Village bargain; it's
the "real thing", right down to the Formica decor and
"barely civil" service.*

**Sel et Poivre**/S (92)        | 16 | 16 | 16 | $38 |

853 Lexington Ave. (bet. 64th & 65th Sts.), 517-5780
*U – A pleasant French neighbor, this "unpretentious"
bistro isn't exciting, but it's "nice" to have around.*

**Sequoia**/S        | 17 | 21 | 16 | $28 |

Pier 17, 89 Fulton St., (South Street Seaport), 732-9090
*M – Casual and "reasonably priced", this American
newcomer gets "thumb's up" for its good seafood, and
"wonderful" waterside setting.*

**Serendipity 3**/LS        | 17 | 19 | 15 | $21 |

225 E. 60th St. (bet. 2nd & 3rd Aves.), 838-3531
*U – A "flashback to childhood", this "cute" restaurant/toy
store is where "kids of all ages" dive into "colossal" ice
cream sundaes and other diet-busting desserts plus
foot-long hot dogs, burgers and the like.*

**Seryna**        | 23 | 22 | 22 | $55 |

11 E. 53rd St. (bet. 5th & Madison Aves.), 980-9393
*U – This "elegant" Midtown Japanese is best known for
serving the "freshest sushi" and house specialty – steak
cooked on a rock; its "beautiful" setting and "royal"
service make its Tokyo prices palatable.*

**Sette Mezzo**/LSX        | 21 | 15 | 16 | $42 |

969 Lexington Ave. (bet. 70th & 71st Sts.), 472-0400
*U – "Always packed", this very "in" Eastsider owes its
popularity to simple but "super" Italian food, served in a
bustling room to an eminently watchable crowd.*

**7th Regiment Mess**        | 11 | 15 | 16 | $27 |

643 Park Ave. (66th St.), 744-4107
*M – "An interesting experience", this Armory room, filled
with military memorabilia, provides "plain American
food" and "no-nonsense" service at "fair prices"; critics
caution "the novelty wears off with the first bite."*

**Sevilla**/LS        | 20 | 12 | 16 | $27 |

62 Charles St. (bet. 7th Ave. & W. 4th St.), 929-3189
*U – As "lively" and "noisy" as a bullfight, this sangria-
dispensing Village Spaniard serves up "huge portions"
of "terrific" paella, mariscada and other "full-flavored"
fare at honest prices; it's "low on decor, high on garlic."*

|  | F | D | S | C |
|--|---|---|---|---|

### Sfuzzi/LS
| 18 | 18 | 16 | $37 |

58 W. 65th St. (bet. CPW & Columbus Ave.), 385-8080
World Financial Ctr., Winter Gdn., 225 Liberty St., 385-8080
*U – At this "slick", "upbeat" Lincoln Center Italian, the
frozen sfuzzi drinks are doozies, the "faux Roman ruin
decor" is "smashing", and the pizza/pasta menu is
rewarding; the new WFC branch has the same menu
minus Uptown's swarming bar scene.*

### Shabu Tatsu
| – | – | – | M |

216 E. 10th St. (bet. 1st & 2nd Aves.), 477-2972
*Exceptionally "warm and winning", this East Village
storefront is a "must try" for anyone interested in
Japanese barbecue; its $3 soups and shabu shabu
dinners are unbelievable buys.*

### Shaliga Thai CuisineS
| 21 | 15 | 18 | $30 |

834 Second Ave. (bet. 44th & 45th Sts.), 573-5526
*U – Get a Thai high at this "impressive" Midtowner that
ranks among "the best in the city", thanks to its "layering
of flavors" and spices; "caring" service adds appeal.*

### Shark Bar/LS
| 19 | 14 | 15 | $29 |

307 Amsterdam Ave. (bet. 74th & 75th Sts.), 874-8500
*U – "Down-home was never so stylish" as at this
"jammed" and "jumping" Westsider, where yuppies line
up to enjoy "terrific" Southern eats, often accompanied
by live music.*

### Sharkey's/S
| – | – | – | E |

239 Third Ave. (bet. 19th & 20th Sts.), 674-0405
*Though too new to call for sure, this Gramercy
American is said to have "great" culinary "promise" and
an attractive setting.*

### Shelby, The/S
| 16 | 16 | 16 | $36 |

967 Lexington Ave. (bet. 70th & 71st Sts.), 988-4624
*U – A preppies-on-parade bar scene, this East Side
American also provides good burgers and other basics
in a "comfortable", high-ceilinged setting.*

### Shinbashi
| 21 | 19 | 20 | $37 |

280 Park Ave. (48th St.), 661-3915
*U – Those seeking "excellent sushi and sashimi" and
other "very good" Japanese food will be more than
satisfied by this "elegant" Midtowner; Japanese clients
outnumber Americans, which is usually a good sign.*

### Shinwa
| 21 | 19 | 18 | $35 |

Olympic Tower, 645 Fifth Ave. (51st St.), 644-7400
*U – This "classy" and "very pretty" Japanese, "hidden"
in Olympic Tower, wins praise for its "excellent sushi",
noteworthy noodles and other "authentic" fare.*

| | F | D | S | C |

**Shun Lee Cafe**/LS    | 21 | 16 | 17 | $30 |

43 W. 65th St. (bet. CPW & Columbus Ave.), 769-3888
*U – A "moving Chinese feast" via rolling carts of "dim sum delights", this "snappy" black-and-white checkerboard-motif Westsider is "great for a quick-dinner meal" when the mood for "fun finger food" strikes.*

**SHUN LEE PALACE**/S    | 24 | 20 | 21 | $40 |

155 E. 55th St. (bet. Lexington & 3rd Ave.), 371-8844
*U – The cream of the Chinese crop, this "sophisticated" Eastsider rates "first class" in all departments, from its "superb" food ("exquisite" Peking duck and seafood) to its "elegant" setting and service, if "pricey for Chinese"; for best results, "follow your captain's suggestions" or try the prix fixes.*

**Shun Lee West**/LS    | 22 | 21 | 20 | $39 |

43 W. 65th St. (bet. CPW & Columbus Ave.), 595-8895
*U – The "best of the East" on the West Side, this Lincoln Center Chinese features "fresh and flavorful" food served in a "knock-your-socks-off" theatrical black setting; it's "crowded and noisy" before performances, but the staff is adept at handling the crush.*

**Siam Inn**/LS    | 20 | 14 | 17 | $25 |

916 Eighth Ave. (bet. 54th & 55th Sts.), 489-5237
854 Eighth Ave. (bet. 51st & 52nd Sts.), 757-3520
*U – "When they say hot, they mean it" at this tried-and-true Thai twosome; both have "tasty" food, "friendly" service and low prices.*

**Sichuan Palace**/S    | 21 | 17 | 18 | $36 |

310 E. 44th St. (bet. 1st & 2nd Aves.), 972-7377
*U – "Serene and superior", this "high-class" U.N.-area Chinese serves excellent Szechuan food in an upscale setting; it's "reliable but somewhat old-fashioned", not to mention "pricey", but most call it a "winner."*

**Sidewalker's**/S    | 17 | 11 | 14 | $31 |

12 W. 72nd St. (bet. CPW & Columbus Ave.), 799-6070
*U – Vent your "frustration on a crustacean" at this West Side version of a Maryland crab house, where diners grab wooden mallets and "smash away" at spicy hard-shell crabs; the rest of the seafood menu is only ok.*

**Sido Abu Salim**/S    | 17 | 10 | 16 | $26 |

81 Lexington Ave. (26th St.), 686-2031
*M – Though not everyone's an admirer ("recommend it to Saddam Hussein"), this "modest" Middle Eastern wins mostly praise for its falafel, couscous and other "good ethnic food"; if its decor is "below average", so are its prices.*

| | F | D | S | C |
|---|---|---|---|---|

### SIGN OF THE DOVE/S   | 23 | 26 | 22 | $57 |
1110 Third Ave. (65th St.), 861-8080
*U – "Prepare to be seduced" by this "oh so romantic"
Eastsider; always "one of NYC's most beautiful"
restaurants, now one of its best too, with "creative"
French-American food that "gets better and better"; the
prices are as "breathtaking" as the decor, but you can
breathe easier in the lower-priced adjacent cafe.*

### Silk Road Palace/SX   | 20 | 10 | 18 | $18 |
447B Amsterdam Ave. (bet. 81st & 82nd Sts.), 580-6294
*U – Westsiders gladly cool their heels waiting outside
this "tiny" Chinese spot because it has "swell food",
"cheap prices" and "hospitable" service; it may look
"humdrum", but it's "always humming."*

### Silverado/LS   | – | – | – | M |
99 E. 19th St. (bet. Park Ave. & Irving Pl.), 505-5500
*Chef Richard Krause goes SW in this new, hip,
adobe Gramercy venture; he's too creative a chef
not to take seriously.*

### Silver Palace/S   | 17 | 10 | 11 | $20 |
50 Bowery (bet. Canal & Hester Sts.), 964-1204
*M – As "massive" as Grand Central and at times just as
"manic", this Chinatown Cantonese is popular for its
"never-ending" midday parade of dim sum, but that's all.*

### Silver Swan*/S   | 16 | 10 | 14 | $25 |
41 E. 20th St. (bet. B'way & Park Ave. So.), 254-3611
*U – German restaurants are in short supply, which is
why this Flatiron District newcomer is a "pleasant
discovery"; ignore the "patched-together" decor and
so-so service and you'll enjoy "good", "rib-sticking" fare.*

### Sirabella's/SX   | 21 | 12 | 19 | $32 |
72 East End Ave. (bet. 82nd & 83rd Sts.), 988-6557
*U – "Tiny" in size but big on taste, this "trendy" Eastsider
serves "terrific pastas" and other "good, honest" Italian
food at fair prices.*

### Siracusa   | 20 | 14 | 16 | $38 |
65 Fourth Ave. (bet. 9th & 10th Sts.), 254-1940
*M – Almost everyone admires this East Villager's pastas
and gelato, but the same can't be said of its "spare"
setting and "brusque" service.*

### Sistina/LS   | 22 | 17 | 19 | $50 |
1555 Second Ave. (bet. 80th & 81st Sts.), 861-7660
*U – "Lusty and inspired" regional Italian cooking is the
hallmark of this attractive, wood-paneled Eastsider; it's
not cheap, but it's "near the top of the Italian pack."*

|  | F | D | S | C |
|---|---|---|---|---|

### Siu Lam Kung/S
**18 | 10 | 13 | $22**

499 Third Ave. (bet. 33rd & 34th Sts.), 696-9099
*U – "Delicious" Cantonese fare makes this "a real find"; both service and setting are bare bones, but it's "priced right", so who's complaining?*

### Sloppy Louie's/S
**17 | 9 | 12 | $31**

92 South St. (bet. Fulton & John Sts.), 509-9694
*M – Part of the South Street Seaport, this old-time fish house serves "good, plain seafood" that's "priced for tourists" and "thrown at you" by "cranky waiters."*

### Small Cafe, The/S
**21 | 15 | 20 | $35**

Sutton New Residence Hotel, 330 E. 56th St. (bet. 1st & 2nd Aves.), 753-2233
*U – Diners are happy to squeeze into this "tiny" but "cute" Eastsider to enjoy American cooking that's big on quantity, quality and variety plus "friendly, willing" service.*

### SMITH & WOLLENSKY/LS
**22 | 16 | 18 | $50**

201 E. 49th St. (3rd Ave.), 753-1530
*U – Exactly "what a steakhouse should be"; with a "fine wine list" as a plus, this "big", "bustling" Midtowner has the formula down pat: it provides "excellent" "elephant"-sized steaks, chops, lobster and trimmings in a handsome "old-boys–club" setting; undoubtedly the most popular steakhouse in town – they've discovered a new way to print money.*

### Snaps
**– | – | – | E**

Helmsley Building, 230 Park Ave. (46th St.), 949-7878
*Given NYC's shortage of Scandinavians, this attractive Aquavit sibling is snapping up clients; scaled down slightly from its sister, it's still a serious place in style and price.*

### SoHo Kitchen and Bar/LS
**16 | 17 | 15 | $26**

103 Greene St. (bet. Prince & Spring Sts.), 925-1866
*U – "SoHo bar and kitchen" is more like it, since the "food (e.g. pizza, pasta, etc.) is secondary" to the "amazing" selection of wines by the glass; stick with "simple" dishes.*

### Sofia's
**– | – | – | M**

221 W. 46th St. (bet. B'way & Eighth Aves.), 719-5799
*In the heart of the Theater District, this spacious multi-level Northern Italian has respectable food at moderate prices, plus a pianist thrown in for good measure.*

### Solera
**23 | 20 | 21 | $45**

216 E. 53rd St. (bet. 2nd & 3rd Aves.), 644-1166
*U – At this "stylish" townhouse, "very good" "Modern Spanish food", "solid" service and a "lovely" setting afford an "escape from the city's hurly-burly."*

| | F | D | S | C |
|---|---|---|---|---|

**Sonia Rose** | 24 | 21 | 23 | $43 |

132 Lexington Ave. (bet. 28th & 29th Sts.), 545-1777
*U – "One of the best-kept secrets in NY", this "tiny jewel" in Murray Hill sparkles in every facet, from its "exceptional" Eclectic cuisine to its "romantic" townhouse setting and "attentive but nonintrusive" service; it's a perfect place to "fall in love all over again."*

**Sotto Cinque**/SX | 13 | 9 | 14 | $14 |

1644 Second Ave. (85th St.), 472-5563
*M – "Who can argue" with a cheerful place that charges $4.95 for all pasta dishes? fans say "it's the best five bucks you can spend on the East Side", but foes rebut "for $4.95, I can buy a frozen dinner that tastes better."*

**Souen**/S | 15 | 11 | 13 | $20 |

210 Ave. of the Americas (Prince St.), 807-7421
28 E. 13th St. (bet. 5th Ave. & University Pl.), 627-7150
*M – These "politically correct" Villagers serve "healthful and filling" vegetarian-seafood fare that leaves you feeling "spiritually pure"; dissenters say the food tastes like "well-prepared cardboard" and service is "sincere" but "spaced-out."*

**Soup Burg**/LS | 12 | 5 | 12 | $14 |

922 Madison Ave. (73rd St.), 734-6964
1026 First Ave. (56th St.), 421-9184
229 Columbus Ave. (bet. 70th & 71st Sts.), 721-3009
1150 Lexington Ave. (bet. 79th & 80th Sts.), 737-0095
1347 Second Ave. (71st St.), 879-4814
*M – For a "quick, cheap, greasy burger" or "sandwich on the run", these "hole-in-the-wall" coffee shops are voted a good bet by most, but definitely not all.*

**SPARKS STEAK HOUSE** | 24 | 18 | 21 | $54 |

210 E. 46th St. (bet. 2nd & 3rd Aves.), 687-4855
*U – Besides steak "done exactly the way you want it", this "top-tier" Midtowner has "terrific lobster", "wonderful" wines, an "elegant, masculine" setting and "first-class" service; waits and noise are the price of popularity.*

**S.P.Q.R.**/LS | 18 | 19 | 18 | $40 |

133 Mulberry St. (bet. Hester & Grand Sts.), 925-3120
*U – This handsome Genovese used to offer more decor than its Little Italy peers, now thanks to a new chef it offers "very good food" as well; put it back on your list.*

**Spring Street Natural**/LS | 17 | 15 | 14 | $24 |

62 Spring St. (Lafayette St.), 966-0290
*U – "Healthy, but not obnoxious about it", this SoHo veggie-and-fish natural pleases the "whole-grain crowd" (and others) with a mellow "'60s feel".*

|   | F | D | S | C |
|---|---|---|---|---|

**Stage Deli**/LS                    | 16 | 8 | 12 | $20 |

834 Seventh Ave. (bet. 53rd & 54th Sts.), 245-7850
M – This off-Broadway version of Guys and Dolls *has
two aspects of its role down pat: sandwiches so big you
can "dislocate your jaw" and waiters typecast as "surly."*

**Stanhope, The**/S                    | 20 | 24 | 20 | $52 |

Stanhope Hotel, 995 Fifth Ave. (81st St.), 288-5800
U – "'Refined' is the word" for this Continental dining
room; while the cuisine is good, the "genteel and
relaxing" ambiance is the main attraction; it's also "a
treat for tea" and has one of the "best sidewalk cafes in
town" opposite the Met.

**Steak Frites**/LS                    | 18 | 15 | 15 | $34 |

9 E. 16th St. (bet. 5th Ave. & Union Sq. W.), 463-7101
M – True to its name, this newcomer provides "great
steak and fries" at fair prices; it's shaping up as a
"Downtown scene" with "lots of energy."

**Steamer's Landing**/S                    | 13 | 17 | 13 | $27 |

1 Esplanade Plaza (bet. Liberty & Albany Sts.), 432-1451
M – The Eclectic food's merely "ok", but "get a table by
the water on a sunny day" and relax – there's "no better
view of the Hudson."

**Stella del Mare**                    | 21 | 19 | 20 | $45 |

346 Lexington Ave. (bet. 39th & 40th Sts.), 687-4425
M – "Surprising seafood" and other "excellent North
Italian food" plus "caring" service win this Murray Hill
"sleeper" a small but devoted following.

**Stellina**/LS                    | 17 | 12 | 17 | $27 |

220 W. 49th St. (bet. B'way & 8th Ave.), 541-6601
U – "Good pastas", low prices and "convenience" are
the main assets of this Theater District Italian; tables are
"tiny" and there's "no atmosphere."

**Stephanie's**/S                    | 17 | 15 | 17 | $34 |

994 First Ave. (bet. 54th & 55th Sts.), 753-0520
M – A "simple, pleasant" neighbor, this "low-key" Sutton
Place American provides "good if not exceptional" food
in a comfortable setting.

**Stick To Your Ribs BBQ***                    | 23 | 9 | 11 | $17 |
(Queens)/SX

5-16 51st Ave. (west of Vernon Blvd.), 718-937-3030
U – Who'd have thought "the best Texas BBQ pit east of
the Mississippi" was in Long Island City? BBQ buffs
say its ribs and smoked brisket are "unequaled"; a real
"hole in the wall" with "no plates, no cutlery", but at least
it's "clean" – just bring "a road map" and a big appetite.

| F | D | S | C |

**Sugah's**
| – | – | – | M |

248 W. 14th St. (bet. 7th & 8thAves.), 255-7735
*Easily affordable Soul Food and "great" soulful live
music à la New Orleans are the draws at this new West
Village joint which is fortunately "too dark to see."*

**Sugar Reef**/LS
| 15 | 16 | 12 | $24 |

93 Second Ave. (bet. 5th & 6th Sts.), 477-8427
*U – "C'mon, mon, check it out": this "fun and funky" East
Villager has "cheap and spicy" Jamaican food, "mind-
altering" tropical drinks, and "goofy" love-shack decor;
"go with 12 close friends" and "party."*

**Sukhothai West**/S
| 18 | 15 | 15 | $25 |

411 W. 42nd St. (bet. 9th & 10th Aves.), 947-1930
*M – This "always tasty Thai" is worth a try when in the
Theater District; besides good food, it has fair prices,
"polite" service and a "relaxing" setting.*

**Sultan**
| – | – | – | I |

1171 Second Ave. (bet. 61st & 62nd Sts.), 319-7180
*A simple storefront houses this low-budget East 60s
Turkish newcomer, its kebabs and Mazeler (appetizers)
come as a relief after all that East Side pasta.*

**Sumptuary, The**/S
| 18 | 19 | 18 | $32 |

400 Third Ave. (bet. 28th & 29th Sts.), 889-6056
*M – "Intimate and cozy" with both a garden and
fireplace, this Midtown hideaway has a "memorable
setting" for its "offbeat", but good, Eclectic menu.*

**Sunny East**/S
| 21 | 17 | 20 | $31 |

21 W. 39th St. (bet. 5th & 6th Aves.), 764-3232
*U – "Superb" Szechuan food and staff that "go out of
their way" make this attractive Garment District–area
spot "sunny, indeed"; it's busy at lunch, not at night.*

**Supper Club**/L
| 15 | 22 | 15 | $51 |

240 W. 47th St. (bet. B'way & 8th Ave.), 921-1940
*M – The "dancing is fabulous", but the same can't
be said of the American food at this large Theater
District spot with "great '40s nightclub decor", live
bands and entertainment.*

**Supreme Macaroni Co.**/X
| 15 | 11 | 14 | $25 |

511 Ninth Ave. (bet. 38th & 39th Sts.), 502-4842
*M – So it's "not supreme", but this "homey", "hearty"
red-sauce Italian "adventure" in the back of an old Hell's
Kitchen pasta shop has plenty of fans.*

|   | F | D | S | C |
|---|---|---|---|---|

### Sushiden
| | 22 | 16 | 19 | $35 |

19 E. 49th St. (bet. 5th & Madison Aves.), 758-2700
123 W. 49th St. (bet. 6th & 7th Aves.), 246-9204
M – "Superior" sushi and solid service make this duo
stand out in Midtown; some feel the tab is a little high,
but most think it's "well-priced" given the quality.

### SUSHISAY
| | 25 | 16 | 20 | $40 |

38 E. 51st St. (bet. Madison & Park Aves.), 755-1780
U – "Afishonados" say this Midtown Japanese serves
"without a doubt, the best sushi in NYC"; "friendly, helpful"
service and a crisp, clean setting add to its appeal.

### Sushi Zen
| | 23 | 17 | 20 | $34 |

57 W. 46th St. (bet. 5th & 6th Aves.), 302-0707
U – "Meticulous preparation" lies behind the "wonderful"
sushi served at this Midtown Japanese; it's like a "spa
for the palate" with a "calming" setting and good service.

### Sweet Basil's (S.I.)/S
| | 19 | 16 | 16 | $31 |

833 Annadale Rd. (bet. Arden & Amboy), 718-317-5885
U – This "intimate" Islander has a Continental menu
featuring wild game specials: "unbelievably good"; "what
a find – alligator and rattlesnake!"

### Sweets
| | 19 | 12 | 13 | $37 |

2 Fulton St., 2nd fl. (South St.), 825-9786
M – Partisans say this Seaport "old-NY fish house" still
"excels in the basics of seafood"; critics say there's
"nothing sweet about it", from high prices to sour waiters.

### Swiss Inn
| | 17 | 14 | 18 | $32 |

311 W. 48th St. (bet. 8th & 9th Aves.), 459-9280
U – "Hearty", "tasty" Swiss fare (cheese fondue, rosti
potatoes and other "artery-clogging" dishes) comes with
genuine hospitality at this "cozy" Theater District spot.

### Sylvia's Restaurant/S
| | 20 | 12 | 17 | $23 |

328 Lenox Ave. (bet. 126th & 127th Sts.), 996-0660
U – Long the "standard-setter" for "down-home"
Uptown, this Harlem Soul Fooder dishes up "amazing"
ribs, fried chicken, collard greens, etc.; it's "homey",
"jam-packed" and "cheerful", but at night, there's one
rule – cab in, cab out.

### Symphony Cafe/LS
| | 18 | 18 | 18 | $34 |

950 Eighth Ave. (56th St.), 397-9595
U – With "appealing" American food, spacious setting
and "smooth" service in complete harmony, this
Midtown cafe "strikes a high note in a dreary area";
check out its prix fixe dinner and music memorabilia.

| | F | D | S | C |
|---|---|---|---|---|

**Szechuan Hunan Cottage/S**  | 20 | 9 | 17 | $16 |
1590 York Ave. (bet. 83rd & 84th Sts.), 535-5223
1433 Second Ave. (bet. 74th & 75th Sts.), 535-1471
U – "Very good" food that "couldn't be cheaper" explains
the lines outside these Eastsiders; there's "not much
elbow room" and zero decor, but you can avoid the line
via "fastest delivery on the planet."

**Szechuan Kitchen/SX**  | 23 | 7 | 15 | $17 |
1460 First Ave. (76th St.), 249-4615
U – This "tiny" East Side Szechuan inspires raves:
"fabulous", "excellent", "none better"; it's like eating in a
"crowded" old kitchen, but it "can't be beaten" for value.

**Table d'Hôte/S**  | 21 | 20 | 21 | $41 |
44 E. 92nd St. (bet. Madison & Park Aves.), 348-8125
U – Diners find it "amazing" that this Carnegie Hill
Contemporary "charmer" turns out such a "good,
imaginative" menu in such small space; the "quaint"
decor and staff make you "feel you're not in NY."

**Tai Hong Lau\*/S**  | 21 | 12 | 14 | $22 |
70 Mott St. (bet. Canal & Bayard Sts.), 219-1431
U – The "big portions" of "superb" "haute Hong Kong"
cooking turned out at this "elemental" Chinatown
storefront are "worth a visit" for sure.

**Take-Sushi**  | 21 | 14 | 17 | $36 |
71 Vanderbilt Ave. (bet. 45th & 46th Sts.), 867-5120
M – "Sushi is serious business" at this Grand Central
Japanese standby that, though "better than most" of its
peers, loses face because of its prices and decor.

**Taliesin/S**  | – | – | – | E |
Millenium Hotel, 55 Church St. (bet. Fulton & Dey), 312-2000
Open breakfast, lunch and dinner, this handsome
newcomer is modeled on Frank Lloyd Wright's master-
piece house right down to the chairs and utensils; it's
one of Downtown's few civilized venues; for more
casual dining there's the Millenium Grill next door.

**Tango**  | 19 | 12 | 17 | $33 |
43 W. 54th St. (bet. 5th & 6th Aves.), 765-4683
U – This "simple" spot's "really good sushi" and location
near major hotels make it "good for business lunches";
however, it's often nearly "empty at dinner."

**Tang Tang/S**  | 17 | 9 | 14 | $19 |
236 E. 53rd St. (bet. 2nd & 3rd Aves.), 355-5096
1700 Second Ave. (88th St.), 360-7252
1328 Third Ave. (76th St.), 249-2102
M – The tangy "Chinese fast food" dished out at these
East Side "noodle nooks" is "plentiful and cheap"; you'll
be impressed "if you don't mind being rushed."

| | F | D | S | C |
|---|---|---|---|---|

**Taormina**/LS     | 21 | 17 | 19 | $39 |

147 Mulberry St. (bet. Grand & Hester Sts.), 219-1007
*U – Surveyors like this "solid Sicilian" in the heart of
Little Italy; though it's "loud" and "tacky" and John G. is
away, it's much "better than most in the area."*

**Tartine**     | – | – | – | M |

253 W. 11th St. (W. 4th St.), 229-2611
*A typical West Village French boîte, this corner spot is
casual and comfortable; though it's still too new to
judge, we hear the food is a cut above the norm.*

**Taste of Tokyo**/LS     | 17 | 11 | 17 | $25 |

54 W. 13th St. (bet. 5th & 6th Aves.), 691-8666
*M – You get "reliably good" bargain sushi at this
Villager; true, "Godzilla has a more appealing interior",
but it's "perfect for a no-frills dinner."*

**Tatany**/S     | 23 | 15 | 18 | $27 |

380 Third Ave. (bet. 27th & 28th Sts.), 686-1871
*U – Because it's "civilized and affordable", with "fresh
sushi" served in "generous portions", this Gramercy
Japanese usually has a "long wait"; decor is "neat" but
plain, and service "eager to please" but "rushed."*

**Tatiana**/L     | 14 | 16 | 15 | $37 |

26 Wooster St. (Grand St.), 226-6644
*M – The major virtues of this "too trendy for words"
SoHo Mediterranean are its good people-watching and
hot "location"; nothing else about the place is notable.*

**Tatou**/L     | 17 | 22 | 16 | $42 |

151 E. 50th St. (bet. Lexington & 3rd Aves.), 753-1144
*U – Besides liking the "dreamy design" and music at
this "jumping", "sumptuous" Midtown supper club, many
are "happily surprised" by the "better than you'd expect"
New American food that's also available at the quieter
lunch, when the "BMW", "B&T" crowd is absent.*

**TAVERN ON THE GREEN**/S     | 15 | 26 | 17 | $46 |

Central Park West & 67th St., 873-3200
*U – Is "NY's quintessential wow" "still magical" or
"strictly for the rubes"?; critics disdain the "banal food",
but they don't get the point: this "Disneyland NY", with
all its "gaudiness" and "glitz", its Crystal Room and
"lovely" garden is simply "a must for celebrations"; even
the food is "surprisingly good", if you keep it simple; P.S.
its prix fixe lunch and pre-theater dinner can't be beat.*

**Teachers Too**/LS     | 15 | 12 | 14 | $24 |

2271 Broadway (bet. 81st & 82nd Sts.), 362-4900
*M – The West Side's "burger fallback" has "adequate if
unimaginative food", a pleasant warm setting and super
early-bird specials; critics call it "barely acceptable."*

| | F | D | S | C |
|---|---|---|---|---|

**Telephone Bar & Grill**/LS ⎿ 15 | 15 | 14 | $22 ⏌
149 Second Ave. (bet. 9th & 10th Sts.), 529-5000
*M – "Anglophiles love" the "pseudo-British pub" feel and
menu (fish 'n' chips, shepherd's pie) at this "casual"
East Villager, especially after a few beers.*

**Temple Bar**/LS ⎿ 15 | 27 | 16 | $26 ⏌
332 Lafayette St. (bet. Bleecker & Houston), 925-4242
*U – At "the most beautiful bar in NY", what matters is
the "elegant", "sexy" setting studded with "fashion
plates, not the "indifferent" service or too-limited menu.*

**Tempo** ⎿ 21 | 16 | 22 | $39 ⏌
30 E. 29th St. (bet. Madison & Park Aves.), 532-8125
*U – Why this "delightful" Northern Italian, with the
"freshest homemade pasta" and "concerned service",
doesn't draw more widely is a mystery.*

**Ten Kai**\*/S ⎿ 22 | 16 | 20 | $36 ⏌
20 W. 56th St. (bet. 5th & 6th Aves.), 956-0127
*U – At this West Side "Mount Fuji of sushi houses", the
"fish is swimming minutes before you eat it"; no wonder
it's a "regular Japanese business place."*

**Tennessee Mountain**/S ⎿ 16 | 11 | 14 | $23 ⏌
143 Spring St. (Wooster St.), 431-3993
*M – That this "hillbilly-ish" "smoky" SoHo BBQ is "in the
running for NYC's best rib joint" is only proof that we fall
short in this area; "mall decor" and questions about
cleanliness don't help, but the pitchers of beer do.*

**Tequila Sunrise** ⎿ 10 | 10 | 11 | $19 ⏌
(fka Tequila Willie's)
99 Park Ave. (39th St.), 922-5680
729 Seventh Ave. (49th St.), 626-7313
12 Vanderbilt Ave. (42nd St.), 922-5664
64 W. 52nd St. (bet. 5th & 6th Aves.), 767-8338
*U – "Only in desperation", these "gringo" Mexicans
specialize in "flavorless food" and "after-work drinks";
at least they're "inexpensive" and "quick."*

**Teresa's**/LSX ⎿ 17 | 8 | 13 | $16 ⏌
103 First Ave. (bet. 6th & 7th Sts.), 228-0604
80 Montague St. (bet. Hicks St. & Montague Terrace),
Brooklyn, 718-797-3996
*U – "Polish food doesn't get much better" or cheaper
than at these "no-frills" shops; you can forget about the
niceties, but the clientele could care less.*

| F | D | S | C |

## TERRACE/S
| 25 | 26 | 23 | $57 |

400 W. 119th St. (bet. Amsterdam & Morningside), 666-9490
*U – A "360-degree view" and "heavenly" Classic French food are the top draws at this "very romantic", "much-ballyhooed" Columbia rooftop; it's "an island of civilization" in a locale where the valet parking after 6 PM is a necessity.*

## Terry Dinan's/S
| 15 | 15 | 17 | $36 |

10 Park Ave. (34th St.), 576-1010
*M – If you "don't expect miracles", this Murray Hill spot can win you over with the "charm and sincerity" its namesake once brought to The "21" Club; naysayers counter "you have to be over 60 to appreciate" its Traditional American menu and setting.*

## Tevere 84/S
| 20 | 16 | 17 | $47 |

155 E. 84th St. (bet. Lexington & 3rd Aves.), 744-0210
*U – "Rome meets Jerusalem" on the East Side at this "tasty kosher Italian"; despite being "small and crowded", it's big on flavor.*

## Texas Cafe & Grill
| 12 | 12 | 13 | $20 |

10 E. 16th St. (bet. 5th Ave. & University Pl.), 255-8880
*M – This Tex-Mex "hangout" is timidly spiced and "inattentive"; however, it's "friendly", has "live country-and-western bands" – and "hey, it's cheap."*

## T.G.I. Friday's/S
| 10 | 11 | 11 | $20 |

1152 First Ave. (63rd St.), 832-8512
1680 Broadway (bet. 52nd & 53rd Sts.), 767-8326/L
21 W. 51st St. (bet. 5th & 6th Aves.), 767-8352
407 Park Ave. (bet. 54th & 55th Sts.), 339-8855
761 Seventh Ave. (bet. 50th & 51st Sts.), 767-8349/L
*M – Though many scorn this red- and white-striped chain's "lowest common denominator" pub grub and "amateur-hour" service, but many go there since it serves "safe" "basics" at "fair value."*

## Thai Chef*/LS
| 21 | 18 | 19 | $27 |

1466 First Ave. (bet. 76th & 77th Sts.), 734-2539
*U – "An interesting attempt at high-concept Thai food", this East Side yearling is still finding itself; despite "difficult-to-understand waiters", the food "shows promise", with some calling it "the find of the year."*

## Thai House Cafe/LX
| 21 | 10 | 18 | $22 |

151 Hudson St. (Hubert St.), 334-1085
*U – "It doesn't look like much", but "Thai food doesn't come much better" than at this "little hideaway" near the Holland Tunnel; the "intelligent service" is an added virtue.*

|   | F | D | S | C |
|---|---|---|---|---|

**Thailand Restaurant**/LS | 22 | 8 | 14 | $19 |

106 Bayard St. (Baxter St.), 349-3132
*U – Diners put up with a "dingy setting" and service, kindly called "variable", because the cheap "snappy, hot Thai food" at this C-town dive is "Thai'd with the best" in NY.*

**Thai Taste**/S | 16 | 12 | 14 | $22 |

208 Seventh Ave. (22nd St.), 807-9872
153 Remsen St. (bet. Court & Clinton Sts.), Brooklyn, 718-875-2420
125 Seventh Ave. (Carroll St.), Bklyn., 718-622-9376
*M – If "spicy fare" at low prices and "no pretense" is what you want, these Thais are "good places to know about"; skeptics say they "need a cleaning" and the cooking offers "no surprises."*

**Third Avenue Cafe**/S | 16 | 14 | 16 | $30 |

1438 Third Ave. (bet. 81st & 82nd Sts.), 988-1421
*M – Although it's "pleasant" and "reasonably priced", this East Side Continental is "not distinguishable from the rest of the pack" but nice to have nearby.*

**Tibetan Kitchen**/X | 16 | 9 | 15 | $18 |

444 Third Ave. (bet. 30th & 31st Sts.), 679-6286
*M – Undeniably "unusual" and "cheap", the only outpost of Himalayan food in NY doesn't scale any peaks; the room is "kind of scuzzy", and the food, a "less robust cousin to Chinese", is basically "uninspired."*

**Time & Again Restaurant**/S | 22 | 23 | 22 | $46 |

Doral Tuscany Hotel, 116 E. 39th St. (bet. Park & Lexington Aves.), 685-8887
*U – For "well-orchestrated dining", with a "serene" wood-paneled setting that's like "an escape to the 19th century", this Murray Hill New American is a "sleeper" that "cries out for recognition"; dissenters say it's "soft-packaged white bread" and "could use more zip."*

**Time Cafe**/LS | 17 | 16 | 13 | $27 |

380 Lafayette St. (bet. Great Jones & E. 4th), 533-7000
*M – This "politically correct", "earth-conscious" cafe inspires debate: yeah-sayers cite "airy space" and "delicious" natural fare; naysayers point to a "weird menu" and service "not for type-A personalities."*

**Tina's**/LS | 17 | 14 | 15 | $25 |

249 Park Ave. So. (20th St.), 477-1761
*M – The "better-than-average", "wholesome Chinese" cooking rates above the "stark" modern decor and "inconsistent service" at this Gramercy "value spot."*

| | F | D | S | C |
|---|---|---|---|---|

**Tirami Su**/LSX  | 17 | 14 | 14 | $29 |

1410 Third Ave. (80th St.), 988-9780
*M – Often "packed", this East Side North Italian offers
"satisfying" thin-crust pizza and pasta, and "the best
tiramisu in NY", but critics, noting "lazy, arrogant waiters"
and "bare-bones decor", say "there's better elsewhere."*

**Tiziano Trattoria**/LS  | 19 | 16 | 17 | $34 |

165 Eighth Ave. (bet. 18th & 19th Sts.), 989-2330
*U – This "lively", "cosmopolitan" Chelsea Italian with
"consistently solid cooking" strikes most as "simple and
delicious", a "cozy little find"; the only quibbling comes
over the sometimes "hectic and confused" service.*

**Tommaso's** (Brooklyn)/S  | 21 | 15 | 20 | $36 |

1464 86th St. (bet. 14th & 15th Sts.), 718-236-9883
*U – In Bensonhurst, this "robust Southern Italian"
offers a singing staff, a "serious wine list" and an
"unsophisticated" but "charming" setting that add up
to "fun fun fun."*

**Tommy Tang's**  | 21 | 17 | 17 | $35 |

323 Greenwich St. (bet. Duane & Reade Sts.), 334-9190
*M – If you want to "see celebrities" and eat "small
portions" of innovative Thai food", check out this "flashy"
LA-originated TriBeCan.*

**Tompkins Park Restaurant***/LS  | 17 | 15 | 15 | $22 |

141 Ave. A (9th St.), 260-4798
*U – For "better-than-average American bistro food at a
below average price", East Villagers suggest this "spot
of civility in an area of chaos."*

**Tony's Di Napoli**  | – | – | – | M |

1602 Second Ave. (83rd St.), 861-8686
*We thought the East Side was spaghettied-out, but this
spacious Carmine's imitator proved us wrong, opening
to a full house serving heaping family-style platters that
two to three people have trouble eating.*

**Tony Roma's**/LS  | 12 | 9 | 12 | $21 |

1600 Broadway (48th St.), 956-7427
565 Third Ave. (bet. 37th & 38th Sts.), 661-7406
*M – Though some find these rib joints "low-key and
fast", "messy but marvelous", most find that "tasteless"
food and "worsening" staff add up to "no bargain."*

**Toons**/LS  | 17 | 15 | 16 | $26 |

417 Bleecker St. (bet. Bank & W. 11th Sts.), 924-6420
363 Greenwich Ave. (bet. Franklin & Harrison), 925-7440
*U – They're pretty cheap, "tasty" and "refined", but
many feel these "comfortable" Thais "could be much
better" and "service could be faster."*

| | **F** | **D** | **S** | **C** |

**Top of the Sixes** (92) | 13 | 20 | 16 | $41 |

666 Fifth Ave. (bet. 52nd & 53rd Sts.), 757-6662
*U – Despite a famous name and "stellar" views, this rooftop Midtown Continental is best for its happy hour and for visitors with minimal culinary expectations.*

**Tortilla Flats**/LS | 15 | 13 | 13 | $20 |

767 Washington St. (W. 12th St.), 243-1053
*M – "Drinking and flirting" beat eating at this "anything goes" West Village "pseudo-Mexican" where "Elvis lives"; the "garage-sale decor", "wacky waiters" and loud music keep it a lively party scene.*

**Totonno Pizzeria** | 25 | 5 | 8 | $14 |
**Napolitano** (Brooklyn)/SX

1524 Neptune Ave. (W. 16th St.), 718-372-8606
*U – "The original is still the original, and nothing's better" say the myriad fans of this landmark brick-oven pizzeria; it's open Thursday to Sunday from 3 PM until the dough runs out; for decor and service, look elsewhere.*

**Tout Va Bien**/LS | 19 | 13 | 18 | $33 |

311 W. 51st St. (bet. 8th & 9th Aves.), 265-0190
*U – A "Theater District tradition", this French bistro "out of another era" is "the real thing" with "solid, plain food" that "never disappoints", "waitresses like family", and a relatively modest tab; P.S. reserve downstairs.*

**Townhouse, The**/S | 16 | 16 | 17 | $36 |

206 E. 58th St. (bet. 2nd & 3rd Aves.), 826-6241
*M – You know "you're not in Kansas anymore" at this East Side Continental "bit of La Cage Aux Folles"; the "warm and friendly" waiters and "pretty setting" are deliberate, the "camp is inadvertent."*

**Trastevere 83**/S | 22 | 18 | 20 | $45 |

309 E. 83rd St. (bet. 1st & 2nd Aves.), 734-6343
*U – "Romantic to the nines", with "excellent food" and "attentive staff", this ranks "among the best Italians on the Italo–East Side"; if it were a bit less noisy and cramped, it might be in NY's big leagues.*

**Trattoria Alba**\*/S | 19 | 16 | 18 | $31 |

233 E. 34th St. (bet. 2nd & 3rd Aves.), 689-3200
*M – This Murray Hill "converted speakeasy" has a good Italian menu that "proves you don't have to overspend to enjoy."*

**Trattoria dell'Arte**/LS | 21 | 21 | 18 | $39 |

900 Seventh Ave. (bet. 56th & 57th Sts.), 245-9800
*U – Near Carnegie Hall, this "popular" Italian offers a "baroque eating experience" with a "spectacular" antipasto bar, "assertively seasoned" pastas and entrees, and decor featuring body parts à la Leonardo.*

|   | F | D | S | C |
|---|---|---|---|---|

**Tre Scalini**/LS | 21 | 19 | 21 | $50 |

230 E. 58th St. (bet. 2nd & 3rd Aves.), 688-6888
*M – Despite praise for cooking in NY's "upper echelon" and a "wonderful staff", many say this "staid" Northern Italian Eastsider would do better if its prices were a bit lower and its ambiance livelier.*

**Triangolo**/LSX | 18 | 15 | 16 | $28 |

345 E. 83rd St. (bet. 1st & 2nd Aves.), 472-4488
*U – "A real find", this Northern Italian Eastsider has a warm, rosy setting and food that's "better than most"; it's not a world-beater, but it fills a need affordably.*

**TriBeCa Grill**/S | 20 | 19 | 18 | $43 |

375 Greenwich St. (Franklin St.), 941-3900
*U – With Robert DeNiro and half of Hollywood's leading men as owners, this Downtown American grill is, by definition, a "happening spot"; it gets thumbs-up for its "absolutely first-rate" kitchen, handsome brick-walled room centered around the old bar from Maxwell's Plum and smooth orchestration by host-owner Drew Nieporent; it gets a few thumbs-down for being "too trendy" and "too noisy", but that comes with the territory.*

**Trionfo**/L | 20 | 18 | 20 | $39 |

224 W. 51st St. (bet. B'way & 8th Ave.), 262-6660
*U – A "polished" Theater District Northern Italian that "aims to please", and mostly does, with "superior service" and "impressive" if "not particularly original food."*

**Triple Eight Palace**/LS | 19 | 13 | 13 | $23 |

78 E. Broadway (bet. Division & Market), 941-8886
*M – "From blood soup to nut dumplings", this Chinatown warehouse of dim sum delights is "a madhouse" at lunch, but dead at night; "garish decor" and "waiters who can't understand" English are drawbacks.*

**Triplet's Roumanian**/S | 18 | 14 | 18 | $40 |

11-17 Grand St. (6th Ave.), 925-9303
*M – "Order prix fixe and pig out" at this SoHo "barrel of fun" whose Jewish cooking ("get the flanken and stuffed derma") "triples your cholesterol level"; "tables creak and patrons groan" as the performing staff keep the merriment level high.*

**Tripoli** (Brooklyn)/S | 17 | 14 | 15 | $24 |

156 Atlantic Ave. (Clinton St.), 718-596-5800
*M – For "decent" Middle Eastern, this old-timer is "the real thing"; though some claim there's "better and cheaper", it's comforting food and belly dancing are a tradition.*

149

| | F | D | S | C |
|---|---|---|---|---|

**Trois Jean**     | – | – | – | E |
154 E. 79th St. (bet. Lexington & 3rd Aves.), 988-4858
*"Très Français, très bistro" – three young French chefs
have joined their talents and charm to produce this very
attractive new Eastsider in the duplex space that once
was Jams; reserve upstairs for a wonderful evening.*

**Tropica**     | 22 | 19 | 19 | $41 |
200 Park Ave. (45th St. & Vanderbilt Ave.), 867-6767
*U – Chef Ed Brown's "terrific seafood" and Caribbean
fare are the lure to this "cheerful" Key West–style
restaurant which has a "nice airy feel" that's refreshing
to find so near Grand Central.*

**TSE YANG**/S     | 24 | 24 | 22 | $49 |
34 E. 51st St. (bet. Madison & Park Aves.), 688-5447
*U – For "haute Chinese dining", you can't beat this
Midtowner's "regal" setting, "out of the ordinary" cookery
and "attractive, helpful" staff; critics say it costs a lot, but
not compared to its French and Italian peers.*

**T.S. Ma**/S     | 16 | 13 | 15 | $24 |
5 Penn Plaza (33rd St. & 8th Ave.), 971-0050
*M – This Madison Square Garden–area place is good
for "fast, reasonable, tasty Chinese" before a game, but
the menu "gets boring after a while."*

**Tutta Pasta**/S     | 17 | 9 | 14 | $20 |
504 La Guardia (bet. Bleecker & Houston), 420-0652
26 Carmine St. (bet. Bleecker & Bedford), 463-9653
*U – "You can't go wrong" at these "lively" Village
Italians, where better-than-average pasta at real "low
prices" produces "long, long waits" and crowding.*

**20 Mott Street**/LS     | 21 | 9 | 13 | $22 |
20 Mott St. (bet. Bowery & Pell Sts.), 964-0380
*M – Welcome to "Dim-Sum-O-Rama", where all three
floors are often "raucous" and the staff "overworked",
but the dim sum is "wonderful"; in other words, it's a
paradigmatic Chinatown experience.*

**"21" CLUB**/L     | 19 | 22 | 20 | $56 |
21 W. 52nd St. (bet. 5th & 6th Aves.), 582-7200
*M – A "NY landmark", this Midtown former speakeasy
has a "vastly improved kitchen" that complements its
"elegant", "clubby" four-story quarters; it also has
"surprisingly pleasant service" for "a place known for its
caste system"; the downstairs barroom is most popular
with its "power-hitting celeb" regulars, but it also does
"well-run parties" upstairs in a choice of rooms; for a
bargain introduction, check out the $19.93 lunch.*

|  F | D | S | C |
|----|----|----|----|

## Twigs/LS
| 18 | 14 | 16 | $25 |

196 Eighth Ave. (20th St.), 633-6735
*U – Chelseans call this an "ideal neighbor" because its "hip bar scene" and "dependable" Italian fare come with "pleasant prices"; ergo, it's often cramped.*

## Two Boots/LS
| 18 | 14 | 14 | $18 |

37 Ave. A (bet. 2nd & 3rd Sts.), 505-2276
*U – With loads of "natural personality", this East Village Cajun pizzeria's "imaginative" pies and "congenial staff" produce crowds despite an iffy locale and "dingy" room.*

## Two Eleven/LS
| 19 | 19 | 18 | $33 |

211 W. Broadway (Franklin St.), 925-7202
*U – A "pleasant find" in TriBeCa, this "relaxing" New American offers a "well-prepared" menu to its "groovy art-world" and Wall Street regulars who like the terrace.*

## Umeda/S
| 22 | 16 | 19 | $40 |

102 E. 22nd St. (bet. Park Ave. S. & Lexington), 505-1550
*U – A "serene" Gramercy Japanese serving standout sushi and intriguing dishes "not found elsewhere" – "you may have to be Japanese to appreciate the subtlety."*

## UNION SQUARE CAFE/S
| 26 | 22 | 23 | $48 |

21 E. 16th St. (bet. 5th Ave. & Union Sq.), 243-4020
*U – Customers of Danny Meyer's "very civilized" cafe – and they are legion – praise this New American as a model of what "the restaurant of the '90s should be", citing its "marvelously creative" yet "consistently excellent" cuisine, "friendly and knowledgeable" staff, "extensive wine list" and "warm", "relaxed" ambiance; among NYC's top restaurants, it's a "great value."*

## Universal Grill/LS
| 18 | 14 | 17 | $26 |

44 Bedford St. (Leroy St.), 989-5621
*M – "Lively and crowded", wild late at night, this "ultragroovy" Village American is "where the boys are"; the food is "good, homey" and "cheap", service "friendly" and the soundtrack includes "great '50s music."*

## Upstairs at the Downstairs*/S
| 15 | 16 | 16 | $29 |

531 Hudson St. (bet. W. 10th & Charles Sts.), 206-7093
*U – Live entertainment and a cozy fireplace add to the "theatrical feel" of this Villager; it's "not inspired", but has good Eclectic food, modest prices and "friendly service."*

## Urban Grill/S
| 16 | 7 | 14 | $17 |

1613 Second Ave. (bet. 83rd & 84th Sts.), 744-2122
330 W. 58th St. (bet. 8th & 9th Aves.), 586-3300
*U – Despite coffee-shop settings, "terrific" burgers and pita sandwiches make these takeout-and-delivery specialists "perfect to have around the corner."*

| | F | D | S | C |
|---|---|---|---|---|

**Urbino**  `19 | 13 | 20 | $37`
78 Carmine St. (7th Ave. S.), 242-2676
*M – While most diners find the Northern Italian food and service at this West Villager "very good", the "tired" and "shabby" decor is a real turnoff.*

**Uskudar**/S  `20 | 12 | 17 | $27`
1405 Second Ave. (bet. 73rd & 74th Sts.), 988-2641
*U – The "unusual, tasty" Turkish home cooking is "a treat" and "a bargain" at this "tiny" East Side storefront; however, the decor "needs help"; BYO.*

**Va Bene\***/S  `22 | 17 | 19 | $41`
1589 Second Ave. (bet. 82nd & 83rd Sts.), 517-4448
*M – "Great for kosher Italian", but "not great Italian", this "rather elegant" Eastsider can be "wonderful", but some say that it's too "pricey" for pasta.*

**Valone's**/S  `17 | 12 | 15 | $26`
1236 Third Ave. (bet. 71st & 72nd Sts.), 288-0202
*U – It's "doggy-bag time" at this huge, "earsplitting" East Side version of Carmine's ("but not nearly as good"); its family-style Italian fare comes in hearty portions, but the service and decor need brightening up.*

**Vasata**/S  `18 | 13 | 17 | $33`
339 E. 75th St. (bet. 1st & 2nd Aves.), 988-7166
*U – Though "dated", "it feels like you're in Prague" at this "homey" old-world Czech; when you want goose or duck and dumplings, this is the place.*

**Vernon's Jerk Paradise**  `15 | 11 | 15 | $21`
252 W. 29th St. (bet. 7th & 8th Aves.), 268-7020
*M – If "not paradise", this bright and cheap Caribbean in Chelsea revives one's "memories of Jamaica" with its "hot, hot" jerk meats and funky "Dating Game" decor.*

**Veselka**/LS  `17 | 8 | 12 | $13`
144 Second Ave. (9th St.), 228-9682
*M – A "cheap, ethnic belly-filler", this 24-hour East Village Ukranian coffee shop draws a colorful crowd; "go when you're hungry" for pierogies, borscht, blintzes and fresh challah at "pre-putsch prices" – but don't cross the "surly waitresses."*

**Vespa\***/LSX  `20 | 16 | 17 | $31`
1625 Second Ave. (84th St.), 472-2050
*U – "Step into Italy" at this "charming" yearling whose kitchen is holding its own with neighbors like Elio's and Azzurro; P.S. "ask the prices of specials before ordering."*

|  | F | D | S | C |
|---|---|---|---|---|

### Viand/SX
`17 | 6 | 14 | $13`

300 E. 86th St. (2nd Ave.), 879-9425/LSX
1011 Madison Ave. (bet. 78th & 79th Sts.), 249-8250/S
673 Madison Ave. (bet. 61st & 62nd Sts.), 751-6622/SX
*U – You'll find "mink coats slumming" in search of the "best turkey sandwich in NY" at these popular East Side coffee shops; they're "quick" and "filling", but "no big deal."*

### Via Via/LS
`15 | 15 | 14 | $31`

1294 Third Ave. (bet. 74th & 75th Sts.), 439-0130
*M – "Good but not overly exciting" is how most regard this "airy", "casual" Northern Italian; though "very pleasant", there are better on the East Side.*

### Vico/LSX
`20 | 15 | 17 | $41`

1302 Madison Ave. (92nd St.), 876-2222
*U – Good food "overcomes cramped quarters" and an "annoying" no-plastic policy at this busy Carnegie Hill Italian; it's "full of 'in' people" foraging for "superb" pastas and mixed grill.*

### Vico Express*/LSX
`19 | 13 | 18 | $37`

1603 Second Ave. (bet. 83rd & 84th Sts.), 772-2161
*M – Despite "fine cooking", this speedier Vico sibling hasn't caught on – perhaps because it's "expensive for express" and its mod-storefront lacks warmth.*

### Victor's/LS
`17 | 14 | 15 | $35`

240 Columbus Ave. (71st St.), 595-8599/LS
236 W. 52nd St. (bet. B'way & 8th), 586-7714/LS
*M – While some call the hearty food "mediocre", excellent sangria and "the best roast suckling pig in NY" keep these two separately owned and "very different" Cubans crowded; West 52nd is "spacious and more elegant", while 71st is casual and far from fancy.*

### View, The/S
`18 | 25 | 18 | $46`

Marriott Marquis Hotel, 1535 Broadway (bet. 45th & 46th Sts.), 704-8900
*U – People expect this French-American revolving high above Times Square to be "only for tourists", but they're pleased to find that it's "surprisingly good", both for brunch and pre-theater.*

### Villa Berulia
`21 | 18 | 21 | $39`

107 E. 34th St. (bet. Park & Lexington Aves.), 689-1970
*U – Offering "personable service" and "delicious food", it's amazing that this Midtown "bella" North Italian isn't better known; try the "king-size veal chops" or cannelloni.*

| F | D | S | C |
|---|---|---|---|

**Villa Lulu** | – | – | – | M |
235 Park Ave. So. (19th St.), 529-4770
*In Cafe Iguana's former space, there's a new cheerful yellow Southern Italian featuring pasta and pizzas, loud music and a bocce ball court upstairs; these people are pros at creating singles scenes.*

**Village Atelier**/LS | 21 | 23 | 20 | $39 |
436 Hudson St. (Morton St.), 989-1363
*U – Set off by "exquisite" flowers, this rustic French Village "sleeper" romances diners with its "intelligent" and "homey" food and "charming setting"; it's so nice, some diners "want to live there."*

**Villa Mosconi** | 19 | 14 | 18 | $33 |
69 MacDougal St. (bet. Bleecker & Houston), 673-0390
*U – An "old-reliable" Village Italian with "heavy portions" of good food; the "old-world decor" and "crowded seating" don't daunt diners who say it has "lots of character."*

**Vince and Eddie's**/LS | 19 | 16 | 16 | $39 |
70 W. 68th St. (bet. Columbus Ave. & CPW), 721-0068
*M – This "busy" Westsider serves homestyle American fare that's also "imaginative"; add "fair prices" and a "cute" Americana setting and you've got crowds all the time.*

**Vinnie's Pizza**/LSX | 20 | 6 | 13 | $10 |
285 Amsterdam Ave. (73rd St.), 874-4382
*U – As always, one of NYC's best dining values, this nothing-fancy-Formica by-the-slice West Side pizzeria offers what its fans insist is "the best pizza in NY", or at least "best on the West Side"; if you like "cheesy", "chewy" pizza, this meal in a slice is for you.*

**Vinsanto**/S | 18 | 18 | 18 | $30 |
1619 Second Ave. (84th St.), 772-3375
*U – Being "sandwiched in between Elio's and Azzurro" could be tough, but this attractive trattoria is "quite crowded" anyway, thanks to "good Italian at reasonable prices"; the $16.50 pre-theater menu is a best buy.*

**Vittorio Cucina***/S | 21 | 19 | 19 | $37 |
308 Bleecker St. (bet. 7th Ave. S. & Grove St.), 463-0730
*U – A "charming" Village Italian that "takes you to a new part of Italy every month" with changing regional menus; though good, it hasn't caught on yet.*

**Vivolo**/L | 20 | 19 | 19 | $39 |
140 E. 74th St. (bet. Park & Lexington Aves.), 737-3533
*U – A "romantic Northern Italian that has everything", including "consistently good" food, an "adorable townhouse" setting and solid service; the $12.95 dinner served upstairs after 9 PM and "the fireplace in the winter" get raves; it has a new takeout next door.*

|  F  |  D  |  S  |  C  |
| --- | --- | --- | --- |

### Volare*                          | 19 | 14 | 21 |$30|
147 W. 4th St. (bet. 6th Ave. & Wash. Sq. Park), 777-2849
*U – At this Carmine's wanna-be, the best advice is to ignore the decor and focus on the "amazing" Italian food and the "friendly" staff.*

### Vong and Kwong*/LS              | 20 |  8 | 15 |$26|
11 Division St. (nr. Market St.), 431-1040
*U – There's no decor at this Chinatown spot, but the authentic Cantonese dishes are "worth the trip"; just close your eyes when you eat.*

### Voulez-Vous/LS                  | 19 | 13 | 18 |$35|
1462 First Ave. (76th St.), 249-1776
*U – "A great neighbor", this "solid French" bistro has avid clients who love its "well-priced", rotating regional menu, "fantastic brunch", "good cheap wine" and "anxious-to-please" service; only the decor has doubters.*

### Vucciria/LS                     | 20 | 19 | 18 |$38|
422 W. Broadway (bet. Prince & Spring Sts.), 941-5811
*U – Featuring "fine pasta at good prices" and "terrific specials", this trompe l'oeil SoHo Sicilian offers the taste, and look, of Palermo; usually "nice", the waiters at times act "like you're bothering them."*

### Walker's/LS                     | 16 | 15 | 15 |$22|
16 N. Moore St. (Varick St.), 941-0142
*U – This "great old-NY saloon" draws "local TriBeCa folk" plus a fair share of "art people" and "Wall Streeters" for its "good pub grub."*

### Wally's and Joseph's/L          | 18 | 13 | 17 |$45|
249 W. 49th St. (bet. B'way & 8th Ave.), 582-0460
*M – Regulars return to this Theater District steakhouse for meats, fish, pasta and house salad in a "clubby", masculine setting, but that "private club feeling may be one you don't belong to."*

### Water Club/LS                   | 20 | 24 | 19 |$51|
500 E. 30th St. (East River), 683-3333
*U – "You can't beat the view" from this elegant East River cafe – that's why the "very good" American food and service sometimes get overlooked; still, all agree that it has one of the "best Sunday brunches in NY" and it's "great for parties" or "cocktails on the deck."*

### Water's Edge (Queens)           | 20 | 26 | 20 |$50|
44th Drive & East River, 718-482-0033
*U – The "great view of the NYC skyline" from this Queens barge is "half the fun", the other half comes from eating the much "improved" New American food; it's so "romantic" it's called "proposal territory."*

|   | F | D | S | C |
|---|---|---|---|---|

### West Broadway Restaurant/S    | 20 | 20 | 18 | $38 |
349 W. Broadway (bet. Grand & Broome Sts.), 226-5885
*U – This SoHo yearling with a "cool, chic crowd" has taken off since chef John Schenk arrived breathing new life into the "lovely bar" and "great lofty dining room."*

### Westside Cafe/S    | 16 | 9 | 14 | $18 |
892 Ninth Ave. (bet. 57th & 58th Sts.), 245-8822
*M – A local Chinese that's "a little above your usual coffee shop" and regulars say it's "a real bargain"; there's "lightning-fast" delivery to solve any aesthetic qualms on premises.*

### Westside Cottage/LS    | 17 | 10 | 15 | $16 |
689 Ninth Ave. (bet. 47th & 48th Sts.), 245-0800
*U – Some rate this busy spot as "one of the best Chinese", but we suspect they were influenced by the "free wine" and "low prices"; still, the food's "fresh" and "good" and they don't waste time serving it.*

### White Horse Tavern/LSX    | 12 | 14 | 12 | $18 |
567 Hudson St. (11th St.), 243-9260
*U – At this 1880 "Village landmark" once frequented by Dylan Thomas, "basic pub food" complements the old-Dublin saloon setting; it's a "favorite local hangout" with outdoor tables affording "great people-watching."*

### Whole Wheat 'n Wildberrys/S    | 17 | 11 | 16 | $19 |
57 W. 10th St. (bet. 5th & 6th Aves.), 677-3410
*M – "Good" vegetarian food, served in a "cozy, homey" setting on a private tree-lined Village street has health-food junkies singing its praises; meat-eaters say "healthy and boring" and ask "when's dinner?"*

### Wilkinson's Seafood Cafe/S    | 22 | 17 | 20 | $46 |
1573 York Avenue (bet. 83rd & 84th Sts.), 535-5454
*U – For "beautifully prepared fresh fish" served in "pleasant surroundings" by "nice staff", you'll be hard-pressed to do better than this pricey Eastsider.*

### Willie's*/LS    | 15 | 11 | 14 | $24 |
1426 Third Ave. (81st St.), 472-4500
*M – This inexpensive Eastsider is too new for many comments other than it's a "good local place for burgers and salads", "nice brunch" and "loud blaring music."*

### Wilson's/LS    | 14 | 13 | 14 | $30 |
201 W. 79th St. (Amsterdam Ave.), 769-0100
*M – The "prix fixe, pre-concert dinner is a bargain" and there's an "excellent brunch" at this "spacious" Westsider; it gets "loud" and you risk "singles overload."*

| **F** | **D** | **S** | **C** |

### WINDOWS ON THE WORLD/S  | 16 | 27 | 19 | $52 |
1 World Trade Ctr., 107th fl., West St. (bet. Liberty &
Vesey Sts.), 938-1111
*M – The view and decor at this "Eighth Wonder of the
World" get all raves: "breathtaking", "spectacular", "20
million sparkling lights", but the Continental food rates
less well: "tourist fare", "doesn't measure up"; still, this
elegant aerie is always "great for drinks", watching the
sunset in the City Lights Bar or for Sunday brunch; the
mimeoed wine list is an oenophile's dream.*

### Winter Garden Cafe/S  | 13 | 22 | 12 | $25 |
2 World Financial Ctr. (West St.), 945-7200
*M – "Palm trees" and four-story ceilings make this "one
of NYC's most impressive spaces", but "unexciting" Cal-
Caribe food doesn't make it an impressive restaurant.*

### Wolf's 6th Ave. Delicatessen/LS  | 15 | 8 | 12 | $20 |
101 W. 57th St. (6th Ave.), 586-1110
*M – "A reliable deli with a coffee-shop atmosphere", a
"convenient" Midtown location and "big sandwiches";
critics call it "a poor man's Carnegie."*

### Wollensky's Grill/LS  | 20 | 16 | 17 | $37 |
205 E. 49th St. (3rd Ave.), 753-0444
*U – The smaller, more casual next door sibling of Smith
& Wollensky, with outdoor seating in summer offers "fast
service" in a "handsome bar setting"; its steaks, burgers
and side dishes have "the same high quality" as S&W,
but are "lower priced."*

### Wong Kee/SX  | 20 | 4 | 10 | $14 |
113 Mott St. (bet. Canal & Hester Sts.), 966-1160
*U – "Forget the stark tables, unrelenting noise and
dreary decor", a lot of people consider this "dirt cheap"
Cantonese "the best in Chinatown"; "they're practically
giving the food away; "long may it bustle."*

### Woo Chon*/LS  | 21 | 14 | 16 | $24 |
8-10 W. 36th St. (bet. 5th & 6th Aves.), 695-0676
*U – As it's "one of the few attractive places in Little
Korea", you can feel comfortable bringing clients to this
"terrific Korean", despite "language difficulties."*

### Woo Lae Oak of Seoul/S  | 19 | 13 | 14 | $29 |
77 W. 46th St. (bet. 5th & 6th Aves.), 869-9958
*M – Do-it-yourselfers "love this noisy Korean" for its
"spicy" food; others deride the "Korea-meets-cafeteria"
decor, and "prefer to have someone else cook when
eating out."*

| | F | D | S | C |
|---|---|---|---|---|

### World Yacht Cruises/S
| 13 | 23 | 15 | $54 |

Pier 62, W. 23rd St. & Hudson River, 929-7090
*M – The package here includes a harbor cruise, music and Continental food with passengers rating the features in that order; though some warn "don't count on good food", for most people this is "a must do in NY."*

### Wylie's Ribs I & II/LS
| 16 | 10 | 14 | $25 |

891 First Ave. (50th St.), 751-0700
*M – Rib-aholics are a contentious lot; they can't agree whether the ribs at this elemental Eastsider are "the best in town" or "insulting" and "awful"; bring the kids and find out for yourself.*

### Yamaguchi/S
| 21 | 16 | 19 | $32 |

35 W. 45th St. (bet. 5th & 6th Aves.), 840-8185
*M – What some hail as an "excellent" Japanese with "great value", others find to be "ordinary" with "depressing decor"; its "lunch boxes" are a bargain compromise.*

### Yankee Clipper, The/S
| 16 | 17 | 17 | $35 |

170 John St. (South St.), 344-5959
*M – "An island of civility", this spacious Seaport fish house appeals to "the Wall Street crowd" with "friendly" service and "fresh" seafood; critics say "sail away."*

### Yellowfingers/LS
| 16 | 13 | 14 | $26 |

200 E. 60th St. (3rd Ave.), 751-8615
*U – "Consistently good", this "post-Bloomie's" or "pre-movies" East Side pit stop is praised for its pasta, salads and "satisfying snacks" plus its "high energy" and entertaining "people-watching", all at low prices.*

### Yellow Rose Cafe/S
| 16 | 11 | 14 | $24 |

450 Amsterdam Ave. (bet. 81st & 82nd Sts.), 595-8760
*M – "Put on your cowboy boots" and "stuff yourself" with "satisfying" chicken-fried steak and other gravy-covered Texas diet-busters at this West Side dive; to naysayers, it's "run-down" with "NY–style Texas cooking."*

### Ying/S
| 18 | 13 | 17 | $25 |

117 W. 70th St. (bet. Columbus & B'way), 724-2031
*M – Whether this affordable but cavelike West Side Szechuan is "first class" or "slipping" and "no longer special" defines our surveyors' debate; most votes are positive.*

### Yuka*/S
| 18 | 10 | 16 | $25 |

1557 Second Ave. (bet. 80th & 81st Sts.), 772-9675
*U – The $18 "all-you-can-eat sushi special" at this "seedy" East Side Japanese means crowds, but it's "worth the wait" and there's always "quick" delivery or takeout.*

| | F | D | S | C |
|---|---|---|---|---|

### ZARELA/S
| 22 | 16 | 17 | $35 |

953 Second Ave. (bet. 50th & 51st Sts.), 644-6740
*U – Satisfied surveyors for the fourth year in a row have rated this colorful and cacophonous Eastsider "NYC's Best Mexican", citing "inventive" dishes with "flavors that explode off the plate"; a "fun crowd" fueled by potent margaritas makes for a "festive atmosphere."*

### Zen Palate/S
| 20 | 20 | 18 | $28 |

663 Ninth Ave. (46th St.), 582-1669
*U – "Unique" is the word for this "stylish, modern" "Zen-atmosphere", "health-conscious" Chinese Vegetarian; its customers say they've "seen the future and it's good."*

### Zephyr Grill*/S
| 17 | 19 | 17 | $34 |

Beekman Tower Hotel, 1 Mitchell Pl. (1st Ave. & 49th St.), 223-4200
*U – Locals root for this U.N.-area art deco American to succeed "where several have failed"; they say it's "great" for lunch or brunch and praise the "spa menu" and "good-value" prix fixe.*

### Zinno/S
| 18 | 18 | 19 | $35 |

126 W. 13th St. (bet. 6th & 7th Aves.), 924-5182
*U – "Terrific" Northern Italian food and "wonderful" jazz make an "unbeatable duo" at this "romantic" West Villager where the mood is "classy" but "low key".*

### Zip City Brewery/S
| 15 | 17 | 14 | $26 |

3 W. 18th St. (bet. 5th & 6th Aves.), 366-6333
*M – This Downtown "microbrewery" is a "new hot spot" for "twenty-something" "singles" who crowd in for its "dark and yeasty" home brews and "good" bar food; critics say "beer and attitude – who needs it?"*

### Zocalo
| – | – | – | M |

302 Columbus Ave. (74th St.), 721-6000
*Still ironing out the wrinkles after a recent opening, this charming West Side SW can "rival Mesa" on one night and "disappoint" the next; after a few potent margaritas from the sleek bar, you won't know the difference.*

### Zoe/S
| 20 | 19 | 17 | $40 |

90 Prince St. (bet. B'way & Mercer Sts.), 966-6722
*U – They've "done everything right" at this new SoHo "fun and friendly" Contemporary American; citing "stunning" modern decor, its admirers consider it the "best new restaurant" of the year.*

| | F | D | S | C |
|---|---|---|---|---|

### Zona Rosa
| | 12 | 11 | 13 | $24 |

211 E. 59th St. (bet. 2nd & 3rd Aves.), 759-4444/S
142 W. 44th St. (bet. 6th Ave. & B'way), 354-4444
*M – "Lively" is an understatement when it comes to these convenient Mexican "after-work haunts"; the "young" crowd understandably favors the disco jukebox and "great" margaritas over the "so-so" food.*

### Zucchero/SX
| | 19 | 12 | 16 | $24 |

1464 Second Ave. (bet. 76th & 77th Sts.), 517-2541
*M – A "favorite new bargain" Italian spot, the pastas and salads at this bright, peach-colored Eastsider "can't be beat for price or taste"; as ratings indicate, the decor and "spotty" service can be beaten.*

### Zucchini/S
| | 16 | 14 | 16 | $24 |

1336 First Ave. (bet. 70th & 71st Sts.), 249-0559
*M – Diners divide on this East Side Vegetarian: to some it's "fantastic", "healthy and low-cal" with a "homey" and "comfortable" feel; others find it a "tasteless" "letdown" with "tacky" decor.*

### Zula/LS
| | 17 | 9 | 17 | $18 |

1260 Amsterdam Ave. (122nd St.), 663-1670
*U – It may be "good for students" but this Uptown Ethiopian's "finger-lickin' good" food and modest setting is unlikely to appeal to any but the most adventurous elder diner.*

### Zutto/LS
| | 17 | 17 | 17 | $29 |

77 Hudson St. (bet. Jay & Harrison Sts.), 233-3287
*U – Neighbors give good marks to this "dependable" TriBeCa Japanese's "excellent sushi", "reasonable" prices, "fast" service and "intimate" "Zen setting."*

# INDEXES TO RESTAURANTS

# SPECIAL FEATURES AND APPEALS

# TYPES OF CUISINE

## Afghan

Afghan Kebab House
Khyber Pass
Pamir

## African

Akadi
Zula

## American
## (Contemporary)

Amazon Village
Ambassador Grill
American Festival Cafe
Amsterdam's
An American Place
Angelica Kitchen
Arcadia
Aureole
Bistro 36
Blue Light
Bridge Cafe
Broadway Diner
Broadway Grill
Buckaroo's
Busby's
Cafe S.F.A.
Cameos
Century Cafe
Charlotte
City Cafe
Country Club
Cupping Room
Donald Sacks
Duane Park
Edwardian Room
Edward Moran
Elephant & Castle
Fisher & Levy
44
Garden Cafe
Gotham Bar/Grill
Henry's End
Hi-Life Bar/Grill
Houlihan's
Hourglass Tavern
Hudson River Club
Island
Josephina
Keens Chop Hse.
Kulu

Lion's Rock
Lora
Louie's Westside
Luxe
Manhattan Plaza Cafe
Man Ray
March
McFeely's
Mesa Grill
Metropolis Cafe
Michael's
Mr. Fuji's Tropicana
Museum Cafe
New Deal
Nosmo King
Odeon
One if by Land, TIBS
Palm Court, The
Park Avenue Cafe
Patric
Planet Hollywood
Polo, The
Prix Fixe
Quilted Giraffe
Rascals
Regency, The
Rose Cafe
Saloon, The
Sam's Cafe
Sam's Restaurant
Sarabeth's
Savoy
Sharkey's
Shelby
Sign of the Dove
Small Cafe
SoHo Kitchen/Bar
Spring St. Natural
Supper Club
Symphony Cafe
Table d'Hote
Tatou
Time & Again
Time Cafe
TriBeCa Grill
Two Eleven
Union Square Cafe
Universal Grill
View, The
Walker's
Water Club
Water's Edge

West Broadway
Wilson's
Yellowfingers
Zephyr Grill
Zoe

## American
## (Traditional)

Aggie's
American Harvest
Aspen Cafe
Beach Cafe
Bellevues
Bill's Gay 90s
Billy's
Boogies Diner
Boulevard
Brighton Grill
Bubby's
Buckaroo's
Bull & Bear
Burger Heaven
Busby's
Cafe Nicholson
Cal's
Charley O's
Chelsea Commons
Christ Cella
Churchill's
Cloister Cafe
Coconut Grill
Common Market Cafe
Condon's
Cornelia St. Cafe
Corner Bistro
Dakota Bar & Grill
Dock's
Ed Debevic's
EJ's Luncheonette
Empire Diner
Fanelli
Fraunces Tavern
Friend of a Farmer
Gallagher's
Good Enough to Eat
Grange Hall
Hard Rock Cafe
Harriet's Kitchen
Harry's
Jerry's
Jerry's 103
Jim McMullen
Lexington Ave. Grill
Lion's Head
Lofland's N.Y. Grill

Luke's Bar & Grill
Mackinac Bar & Grill
Maryland Crab House
Mayfair
McDonald's
Merchants
Mezzanine
Mickey Mantle's
Moran's
Mortimer's
Mulholland Drive
Nadine's
Nick & Eddie
N.Y. Deli
Oak Bar
Old Bermuda Inn
Old Town Bar
Orson's
Papaya King
Park Ave. Country Club
Pen & Pencil
Pete's Tavern
Phoebe's
Pietro & Vanessa
Popover Cafe
Post House
Rascals
Ratner's
R.H. Tugs
Roebling's
Rogers & Barbero
Royal Canadian
Rumpelmayer's
Ruppert's
Russell's
Saranac
Sequoia
Serendipity 3
7th Regiment Mess
Smith & Wollensky
SoHo Kitchen/Bar
Soup Burg
Stephanie's
Teachers Too
Terry Dinan's
T.G.I. Friday's
Tompkins Park
"21" Club
Urban Grill
Vince & Eddie's
Walker's
Willie's
Yankee Clipper

## Argentinean

La Fusta

## Bar-B-Q

Atomic Wings
Brother Jimmy's BBQ
Brother's BBQ
Buckaroo's
Chicken Chef
Dallas BBQ
Hard Rock Cafe
Levee, The
R.H. Tugs
Stick to Ribs BBQ
Sylvia's
Tennessee Mountain
Tony Roma's
Wylie's Ribs

## Belgian

Cafe de Bruxelles

## Brazilian

Banana Cafe
Brazilian Pavilion
Cabana Carioca
Coffee Shop

## Burmese

Bali Burma
BTI
Mingala Burmese
Road to Mandalay

## Cajun/Creole

Acme Bar & Grill
Fannie's Oyster Bar
Great Jones Cafe
Gulf Coast
Hows Bayou
Memphis
107 West
Sazarac House
Two Boots

## Californian

Benny's Burritos
Bertha's
Cafe Botanica
Coastal
Lora
Lucy's
Metro C.C.
Michael's

New Prospect Cafe
Original Taqueria
Rose Cafe
Winter Garden Cafe

## Caribbean

Bimini Twist
Caribe
Day-O
Flying Fish
Island Spice
Mr. Fuji's Tropicana
R.H. Tugs
Sabor
Sugar Reef
Tropica
Vernon's
Winter Garden Cafe

## Caviar

Petrossian
Russian Tea Room

## Chinese

Au Mandarin
Beijing Duck House
Bo Ky
Canton
Chao Chow
Chef Ho's
Chiam
China Grill
Chin Chin
Chop Suey Looey's
Cho-Sen Garden
Columbia Cottage
David Keh's N.R.
Dish of Salt
Empire Szechuan
1st Wok
Fu's
Golden Unicorn
Great Shanghai
H.S.F.
Hunan Balcony
Hunan Garden
Hwa Yuan Szechuan
J. Sung Dynasty
Keewah Yen
La Caridad
Lai Lai West
Little Shanghai
Lum Chin
Mandarin Court
Marnie's Noodle Shop

Mr. Chow
Mr. Tang's
Nice Restaurant
Ollie's
Oriental Pearl
Oriental Town
Our Place
Pig Heaven
Shun Lee Cafe
Shun Lee Palace
Shun Lee West
Sichuan Palace
Silk Road Place
Silver Palace
Siu Lam Kung
Sunny East
Szechuan Hunan
Szechuan Kitchen
Tai Hong Lau
Tang Tang
Tina's
Triple Eight Palace
Tse Yang
T.S. Ma
20 Mott Street
Vong & Kwong
Westside Cafe
Westside Cottage
Wong Kee
Ying

## Coffee Houses

Algonquin Lobby*
Anglers & Writers
Au Cafe
Cafe Bel Canto
Cafe Lalo
Cafe Word of Mouth
Caffe Bianco
Caffe Biondo
Caffe Vivaldi
Cooper's Coffee
Cornelia St. Cafe
Cupcake Cafe
Ferrara
La Boulangere
Les Friandises
Lipstick Cafe
Mayfair Lobby*
Patisserie Lanciani
Sarabeth's
(*Not in *Survey*)

## Coffee Shops

Bendix Diner
Broadway Diner

Burger Heaven
Conservatory Cafe
E.A.T.
Edison Cafe
Eighteenth & Eighth
Pete's Place
2nd Ave. Brasserie
Soup Burg
Viand

## Colombian

Casa Colombia

## Continental

Algonquin Hotel
Blue Light
Box Tree
Carlyle Dining Rm.
Cellar in the Sky
Copacabana
Cupping Room
Delmonico's
Four Seasons
Giando
Grove Street Cafe
Halcyon
Harbour Lights
Jockey Club
Leopard
Le Train Bleu
Levana
Lion's Rock
Marion's
Mark's
Marylou's
Metropolitan Cafe
Mme. Romaine
Nicola Paone
One Hudson Cafe
One if by Land, TIBS
Palm Court
Peacock Alley
Pembroke Room
Rainbow Room
Rao's
River Cafe
Stanhope, The
Sweet Basil's
Swiss Inn
Tavern on the Green
Third Ave. Cafe
Top of the Sixes
Townhouse
Water Club
Windows on the World
World Yacht

## Cuban

Bayamo
La Caridad
La Taza de Oro
Sabor
Victor's

## Czech

Vasata

## Delis

Barney Greengrass
Bloom's Delicatessen
Carnegie Deli
Fine & Schapiro
Katz's Deli
Second Ave. Deli
Stage Deli
N.Y. Deli
Wolf's 6th Ave. Deli

## Dim Sum

Chin Chin
Golden Unicorn
H.S.F.
Mandarin Court
Silver Palace
Shun Lee Cafe
Triple Eight Palace
20 Mott Street

## Diners

Bendix Diner
Boogies Diner
Eighteenth & Eighth
EJ's Luncheonette

## Eclectic

Aggie's
America
Anglers & Writers
Au Cafe
Aunt Sonia's
Back Porch
Ballroom, The
Bell Caffe
Bendix Diner
Bloom's Delicatessen
Boom
Boxers
Broadway Diner
B. Smith's
Cafe Word of Mouth
Camelback & Central

Chefs & Cuisiniers
Coming or Going
Flamingo East
44 Southwest
Groceries
Hourglass Tavern
Jekyll & Hyde
King Crab
Kitchen Club
La Goulue
Laura Belle
Lipstick Cafe
Ludlow St. Cafe
NoHo Star
Nosmo King
Sonia Rose
Steamer's Landing
Sumptuary
Temple Bar
Upstairs/Downstairs

## English

Telephone Bar/Grill

## Ethiopian

Zula

## Frankfurters

Carnegie Deli
Gray's Papaya
Katz's Deli
Papaya King

## French

Akadi
Aureole
Bouley
Brasserie des Theatres
Cafe des Artistes
Cafe Metairie
Cafe Pierre
Can
Chanterelle
Chez Brigitte
Chez Napoleon
Gibbon
Kulu
La Caravelle
La Cote Basque
Lafayette
La Fondue
La Grenouille
La Maison Japonaise
La Petite Ferme
La Reserve

Le Bernardin
Le Chantilly
Le Cirque
Le Pactole
Le Perigord
Leopard
Le Refuge
Le Regence
Les Celebrites
Lespinasse
Les Pyrenees
Les Sans Culottes
Lutece
Mme. Romaine
One Hudson Cafe
Pastis
Petrossian
Pigalle
Polo
Raphael
Sonia Rose
Terrace
View, The
Village Atelier

## French Bistro

Alison
Au Troquet
Bellevues
Bienvenue
Bistro 790
Bistro 36
Bistro Bamboche
Bistro du Nord
Bistrovia
Black Sheep
Brasserie
Cafe
Cafe des Sports
Cafe Europa
Cafe Loup
Cafe Luxembourg
Cafe St. John
Cafe Tabac
Cafe Un Deux Trois
Capsouto Freres
Chantal Cafe
Chez Jaqueline
Chez Josephine
Chez Ma Tante
Chez Michallet
Cite
Cite Grille
City Cafe
Collage

Crepes Suzette
Demarchelier
Felix
Ferrier
Flourent
Gascogne
Hulot's
Jean Claude
Jean Lafitte
Jo Jo
Jour et Nuit
Koo Koo's Bistro
La Boheme
La Boite en Bois
La Bonne Soupe
La Boulangere
L'Acajou
La Colombe d'Or
La Jumelle
La Luncheonette
La Mangeoire
La Mediterranee
La Metairie
La Mirabelle
La Petite Auberge
La Ripaille
La Topiaire
L'Auberge du Midi
La Vieille Auberge
Le Bilboquet
Le Boeuf a la Mode
L'Ecole
Le Comptoir
Le Madeleine
Le Max
L'Entrecote
Le Pescadou
Le Pistou
Le Quercy
Le Relais
Le Rivage
L'Escale
Les Halles
Les Routiers
Le Steak
Le Veau d'Or
Lucky Strike
Luxe
Montrachet
Nicole Brasserie
Odeon
Paris Commune
Park Bistro
Pierre au Tunnel
Pierre's

Poiret
Provence
Quatorze
Quatorze Bis
Raoul's
Raoul's Brasserie
Raymond's Cafe
Rendez-vous
Rene Pujol
Sel et Poivre
Sultan
Table d'Hote
Tartine
Tout Va Bien
Trois Jean
Voulez-Vous

## French-Japanese

Gibbon
Indochine
Kulu
La Maison Japonaise

## German

Rolf's
Silver Swan

## Greek

Greek Village
Karyatis
Periyali
Pier 25A
Roumeli Taverna

## Grills

Billy's
Brighton Grill
Broadway Grill
Century Cafe
Chicken Chef
Coconut Grill
Gotham Bar/Grill
Lexington Ave. Grill
Lofland's N.Y. Grill
Mackinac Bar & Grill
TriBeCa Grill
Urban Grill
Wollensky's Grill

## Hamburgers & Beer

Billy's
Boxers
Broome St. Bar
Burger Heaven
Charley O's

Chelsea Commons
Chumley's
Churchill's
Clarke's P.J.
Corner Bistro
Hamburger Harry's
Harbour Lights
Hard Rock Cafe
Harry's
Houlihan's
Jackson Hole
Jim McMullen
Joe Allen
Keens Chop Hse.
Luke's Bar & Grill
Melon, J.G.
Old Town Bar
Ottomanelli's Cafe
Pete's Tavern
Planet Hollywood
Ruppert's
SoHo Kitchen
Soup Burg
Telephone Bar
T.G.I Friday's
Walker's
White Horse Tavern
Wollensky's Grill
Zip City Brewing

## Health Food

Angelica Kitchen
Bell Caffe
Bubby's
Great Am. Health
Health Pub
Luma
Nosmo King
Spring St. Natural
Souen
Whole Wheat 'n Berrys
Zen Palate

## Hungarian

Eva's Cafe
Mocca Hungarian
Red Tulip

## Indian

Akbar
Bombay Palace
Darbar
Dawat
Haveli
Indian Cafe

Indian Oven
India Pavilion
Jewel of India
Maurya
Mitali East
Mitali West
Mughlai
Nawab
Nirvana
Pandit
Passage to India

## Indonesian

BTI
Nusantara

## Irish

Charley O's
Neary's

## Italian (Northern)

Allegria
Alo Alo
Anche Vivolo
Antolotti's
Aperitivo
Appetito
Arcobaleno
Aria
Baci
Barbetta
Barolo
Bella Donna
Bellini by Cipriani
Bellisimo
Benvenuti Ristorante
Boathouse Cafe
Bondini
Bora
Borsalino
Braque
Bravo Gianni
Cafe Bel Canto
Cafe Lucas
Cafe Trevi
Caffe Cielo
Caffe La Strada
Caffe Rosso
Campagnola
Canastel's
Capriccio
Capriccioso
Castellano
Cent' Anni
Cesarina

Chelsea Trattoria
Ciaobella
Col Legno
Corrado
Cucina Della Fontana
Da Silvano
Da Tommaso
Da Umberto
DeGrezia
Divino
Dolce
Due
Ecco-La
Elaine's
Elio's
Ernie's
Est Est Est
Fagiolini
Felidia
Fino
Firenze
5 & 10
Frank's
Gabriel's
Giambelli
Gian Marino
Giando
Gianni's
Gijo's
Giordano
Girafe
Girasole
Grifone
Harry Cipriani
Il Giglio
Il Menestrello
Il Monello
Il Mulino
Il Nido
Il Nonno
Il Tinello
Isabella's
I Tre Merli
La Barca
La Collina
La Focaccia
La Primavera
La Strada
Lattanzi
Lello
Letizia
Lusardi's
Mappamondo
Mary's
Mezzaluna

Montebello
Moreno
Nanni Il Valletto
Nanni's
Nicola's
Olio
101
Orso
Osso Buco
Palio
Paper Moon Milano
Pappardella
Parioli Romanissimo
Parma
Piccola Venezia
Piccolo Mondo
Primavera
Remi
Romeo Salta
Rosemarie's
Rosolio
San Giusto
Scaletta
Scalinatella
Scarlatti
Sfuzzi
Sirabella's
Sofia's
Stella del Mare
Tempo
Tiramisu
Trattoria Alba
Triangolo
Trionfo
Urbino
Vespa
Via Via
Villa Berulia
Vivolo
Volare

## Italian (Southern)

Angelo's
Azzurro
Barocco
Bella Mama
Benito I
Benito II
Caffe Cefalu
Caffe Cielo
Caffe Florence
Carino
Carmine's
Casalone
Crisci's

Da Noi
Dominick's
Fiorello's
Follonico
Garibaldi
Grotto Azzurra
Il Cantinori
Il Vagabondo
John's of 12th St.
Lamarca
Las Marcias
Paul & Jimmy's
Positano
Rao's
Ronasi
Sambuca
Siracusa
Taormina
Tommaso's
Tony's di Napoli
Tre Scalini
Villa Lulu
Vucciria

## Italian (North & South)

Aglio e Olio
Amici Miei
Andiamo
Angels
Antico Caffee
Arlecchino
Arqua
Artepasta
Arturo's Pizzeria
Asti
Bacchus
Ballato's
Basta Pasta
Beach Cafe
Becco
Bella Luna
Bice
Brio
Bruno Ristorante
Buona Sera
Cafe Buon Gusto
Caffe Bianco
Caffe Biondo
Caffe Bondi
Caffe Vivaldi
Carosello
Casa di Pre
Cavaliere
Ciaobella

170

Cinquanta
Ci Vediamo
Coco Pazzo
Contrapunto
Courtyard Cafe
Cucina
Cucina & Co.
Cucina di Pesce
Cucina Stagionale
Denino's Tavern
Ecco
Ennio & Michael
Erminia
Fiori
Fishin Eddies
Frutti di Mare
Fusillo
Gabriel
Gino
Grand Ticino
Grappino
Hosteria Fiorella
Il–Corallo
Il Cortile
Il Gabbiano
Il Gattopardo
Il Ponte Vecchio
Isle of Capri
Isola
La Fusta
Laguna
La Rivista
Le Madri
Lido's
Little Mushroom Cafe
Mamma Leone's
Manganaro's Hero-Boy
Mario's
Mazzei
Mediterraneo
Meridiana
Mezzogiorno
Minetta Tavern
Monreale
Natalino
Nello
Nicola Paone
Ottomanelli's Cafe
Panarella
Paola's
Paolucci's
Park Side
Pasta Lovers
Pasta Place, A
Pasta Presto

Pasta Roma
Pasta Supreme
Pasta Vicci
Pasticcio
Patriccio's
Patrissy's
Patsy's
Patzo
Pellegrino
Perretti
Petaluma
Piccolino
Piccolo Pomodoro
Pietro & Vanessa
Pietro's
Pinocchio
Ponte's
Ponticello
Portico
Presto's
Primola
Quartiere
Sal Anthony's
San Domenico
San Pietro
Sandro's
Sant Ambroeus
Santerello
Sardi's
Scalinatella
Scoop
Sette Mezzo
Sistina
Sotto Cinque
S.P.Q.R.
Stellina
Supreme Macaroni Co.
Tevere 84
Tiziano Trattoria
Trastevere 83
Trattoria dell'Arte
Tutta Pasta
Twigs
Va Bene
Valone's
Vico
Vico Express
Villa Mosconi
Vinsanto
Vittorio Cucina
Zucchero

## Japanese

Asia
Benihana of Tokyo

Chikubu
Choshi
Dosanko
East
Four Winds
Fujiyama Mama
Genji
Gibbon
Hamachi
Hasaki
Hatsuhana
Honmura An
Inagiku
Iso
Itcho
Japanese on Hudson
Japonica
Kan Pai
Kiiroi Hana
Kinoko
Kurumazushi
La Maison Japonaise
Lenge
Menchanko-tei
Meriken
Mitsukoshi
Nippon
Omen
Sakura of Japan
Seryna
Shabu Tatsu
Shinbashi
Shinwa
Sushi Zen
Sushiden
Sushisay
Take-Sushi
Tango
Taste of Tokyo
Tatany
Ten Kai
Umeda
Yamaguchi
Yuka
Zutto

## Jewish

Barney Greengrass
Cafe Andrusha
Carneigie Deli
Fine & Schapiro*
Grand Dairy*
Katz's Deli
Lattanzi Ristoranti*
Lou G. Siegel*

Ossie's Table*
Ratner's*
Sammy's Roumanian
Second Ave. Deli
Stage Deli
Tevere 84*
Triplet's Roumanian
Va Bene*
(*Kosher)

## Korean

Kom Tang Soot Bul
Woo Chon
Woo Lae Oak

## Lebanese

Al Bustan
Cedars of Lebanon
Eden Rock
Tripoli

## Mediterranean

Adrienne
Alison
Cafe
Cafe Crocodile
Cafe Greco
Casa La Femme
Gus' Place
La Chandelle
May We
Mimosa
Savoy
Stanhope, The
Tatiana

## Mexican/Tex-Mex

Albuquerque Eats
Arriba Arriba
Benny's Burritos
Bertha's
Blue Moon Cafe
Bright Food Shop
Caliente Cab Co.
Cantina
Canyon Road
Cottonwood Cafe
Cowgirl Hall of Fame
Do Da's
El Parador
El Rio Grande
El Teddy's
Fiesta Mexicana
Gonzalez y Gonzalez
Juanita's

Lucy's
Lupe's East L.A.
Manhattan Chili Co.
Mary Ann's
Maz Mescal
Mi Cocina
Mi Tierra
Original Taqueria
Passports
Pedro Paramo
Rocking Horse Cafe
Rosa Mexicano
Santa Fe
Tequila Sunrise
Texas Cafe/Grill
Tortilla Flats
Yellow Rose Cafe
Zarela
Zona Rosa

## Middle Eastern

Al Bustan
Amir's Falafel
Cedars of Lebanon
Cleopatra's Needle
Eden Rock
Galil
Marti Kebab
Masada Cafe
Nazareth Restaurant
Sabra Kitchen
Sido Abu
Tripoli

## Omelettes

Elephant & Castle
Mme. Romaine

## Pancakes

Anglers & Writers
Royal Canadian
Sarabeth's

## Pasta
(All Italians and
 the following)

Angels
Azzurro
Bella Donna
Ernie's
Mezzogiorno
Pasta Lovers
Pasta Place
Pasta Presto
Pasta Roma

Pasta Vicci
Pasticcio
Sotto Cinque

## Pastries

Bubby's
Cafe Lalo
Caffe Vivaldi
Cooper's Coffee
Ferrara
Rumpelmayer's
Sarabeth's
Serendipity 3

## Peruvian

El Pollo
Peruvian Restaurant

## Pizza

Arturo's Pizzeria
Freddie & Pepper
Fusillo
John's Pizzeria
Patsy's
Pizzapiazza
Pizzeria Uno
Totonno
Two Boots
Vinnie's Pizza

## Polish

Christine's
Little Poland
Teresa's
Veselka

## Romanian

Triplet's Roumanian

## Rotisseries

Amsterdam's

## Russian

Cafe Andrusha
Kalinka
Kiev
National
Petrossian
Pie, The
Russian Samovar
Russian Tea Room

## Scandinavian

Aquavit
Snaps

## Seafood

Captain's Table
Claire
Coastal
Dock's
Fannie's Oyster Bar
Fishin Eddie
Gage & Tollner
Hosteria Fiorella
Jane St. Seafood
John Clancy's
King Crab
La Sarten
Le Bernardin
Le Pescadou
Lobster Box
Lola
Luma
Mambo Grill
Manhattan Cafe
Manhattan Ocean Club
Maryland Crab House
Marylou's
Oceana
101 Seafood
Ossie's Table
Oyster Bar
Parker's Lighthouse
Pen & Pencil
Plaza Oyster Bar
Presto's
Sea Grill
Seafood Palace
Sidewalker's
Sloppy Louie's
Souen
Sumptuary
Sweets
Water Club
Wilkinson's
Yankee Clipper

## South American

Boca Chica

## Southern/Soul

Acme Bar & Grill
Brother Jimmy's BBQ
Brother's BBQ
Claire
Coach House, The
Copeland's
Cottonwood Cafe
Gage & Tollner
Gulf Coast

Honeysuckle
Hows Bayou
Jezebel
Levee, The
Live Bait
Lola
Memphis
107 West
Perk's Fine Cuisine
Shark Bar
Sugah's
Sylvia's

## Southwestern

Arizona 206
Automatic Slim's
Manhattan Chili Co.
Mesa Grill
Miracle Grill
Silverado
Tequila Sunrise
Yellow Rose Cafe
Zocalo

## Spanish

Alcala
Cafe Espanol
Cafe San Martin
El Charro
El Faro
El Rincon de Espana
Eldorado Petit
Flying Fish
Harlequin
Malaga
Mesa de Espana
Meson Botin
Paradis Barcelona
Rio Mar
Sevilla
Solera

## Steakhouses

Abe's Steak House
Assembly, The
Ben Benson's
Billy's
Bull & Bear
Christ Cella
Embers
Frank's
Gage & Tollner
Gallagher's
Keens Chop Hse.
L'Entrecote

Le Steak
Manhattan Cafe
Neary's
Oak Bar
Old Homestead
Palm, The
Palm Too
Pen & Pencil
Peter Luger
Post House
S.P.Q.R.
Smith & Wollensky
Sparks
Steak Frites
Wally's & Joseph's
Wollensky's Grill

## Swiss

Roettelle A. G.
Swiss Inn

## Thai

Bangkok Cuisine
Bangkok House
Boonthai
BTI
Jai Ya Thai
Kodnoi
Little Mushroom Cafe
Mueng Thai
Pongsri Thai
Puket
Regional Thai Taste
Sala Thai
Sawadee Thai
Shaliga Thai
Siam Inn
Sukhothai West
Thai Chef
Thai House Cafe
Thailand Restaurant

Thai Taste
Tommy Tang's
Toons

## Tibetan

Tibetan Kitchen

## Turkish

Marti Kebab
Sultan
Uskudar

## Ukranian

Kiev
Little Poland
Odessa
Sweet Basil's
Veselka

## Vegetarian
(Most Chinese, Indian
and Thai restaurants)

Angelica Kitchen
Great Am. Health
Health Pub
Luma
Regional Thai Taste
Souen
Spring St. Natural
Whole Wheat 'n Berrys
Zen Palate
Zucchini

## Vietnamese

Bo Ky
Can
Cuisine de Saigon
Indochine
Le Bar Bat
Saigon

# NEIGHBORHOOD LOCATIONS

## East 80s & Up
(East of Fifth Avenue)

Abe's Steak House
Arriba Arriba
Atomic Wings
Azzurro
Bistro Bamboche
Bistro du Nord
BTI
Busby's
Cafe Andrusha
Cafe Metairie
Cafe Trevi
Carino
Casalone
Chef Ho's
Chicken Chef
Ci Vediamo
Country Club
Dakota Bar & Grill
Demarchelier
Divino
East
E.A.T.
Ecco-La
El Pollo
Elaine's
Elio's
Erminia
Firenze
1st Wok
Gabriel
Galil
Gibbon
Gijo's
Girasole
Houlihan's
Island
Jackson Hole
Kalinka
Koo Koo's Bistro
Kulu
La Collina
Laguna
Le Boeuf a la Mode
Le Refuge
Lenge
Mambo Grill
Maz Mescal
Mazzei
Mocca Hungarian
Monreale

Nazareth Restaurant
Nicola's
Ottomanelli's Cafe
Our Place
Paola's
Papaya King
Parioli Romanissimo
Patsy's
Perk's Fine Cuisine
Piccolo Pomodoro
Pie
Pig Heaven
Pinocchio
Primavera
Rao's
Ruppert's
Sala Thai
Sam's Cafe
Sarabeth's
Saranac
Sirabella's
Sistina
Sotto Cinque
Soup Burg
Stanhope
Szechuan Hunan
Table d'Hote
Tang Tang
Tevere 84
Third Ave. Cafe
Tiramisu
Tony's di Napoli
Trastevere 83
Trianglo
Urban Grill
Va Bene
Vespa
Viand
Vico
Vico Express
Vinsanto
Wilkinson's
Willie's
Yuka

## East 70s
(East of Fifth Avenue)

Afghan Kebab House
Antico Caffee
Atomic Wings
Bangkok House
Beach Cafe

176

Bella Donna
Bistrovia
Blue Moon Cafe
Boathouse Cafe
Boonthai
Brighton Grill
Brother Jimmy's BBQ
Buckaroo's
Cafe Buon Gusto
Cafe Crocodile
Cafe Greco
Cafe Lucas
Cafe San Martin
Cafe Word of Mouth
Caffe Bianco
Camelback & Central
Campagnola
Canyon Road
Carlyle Dining Rm.
Churchill's
Ciaobella
City Cafe
Coastal
Coconut Grill
Coco Pazzo
Dallas BBQ
Da Noi
Due
E.J.'s Luncheonette
Fagiolini
1st Wok
Fu's
Fusillo
Greek Village
Hulot's
Hunan Balcony
Il Monello
Itcho
Jim McMullen
Juanita's
Kan Pai
La Goulue
La Petite Ferme
Les Friandises
Letizia
Lion's Rock
Luke's Bar & Grill
Lusardi's
Malaga
Mark's
Mary Ann's
May We
Melon, J.G.
Mezzaluna
Mimosa

Mortimer's
Natalino
Ottomanelli's Cafe
Pamir
Parma
Pastis
Petaluma
Portico
Quatorze Bis
Red Tulip
Sant Ambroeus
Sarabeth's
Sette Mezzo
Shelby
Soup Burg
Szechuan Hunan
Szechuan Kitchen
Trois Jean
Uskudar
Valone's
Vasata
Vespa
Via Via
Viand
Vivolo
Voulez-Vous
Zucchero

**East 60s**
(East of Fifth Avenue)

Alo Alo
Angels
Arcadia
Arizona 206
Asia
Aureole
Bravo Gianni
Brio
Burger Heaven
Cafe Pierre
Capriccio
Chicken Chef
Contrapunto
Copacabana
Empire Szechuan
Ferrier
Four Winds
Gino
Hosteria Fiorella Fiorella
Il Vagabondo
Isle of Capri
Jackson Hole
John Clancy's
John's Pizzeria
Kodnoi

Le Bilboquet
Le Cirque
Le Comptoir
Le Pistou
Le Regence
Le Relais
Le Veau d'Or
Manhattan Cafe
Masada Cafe
Mediterraneo
Mme. Romaine
Mulholland Drive
Nanni Il Valletto
Nello
Olio
Ottomanelli's Cafe
Park Avenue Cafe
Pembroke Room
Piccolo Mondo
Polo
Post House
Primola
Regency
Ronasi
Scalinatella
Sel et Poivre
Serendipity 3
7th Regiment Mess
Sign of the Dove
Sultan
Tang Tang
T.G.I. Friday's
Thai Chef
Viand
Yellowfingers

## East 50s
(East of Fifth Avenue)

Akbar
Al Bustan
Allegria
Anche Vivolo
Aria
Beijing Duck House
Benihana of Tokyo
Bice
Bill's Gay 90s
Billy's
Blue Light
Boogies Diner
Brasserie
Brazilian Pavilion
Broadway Diner
Bruno Ristorante
Burger Heaven

Cafe Europa
Cafe Nicholson
Carosello
Charley O's
Cinquanta
Clarke's P.J.
Coming or Going
Common Market Cafe
Dawat
DeGrezia
Dosanko
Felidia
Fisher & Levy
Four Seasons
Giambelli
Girafe
Harry Cipriani
Houlihan's
Hwa Yuan Szechuan
Il Gabbiano
Il Menestrello
Il Nido
L'Entrecote
La Cote Basque
La Grenouille
La Mangeoire
La Mediterranee
Lafayette
Le Chantilly
Leopard
Le Perigord
Lespinasse
Le Steak
Le Train Bleu
Lello
Les Sans Culottes
Lexington Ave. Grill
Lipstick Cafe
Lutece
March
Mayfair
Metropolitan Cafe
Mitsukoshi
Montebello
Mr. Chow
Neary's
Nippon
Oceana
Pamir
Papaya King
Paper Moon Milano
Paradis Barcelona
Pasta Presto
Puket
Quilted Giraffe

Rendez-Vous
Rosa Mexicano
Royal Canadian
San Pietro
Sandro's
Scarlatti
2nd Ave. Brasserie
Seryna
Shaliga Thai
Shinwa
Shun Lee Palace
Small Cafe
Solera
Soup Burg
Stephanie's
Sushisay
Tang Tang
Tatou
T.G.I. Friday's
Tre Scalini
Tse Yang
Westside Cafe
Wylie's Ribs
Zarela
Zona Rosa

## East 40s
(East of Fifth Avenue)

Ambassador Grill
Antolotti's
Aurora
Bloom's Delicatessen
Box Tree
Bull & Bear
Burger Heaven
Cafe S.F.A.
Captain's Table
Charley O's
Chiam
Chikubu
Chin Chin
Christ Cella
Cucina & Co.
David Keh's N.R.
Dock's
Dolce
Dosanko
East
Grifone
Hatsuhana
Houlihan's
Inagiku
J. Sung Dynasty
Nanni's
Nawab

Nusantara
Oyster Bar
Palm
Palm Too
Peacock Alley
Pen & Pencil
Pietro's
San Giusto
Scoop
Shinbashi
Sichuan Palace
Smith & Wollensky
Snaps
Sparks
Sushiden
Take-Sushi
Tequila Sunrise
Tropica
Westside Cottage
Wollensky's Grill
Zephyr Grill

## West 70s & Up
(West of Fifth Avenue)

Alcala
Amir's Falafel
Amsterdam's
Arriba Arriba
Aspen Cafe
Atomic Wings
Baci
Barney Greengrass
Bella Luna
Bertha's
Bimini Twist
Blue Moon Cafe
Boulevard
BTI
Cafe Lalo
Cafe Luxembourg
Cafe St. John
Cantina
Capriccioso
Carmine's
Cavaliere
Cleopatra's Needle
Coastal
Columbia Cottage
Cooper's Coffee
Copeland's
Dallas BBQ
Dock's
Eden Rock
E.J.'s Luncheonette
Empire Szechuan

Ernie's
Fiesta Mexicana
Fine & Schapiro
Fishin Eddie
Freddie & Pepper
Fujiyama Mama
Good Enough to Eat
Gray's Papaya
Harriet's Kitchen
Hi-Life Bar/Grill
Honeysuckle
Hunan Balcony
Indian Cafe
Indian Oven
Isabella's
Isola
Jackson Hole
Kinoko
La Caridad
La Chandelle
La Mirabelle
Las Marcias
Les Routiers
Louie's Westside
Lucy's
Mackinac Bar & Grill
Melon, J.G.
Memphis
Meridiana
Mingala Burmese
Mughlai
Museum Cafe
Ollie's
107 West
Ottomanelli's Cafe
Panarella
Pandit
Pappardella
Pasta Vicci
Patzo
Perretti
Phoebe's
Piccolino
Pizzeria Uno
Poiret
Popover Cafe
Presto's
Ruppert's
Sabra Kitchen
Sakura of Japan
Sambuca
Santerello
Sarabeth's
Sawadee Thai
Scaletta

Shark Bar
Sidewalker's
Silk Road Palace
Soup Burg
Sylvia's
Teachers Too
Terrace
Victor's
Vinnie's Pizza
Wilson's
Yellow Rose Cafe
Ying
Zocalo
Zula

## West 60s
(West of Fifth Avenue)

Andiamo
Cafe Bel Canto
Cafe des Artistes
Cameos
Conservatory Cafe
Empire Szechuan
Fiorello's
Gabriel's
Houlihan's
Josephina
La Boite en Bois
Lenge
Levana
Saloon
Santa Fe
Sfuzzi
Shun Lee Cafe
Shun Lee West
Tavern on the Green
Vince & Eddie's

## West 50s
(West of Fifth Avenue)

Adrienne
Afghan Kebab House
Aglio e Olio
Allegria
American Festival Cafe
Aperitivo
Aquavit
Arriba Arriba
Assembly
Au Cafe
Bangkok Cuisine
Bellini by Cipriani
Ben Benson's
Benihana of Tokyo
Bistro 790

Bombay Palace
Borsalino
Broadway Diner
Cafe Botanica
Cafe des Sports
Caffe Cielo
Carnegie Deli
Castellano
Cesarina
Chantal Cafe
Chez Napoleon
China Grill
Chop Suey Looey's
Cite
Cite Grille
Corrado
Da Tommaso
Darbar
Dosanko
East
Edwardian Room
Eldorado Petit
Gallagher's
Gian Marino
Great Am. Health
Halcyon
Hard Rock Cafe
Il Gattopardo
Il Tinello
India Pavilion
Jean Lafitte
Jockey Club
Keewah Yen
Kiiroi Hana
King Crab
Kurumazushi
La Bonne Soupe
La Caravelle
La Fondue
Lai Lai West
Le Bar Bat
Le Bernardin
Le Quercy
Les Celebrites
Les Pyrenees
Manhattan Ocean Club
Menchanko-tei
Meson Botin
Michael's
Mickey Mantle's
Nicole Brasserie
N.Y. Deli
Nirvana
Oak Bar
Palio

Palm Court
Pasta Lovers
Pasta Roma
Petrossian
Planet Hollywood
Plaza Oyster Bar
Raphael
Remi
Rene Pujol
Romeo Salta
Rumpelmayer's
Russian Samovar
Russian Tea Room
Sam's Cafe Restaurant
San Domenico
Sawadee Thai
Siam Inn
Stage Deli
Symphony Cafe
Tango
Ten Kai
Tequila Sunrise
T.G.I. Friday's
Top of the Sixes
Tout Va Bien
Trattoria dell'Arte
Trionfo
"21" Club
Urban Grill
Victor's
Wolf's 6th Ave. Deli

## West 40s
(West of Fifth Avenue,
  incl. Theater District)

Afghan Kebab House
Algonquin Hotel
Bali Burma
Barbetta
Becco
Brasserie des Theatres
Broadway Grill
B. Smith's
Cabana Carioca
Cafe Un Deux Trois
Carmine's
Century Cafe
Charley O's
Charlotte
Chez Josephine
Crepes Suzette
Dish of Salt
Dosanko
Edison Cafe
44

44 Southwest
Hamburger Harry's
Houlihan's
Hourglass Tavern
Island Spice
Jewel of India
Jezebel
Joe Allen
La Primavera
La Reserve
La Rivista
La Topiaire
Laura Belle
La Vieille Auberge
Lattanzi
Le Madeleine
Le Max
Le Rivage
Mamma Leone's
Manhattan Plaza Cafe
Mezzanine
Ollie's
Orso
Peruvian Restaurant
Pierre au Tunnel
Pongsri Thai
Rainbow Room
Sardi's
Sea Grill
Sofia's
Stellina
Sukhothai West
Supper Club
Sushi Zen
Sushiden
Swiss Inn
Tony Roma's
View
Wally's & Joseph's
Woo Lae Oak
Yamaguchi
Zen Palate
Zona Rosa

**Murray Hill –
Gramercy Park**
(40th to 14th Streets,
East of Fifth Avenue)

Albuquerque Eats
America
An American Place
Back Porch
Banana Cafe
Bellisimo
Bienvenue

Bora*
Canastel's
Cedars of Lebanon
Charley O's
Chefs & Cuisiniers
Choshi
Christine's
Coffee Shop
Condon's
Courtyard Cafe
Dosanko
East
El Charro
El Parador
El Rio Grande
Fagiolini
Fino
Fiori
1st Wok
Friend of a Farmer
Great Am. Health
Hamachi
Health Pub
Houlihan's
H.S.F.
Jackson Hole
Kan Pai
La Boulangere
La Colombe d'Or
La Maison Japonaise
Lamarca
La Petite Auberge
L'Escale
Les Halles
Live Bait
Luxe
Marti Kebab
Maryland Crab House
Maurya
Mesa de Espana
Mesa Grill
Metropolis Cafe
Moreno
Nicola Paone
Old Town Bar
Ottomanelli's Cafe
Park Ave. Country Club
Park Bistro
Pasta Presto
Pasta Vicci
Pasticcio
Paul & Jimmy's
Pete's Place
Pete's Tavern
Pigalle

Positano
Rascals
Rolf's
Russell's
Sakura of Japan
Sal Anthony's
Sharkey's
Sido Abu
Silver Swan
Silverado
Siu Lam Kung
Sonia Rose
Stella del Mare
Sumptuary
Tatany
Tempo
Tequila Sunrise
Terry Dinan's
Texas Cafe/Grill
Tibetan Kitchen
Time & Again
Tina's
Tony Roma's
Trattoria Alba
Umeda
Union Square Cafe
Via Via
Villa Berulia
Villa Lulu
Water Club

## Garment District –
## Chelsea
(40th to 14th Streets,
 West of Fifth Avenue)

Akadi
Appetito
Bacchus
Ballroom
Basta Pasta
Beijing Duck House
Bellevues
Bendix Diner
Benvenuti Ristorante
Blue Moon Cafe
Bright Food Shop
Caffe Bondi
Cal's
Charley O's
Chelsea Commons
Chelsea Trattoria
Claire
Cupcake Cafe
Da Umberto
Do Da's

Eighteenth & Eighth
Empire Diner
Empire Szechuan
Follonico
Gascogne
Giordano
Grappino
Houlihan's
Keens Chop Hse.
Kom Tang Soot Bul
L'Acajou
La Luncheonette
La Taza de Oro
Le Madri
Lofland's N.Y. Grill
Lola
Lou G. Siegel
Luma
Man Ray
Manganaro's Hero-Boy
Mary Ann's
Merchants
Meriken
Metro C.C.
Mi Tierra
Moran's
Old Homestead
Periyali
Pizzeria Uno
Prix Fixe
Raymond's Cafe
Regional Thai Taste
Rocking Horse Cafe
Rogers & Barbero
Steak Frites
Sunny East
Supreme Macaroni Co.
T.S. Ma
Thai Taste
Tiziano Trattoria
Twigs
Vernon's
Woo Chon
World Yacht
Zip City Brewing

## Greenwich Village
(14th to Houston Sts.,
 West of Third Avenue)

Acme Bar & Grill
Aggie's
Anglers & Writers
Arcobaleno
Arlecchino
Artepasta

| | |
|---|---|
| Asti | Grand Ticino |
| Atomic Wings | Grange Hall |
| Automatic Slims | Gray's Papaya |
| Au Troquet | Great Jones Cafe |
| Bayamo | Groceries |
| Benny's Burritos | Grove Street Cafe |
| Black Sheep | Gulf Coast |
| Bondini | Gus' Place |
| Boxers | Hamburger Harry's |
| Braque | Harlequin |
| Buona Sera | Houlihan's |
| Cafe de Bruxelles | Il Cantinori |
| Cafe Espanol | Il Mulino |
| Cafe Loup | Il Nonno |
| Caffe Cefalu | Il Ponte Vecchio |
| Caffe Florence | India Pavilion |
| Caffe Rosso | Indochine |
| Caffe Vivaldi | Jane St. Seafood |
| Caliente Cab Co. | Japanese on Hudson |
| Caribe | Japonica |
| Casa di Pre | Jekyll & Hyde |
| Cent' Anni | John Clancy's |
| Chez Brigitte | John's Pizzeria |
| Chez Jacqueline | La Boheme |
| Chez Ma Tante | La Focaccia |
| Chez Michallet | La Metairie |
| Chicken Chef | La Ripaille |
| Chumley's | L'Auberge du Midi |
| Coach House | Lion's Head |
| Collage | Little Mushroom Cafe |
| Cornelia St. Cafe | Lora |
| Corner Bistro | Manhattan Chili Co. |
| Cottonwood Cafe | Mappamondo |
| Cowgirl Hall of Fame | Marnie's Noodle Shop |
| Cucina della Fontana | Marylou's |
| Cucina Stagionale | Mary's |
| Cuisine de Saigon | Mi Cocina |
| Dallas BBQ | Minetta Tavern |
| Da Silvano | Mingala West |
| Day-O | Mitali West |
| Ed Debevic's | Mr. Fuji's Tropicana |
| El Charro | Nadine's |
| Elephant & Castle | NoHo Star |
| El Faro | One If by Land, TIBS |
| El Rincon de Espana | Osso Buco |
| Empire Szechuan | Ottomanelli's Cafe |
| Ennio & Michael | Paris Commune |
| Est Est Est | Pasta Presto |
| Fannie's Oyster Bar | Pasta Supreme |
| Florent | Pasta Vicci |
| Flying Fish | Patisserie Lanciani |
| Frank's | Pierre's |
| Garibaldi | Pizzapiazza |
| Gonzalez y Gonzalez | Pizzeria Uno |
| Gotham Bar/Grill | Quatorze |

Rio Mar
Rose Cafe
Rosolio
Sabor
Sazarac House
Sevilla
Siracusa
Souen
Sugah's
Tartine
Taste of Tokyo
Toons
Tortilla Flats
Tutta Pasta
Universal Grill
Upstairs/Downstairs
Urbino
Villa Mosconi
Village Atelier
Vittorio Cucina
Volare
Zinno

## East Village
(14th to Houston Sts.,
East of Third Avenue)

Angelica Kitchen
Benny's Burritos
Boca Chica
Cafe Tabac
Caffe La Strada
Caribe
Christine's
Ci Vediano
Cloister Cafe
Col Legno
Cucina di Pesce
Dallas BBQ
Flamingo East
Frutti di Mare
Genji
Hasaki
Haveli
Iso
Jerry's 103
John's of 12 St.
Khyber Pass
Kiev
Levee
Little Poland
Marion's
Mary Ann's
Mingala Burmese
Miracle Grill
Mitali East

Odessa
Orson's
Passage to India
Passports
Pedro Paramo
Pizzeria Uno
Roettelle A.G.
Second Ave. Deli
Shabu Tatsu
Sugar Reef
Telephone Bar
Temple Bar
Teresa's
Time Cafe
Tompkins Park
Two Boots
Veselka

## Lower East Side
(Houston to Canal Streets,
East of Bowery)

Grand Dairy
Katz's Deli
Ludlow St. Cafe
Ratner's
Sammy's Roumanian

## SoHo – Little Italy
(Houston to Canal Streets,
West of Bowery)

5 & 10
Alison
Amici Miei
Amsterdam's
Angelo's
Arturo's Pizzeria
Ballato's
Barolo
Bell Caffe
Benito I
Benito II
Boom
Broome St. Bar
Brother's BBQ
Cafe
Cafe Biondo
Can
Casa La Femme
Cupping Room
Elephant & Castle
Fanelli
Felix
Ferrara
Grotta Azzurra
Honmura An

Il Cortile
Il–Corallo
I Tre Merli
Jean Claude
Jerry's
Jour et Nuit
La Jumelle
L'Ecole
Le Pescadon
Lucky Strike
Lupe's East L.A.
Mezzogiorno
New Deal
Nick & Eddie
Omen
Paolucci's
Patrissy's
Pellegrino
Pietro & Vanessa
Provence
Raoul's
Raoul's Brasserie
Savoy
SoHo Kitchen/Bar
S.P.Q.R.
Spring St. Natural
Taormina
Tatiana
Tennessee Mountain
Triplet's Roumanian
Vucciria
West Broadway
Zoe

## Chinatown

Beijing Duck House
Bo Ky
Canton
Chao Chow*
Golden Unicorn
Great Shanghai
H.S.F.
Hunan Garden
Hwa Yuan Szechuan
Kitchen Club
Little Shanghai
Mandarin Court
Mueng Thai
Nice Restaurant
Oriental Pearl
Oriental Town
Road to Mandalay
Saigon
Seafood Palace
Silver Palace

Tai Hong Lau
Thailand Restaurant
Triple Eight Palace
20 Mott Street
Vong & Kwong
Wong Kee

## TriBeCa – Downtown
(South of Canal Street,
 including Wall St. area)

Amazon Village
American Harvest
Arqua
Au Mandarin
Barocco
Bouley
Bridge Cafe
Bubby's
Capsouto Freres
Cellar in the Sky
Chanterelle
Delmonico's
Donald Sacks
Duane Park
Ecco
Edward Moran
El Teddy's
Fraunces Tavern
Gianni's
Harbour Lights
Harry's
Houlihan's
Hows Bayou
Hudson River Club
Il Giglio
La Barca
Le Pactole
McDonald's
Montrachet
Nice Restaurant
Nosmo King
Odeon
One Hudson Cafe
Patric
Ponte's
Roebling's
Rosemarie's
Royal Canadian
Sequoia
Sfuzzi
Sloppy Louie's
Steamer's Landing
Sweets
Taliesin
Thai House Cafe

186

Tommy Tang's
Toons
TriBeCa Grill
Two Eleven
Walker's
Windows on the World
Winter Garden Cafe
Yankee Clipper
Zutto

## Brooklyn

Aunt Sonia's
Bistro 36
Crisci's
Cucina
Embers
Gage & Tollner
Garden Cafe
Giando
Henry's End
Lum Chin
McFeely's
Mr. Tang's
National
New Prospect Cafe
101
101 Seafood
Original Taqueria
Ossie's Table
Parker's Lighthouse
Patsy's
Peter Luger
River Cafe
Teresa's
Thai Taste
Tommaso's

Totonno
Tripoli

## Queens

Casa Colombia
Cho-Sen Garden
Jai Ya Thai
Karyatis
La Fusta
Ottomanelli's Cafe
Park Side
Piccola Venezia
Pier 25A
Pizzeria Uno
Ponticello
Quartiere
Roumeli Taverna
Stick to Ribs BBQ
Water's Edge

## Bronx

Dominick's
Lobster Box
Mario's

## Staten Island

Bella Mama
Denino's Tavern
La Strada
Lido's
Lum Chin
Old Bermuda Inn
Pasta Place, A
Patriccio's
Sweet Basil's

# SPECIAL FEATURES AND APPEALS

## Braille Menus

America
Brighton Grill
Cafe Pierre
Christine's
Cucina
Dock's
Edwardian Room
Ernie's
El Rio Grande
Oak Bar
Palm Court
Plaza Oyster Bar
San Domenico
Sarabeth's
Sardis
Union Square Cafe
Windows on the World

Kiev
Les Friandises
Lipstick Cafe
Louie's Westside
NoHo Star
Odessa
Patisserie Lanciani
Peacock Alley
Popover Cafe
Ratner's
Royal Canadian
Sarabeth's
Taliesin
Tartine
Teresa's
Veselka
Viand
Winter Garden Cafe

## Breakfast
(All hotels and the
following standouts)

Aggie's
Ambassador Grill
American Festival Cafe
Anglers & Writers
Bendix Diner
Bloom's Delicatessen
Brasserie
Cafe Pierre
Cafe Word of Mouth
Caffe Bianco
Caffe Bondi
Carlyle Dining Room
Christine's
Coming or Going
Common Market Cafe
Conservatory Cafe
Cooper's Coffee
Cupcake Cafe
Cupping Room
E.A.T.
Edwardian Room
Eighteenth & Eighth
EJ's Luncheonette
Elephant & Castle
Empire Diner
Fraunces Tavern
Friend of a Farmer
Good Enough to Eat
Grand Dairy
Great Am. Health

## Brunch
(Best of the many)

Aggie's
Ambassador Grill
Anglers & Writers
Barney Greengrass
Bell Caffe
Black Sheep
Boulevard
Brighton Grill
Bubby's
Busby's
Cafe Botanica
Cafe des Artistes
Cafe Luxembourg
Cafe St. John
Cafe Un Deux Trois
Caffe Vivaldi
Cameos
Capsouto Freres
Carlyle Dining Rm.
Casa La Femme
Chelsea Commons
Chez Michallet
Churchill's
City Cafe
Claire
Coastal
Coconut Grill
Coffee Shop
Conservatory Cafe
Cornelia St. Cafe
Cottonwood Cafe

188

Cupcake Cafe
Cupping Room
Demarchelier
Due
EJ's Luncheonette
Elephant & Castle
El Rio Grande
Empire Diner
Florent
Friend of a Farmer
44
Gage & Tollner
Good Enough to Eat
Gus' Place
Hudson River Club
Isabella's
Island
Jerry's
Jim McMullen
Jockey Club
La Goulue
Le Pactole
Le Refuge
Le Regence
Lion's Head
Lion's Rock
Lola
Ludlow St. Cafe
Manhattan Plaza Cafe
Mark's
Mayfair
Metropolis Cafe
Metropolitan Cafe
Michael's
New Prospect Cafe
NoHo Star
Odeon
Park Avenue Cafe
Pembroke Room
Perk's Fine Cuisine
Petaluma
Phoebe's
Polo
River Cafe
Rogers & Barbero
Rose Cafe
Royal Canadian
Sarabeth's
Serendipity 3
Sign of the Dove
Stanhope
Stephanie's
Sylvia's
Symphony Cafe
Table d'Hote

Tavern on the Green
Teachers Too
Time Cafe
Tompkins Park
TriBeCa Grill
Twigs
Victor's
View
Vince & Eddie's
Water Club
West Broadway
Whole Wheat 'n Berrys
Windows on the World
Zoe

## Dancing
(Nightclubs and the
following; check times)

Amazon Village
Country Club
Do Da's
Laura Belle
Le Bar Bat
Lola
Mr. Fuji's Tropicana
Rainbow Room
Rascals
Red Tulip
Sequoia
Supper Club
Tatou
Tavern on the Green
View
Windows on the World
World Yacht

## Delivers
(Almost all Chinese,
delis and pizzerias
deliver; here are
some good bets;
call to check range
and charges, if any)

Abe's Steak House
Aglio e Olio
American Festival Cafe
Arturo's Pizzeria
Au Mandarin
Balducci's*
Bangok House
Barney Greengrass
Barocco
Bellevues
Benny's Burritos
Bertha's

Bloom's Delicatessen
Bondini
Braque
B. Smith's
BTI
Bubby's
Cafe Andrusha
Cafe Word of Mouth
Carmine's
Carnegie Deli
Chef Ho's
Chicken Chef
Cite Grille
City Cafe
Coming or Going
Cucina & Co.
Darbar
Dawat
Dean & DuLuca*
Divino
Donald Sacks
Duane Park
Empire Diner
Empire Szechuan
Friend of a Farmer
Fu's
Grace's Marketplace*
Good Enough to Eat
Great Am. Health
Hamburger Harry's
Harriet's Kitchen
Hwa Yuan Szechuan
India Pavilion
Jackson Hole
Jai Ya Thai
Japonica
Jefferson Market*
Jewel of India
Jim McMullen
John's Pizzeria
Katz's Deli
La Boulaugere
Les Friandises
Manganaro's Hero-Boy
Manhattan Chili Co.
Mezzogiorno
Mi Cocina
Nusantara
N.Y. Deli
One Hudson Cafe
Our Place
Pasta Roma
Patisserie Lanciani
Pedro Paramo
Pen & Pencil

Petak's*
Petaluma
Pete's Place
Pig Heaven
Quilted Giraffe
Ratner's
Sala Thai
Sant Ambroeus
Sawadee Thai
Second Ave. Deli
Shaliga Thai
Shark Bar
Shun Lee Palace
Shun Lee West
Siam Inn
Souen
Stage Deli
Steak Frites
Sultan
Sunny East
Todaro Brothers*
Twigs
Two Boots
Vernon's
Viand
Vinnie's Pizza
Wilson's
Yankee Clipper
Yellowfingers
Zabar's*
Zen Palate
(*Listed in *Zagat NYC
Marketplace* Survey)

## Dessert (D) and
## Ice Cream (I)
(Besides Baskin
Robbins, David's
Cookies; Haagen-
Dazs; Sedutto;
Steve's)

Au Cafe (D)
Cafe Lalo (D,I)
Cafe S.F.A. (D,I)
Caffe Bianco (D)
Caffe Biondo (D)
Caffe Bondi (D)
Caffe Vivaldi (D,I)
Cooper's Coffee (D)
Cupcake Cafe (D)
Empire Diner (D,I)
Ferrara (D)
Hard Rock Cafe (D,I)
Jim McMullen (D)
Le Train Bleu (D,I)

190

Les Friandises (D,I)
Palm Court (D)
Patisserie Lanciani (D)
Rumpelmayer's (I)
Sant Ambroeus (D,I)
Sarabeth's (D)
Serendipity 3 (D,I)
Trois Jean (D)

## Dining Alone
(Other than hotels,
 coffee shops, sushi
 bars and places
 with counter service)

Asia
Au Cafe
Basta Pasta
Bistrovia
Bloom's Delicatessen
Brighton Grill
Cafe Bel Canto
Cafe Botanica
Cafe Pierre
Cafe S.F.A.
Caffe Bondi
Caffe Vivaldi
Carnegie Deli
Chez Brigitte
Chicken Chef
Christine's
Common Market Cafe
Conservatory Cafe
Cooper's Coffee
E.A.T.
EJ's Luncheonette
Elephant & Castle
Empire Diner
Eva's Cafe
Follonico
Garibaldi Ristorante
Gus' Place
Hatsuhana
Honomura An
Hosteria Fiorella
Inagiku
Jackson Hole
Kalinka
Kan Pai
Kitchen Club
La Boulangere
La Brochette
La Taza de Oro
Las Marcias
Le Train Bleu
Les Routiers

Lipstick Cafe
Lum Chin
Marnie's Noodle
McDonald's
Melon, J.G.
Meridiana
Mme. Romaine
Museum Cafe
Neary's
Pete's Place
Rendez-Vous
Russell's
Sant Ambroeus
Sarabeth's
Second Ave. Deli
Stage Deli
Stick to Ribs BBQ
Sushisay
Tango
Trattoria dell 'Arte
Urban Grill
Viand
Wolf's 6th Ave. Deli

## Entertainment
(Check days, times
 and performers)

Albuquerque (country)
Algonquin Hotel (cabaret)
Ambassador Grill (piano)
American Harvest (piano)
Asti (opera)
Bacchus (bands)
Ballroom (cabaret)
Bill's Gay (sing-a-long)
Boca Chica (salsa)
Brother's BBQ (varies)
Bruno Ristorante (piano)
B. Smith's (piano)
Cafe Pierre (piano)
Cafe San Martin (piano)
Cameos (piano)
Chelsea Commons (jazz)
Chez Josephine (piano)
Coffee Shop (samba)
Condon's (jazz)
Copeland's (jazz/Gospel)
Cornelia St. Cafe (varies)
Cottonwood (country)
Country Club (D.J.)
Cupping Room (jazz)
Da Noi (piano/singer)
Do Da's (country/western)
Ed Debevic's (D.J.)
5 & 10 (varies)

Gulf Coast (varies)
Harbour Lights (varies)
Honeysuckle (jazz/r&b)
Jezebel (jazz/piano)
J. Sung Dynasty (piano)
Laura Belle (D.J./band)
Le Bar Bat (jazz/blues)
Lespinasse (piano)
Levee (band)
Lola (jazz/Gospel)
Ludlow St. Cafe (band)
McDonald's (piano)
Mesa de Espana (guitar)
Metro C.C. (band)
Metropolis Cafe (piano)
National (Russian)
Nosmo King (varies)
Oak Bar (piano)
One if by Land (piano)
Palm Court (piano)
Passports (jazz)
Peacock Alley (piano)
Perk's Fine Cuisine (jazz)
Pierre's (accordion)
Rainbow Room (band)
Raoul's Brasserie (varies)
Red Tulip (Hungarian)
River Cafe (piano)
Russian Samovar (piano)
Sammy's Roum. (varies)
Savoy (jazz)
Sequoia (band)
Shark Bar (jazz/Gospel)
Sharkey's (varies)
Sign of the Dove (piano)
Stella del Mare (piano)
Sugah's (jazz)
Supper Club (band)
Tatou (band/singers)
Terrace (piano)
Thai House Cafe (band)
Tommaso's (opera)
Top of the Sixes (piano)
Townhouse (piano)
Tripoli (belly dancer)
Triplet's Roumanian (piano)
Vernon's (calypso)
View (jazz)
Water Club (piano)
Water's Edge (piano)
Wilson's (jazz)
World Yacht (band)
Yokohama Mamma (D.J.)

## Fireplaces

Alcala
Arcobaleno
Arizona 206
Black Sheep
Box Tree
Bruno Ristorante
Cafe Metairie
Caffe Vivaldi
Chelsea Commons
Col Legno
Cornelia St. Cafe
Fraunces Tavern
Friend of a Farmer
Gibbon
Harbour Lights
Hosteria Fiorella
Jane St. Seafood
Jekyll & Hyde
Jockey Club
Keens Chop Hse.
La Ripaille
Les Pyrenees
Lion's Rock
Lobster Box
Mackinac Bar & Grill
March
Mary's
Old Bermuda Inn
One if by Land, TIBS
Paris Commune
Pastis
Phoebe's
Pierre au Tunnel
Raphael
Rene Pujol
Santa Fe
Savoy
Sazarac House
Sign of the Dove
Sumptuary
Telephone Bar/Grill
Tiramisu
Tiziano Trattoria
"21" Club
Upstairs/Downstairs
Vince & Eddie's
Vittorio Cucina
Vivolo
Water Club
Water's Edge

## Game in Season

Alison
Ambassador Grill

American Harvest
Aquavit
Barbetta
Bouley
Box Tree
Bruno Ristorante
Cafe Botanica
Cafe Crocodile
Chanterelle
Chefs & Cuisiniers
Chez Michallet
Felidia
Four Seasons
Gascogne
Gotham Bar/Grill
Hudson River Club
Il Mulino
Il Ponte Vecchio
Jo Jo
La Caravelle
La Cote Basque
Lafayette
La Reserve
La Ripaille
Le Cirque
Le Madri
Le Pactole
Les Celebrites
Les Halles
Le Veau d'Or
Lutece
Mesa Grill
New Deal
One Hudson Cafe
Park Bistro
Primavera
Roumeli Taverna
San Domenico
Sette Mezzo
Stanhope
Terrace
"21" Club
Union Square Cafe

## Grand Cafes

America
An American Place
Banana Cafe
Boulevard
Brasserie des Theatres
Cafe Botanica
Cafe Un Deux Trois
Canastel's
China Grill
Cite

Dolce
Ernie's
Gianni's
Gotham Bar/Grill
Hard Rock Cafe
Harry Cipriani
Hosteria Fiorella
Le Max
Le Relais
Metropolis Cafe
Metropolitan Cafe
Park Avenue Cafe
Petaluma
Positano
Remi
River Cafe
Russian Tea Room
Saloon
Sam's Cafe Restaurant
Tavern on the Green
Trattoria dell'Arte
TriBeCa Grill
Union Square Cafe
Villa Lulu
Water Club
Water's Edge
West Broadway

## Health/Spa Menus
(Most places cook
to order to meet
any dietary request;
call in advance to
check; almost all
health food spots,
Chinese, Indian and
other ethnics have
health-conscious meals,
as do the following)

Akbar
Algonquin Hotel
Angelica Kitchen
Arcadia
Aria
Bell Caffe
Bellevues
Bo Ky
Braque
Cafe Pierre
Canastel's
Carnegie Hill Cafe
Charlotte
Cleopatra's Needle
Darbar
Dawat

Edwardian Room
Four Seasons
Great Am. Health
Harbour Lights
Health Pub
Il Nido
Jewel of India
Kitchen Club
Le Train Bleu
Luma
Luxe
Manhattan Plaza Cafe
Marylou's
Michael's
Mr. Fuji's Tropicana
Mueng Thai
Nosmo King
Pigalle
Quilted Giraffe
Rio Mar
Souen
Spring St. Natural
Sultan
Symphony Cafe
Taliesin
Thai Chef
Time Cafe
"21" Club
Whole Wheat 'n Berrys
Zen Palate
Zephyr Grill
Zocalo
Zucchini

## Hotel Dining

Algonquin Hotel
  Algonquin Dining Rm.
Beekman Tower Hotel
  Zephyr Grill
Box Tree
  Box Tree
Cambridge Hotel
  La Mirabelle
Carlyle Hotel
  Carlyle Dining Room
Doral Court Hotel
  Courtyard Cafe
Doral Tuscany
  Time & Again
Drake Hotel
  Lafayette
Dumont Plaza Hotel
  Harold's*
Edison Hotel
  Edison Cafe

Essex House
  Cafe Botanica
  Les Celebrites
Franconia Hotel
  Sambuca
Holiday Inn Crowne Pl.
  Broadway Grill
Hotel Lexington
  J. Sung Dynasty
Hotel Plaza Athenee
  Le Regence
Loews N.Y. Hotel
  Lexington Ave. Grill
Lowell Hotel
  Pembroke Room
  Post House
Macklowe Hotel
  Charlotte
Mark Hotel
  Mark's
Marriott Marquis
  View
Mayfair Hotel
  Le Cirque
  Lounge*
Mayflower Hotel
  Conservatory Cafe
Michelangelo Hotel
  Bellini by Cipriani
Milford Plaza
  Mamma Leone's
Millenium Hotel
  Grill*
  Taliesin
Omni Berkshire Place
  Rendez-vous
Omni Park Central
  Nicole Brasserie
Paramount Hotel
  Brasserie des Theatres
  Mezzanine
Peninsula Hotel
  Adrienne
Pierre Hotel
  Cafe Pierre
Plaza Hotel
  Edwardian Room
  Oak Room/Bar
  Palm Court
  Plaza Oyster Bar
Regency
  Regency (aka 540 Park)
Rihga Royal Hotel
  Halcyon

Ritz-Carlton Hotel
  Jockey Club
Royalton
  44
Sheraton Park Avenue
  Russell's
Sherry Netherland
  Harry Cipriani
Sheraton Manhattan
  Bistro 790
Stanhope Hotel
  Stanhope
St. Moritz Hotel
  Cafe de la Paix*
  Rumpelmayer's
St. Regis
  King Cole Room*
  Lespinasse
Surrey Hotel
  Restaurant Daniel**
Sutton New Residence
  Small Cafe
U.N. Plaza-Park Hyatt
  Ambassador Grill
Vista Int't Hotel
  American Harvest
Waldorf Astoria
  Bull & Bear
  Inagiku
  Peacock Alley
Westbury Hotel
  Polo
(*Not listed in *Survey*)
(**Not open as of press time)

## "In" Places

Aureole
Banana Cafe
Bice
Bouley
Brasserie des Theatres
B. Smith's
Cafe des Artistes
Carlyle Dining Rm.
Carmine's
Da Umberto
Felix
Ferrier
Four Seasons
Gotham Bar/Grill
Grange Hall
Il Mulino
I Tre Merli
Jim McMullen
La Grenouille

Le Cirque
Les Celebrites
Mappamondo
Mesa Grill
Park Avenue Cafe
Peter Luger
Provence
Raoul's
Regency
River Cafe
Silverado
Smith & Wollensky
TriBeCa Grill
Union Square Cafe
West Broadway
Wollensky's Grill
Zoe

## Late Late –
## After 12:30
(All hours are AM)

Acme Bar & Grill (1)
Allegria (1)
Amici Miei (1)
Arturo's Pizzeria (1)
Ballroom (1)
Bell Caffe (2)
Bertha's
Brasserie (24hrs)
Broome St. Bar (1:30)
Buckaroo's (12;30)
Cafe des Artistes (12:30)
Cafe Lalo (2)
Cafe Tabac (1)
Caliente Cab Co. (2)
Casa Colombia (24 hrs.)
Charley O's (1)
Churchill's (1)
Ciaobella (1)
Clarke's P.J. (4)
Coffee Shop (24 hrs.)
Corner Bistro (4)
Cupping Room (1)
Do Da's (1)
Due (1)
Empire Diner (24hrs)
Empire Szechuan (1)
Fanelli (12:30)
Ferrier (1)
Fisher & Levy (3:30)
Flamingo East (12:30)
Florent (24hrs)
Fusillo (2)
Gray's Papaya (24 hrs.)
Halcyon (1)

Honeysuckle (2)
Hunan Balcony (1)
Isabella's (12:30)
I Tre Merli (1)
Jackson Hole (1)
Jekyll & Hyde (4)
La Caridad (1)
La Jumelle (4)
La Metairie (1)
Laura Belle (2)
Lion's Head (1)
Live Bait (2)
Lucky Strike (4)
Luke's Bar & Grill (2)
Marylou's (1)
Melon, J.G. (2:30)
Menchanko-tei (12:30)
Merchants
Metro C.C. (1)
Metropolis Cafe (12:30)
Metropolitan Cafe (1)
Mezzaluna (1)
Mezzogiorno (1)
Mr. Fuji's Tropicana (24 hrs.)
Museum Cafe (12:30)
Neary's (1:30)
Nicola's (12:30)
Nirvana (1)
N.Y. Deli (24 hrs.)
Odeon (2)
Oriental Town (2)
Orson's (2)
Oyster Bar (12:15)
Papaya King (1)
Patsy's (Bklyn) (1)
Patzo (12:45)
Pizzeria Uno (1)
Planet Hollywood (1)
Rio Mar (2)
Ruppert's (12:45)
Sardi's (12:30)
Seafood Palace (4)
Serendipity 3 (12:30)
Siam Inn (1:30)
Supper Club (1)
Tatiana (1)
Temple Bar (1)
T.G.I. Friday's (12:30)
Time Cafe (1)
Tompkins Park (1)
Veselka (24hrs)
Viand (24 hrs.)
Victor's (12:45)
Vong & Kwong (4)
Walker's (1)

White Horse Tavern (1:30)
Wilson's (12:30)
Wolf's 6th Ave. Deli (1)
Wollensky's Grill (2)
Woo Chon (24 hrs.)

## Noteworthy Newcomers (145)

Ahnell*
Akadi
Allegria
Appetito
Ariel & Mike*
Asia
Aspen Cafe
Au Cafe
Bali Burma
Banana Cafe
Becco
Bellisimo
Bendix Diner
Bertha's
Bistro 790
Bistrovia
Bloom's Delicatessen
Blue Ribbon*
Boca Chica
Boom
Boonthai
Bora
Braque
Brasserie des Theatres
Brasserie Pascal*
BTI
Cafe Tabac
Cafe Word of Mouth
Caffe Cefalu
Caffe Florence
Caffe Rosso
Canyon Road
Capriccioso
Carosello
Casa La Femme
Casalone
Chao Chow
Charivari Cafe*
Chop Suey Looey's
Ciccio & Tony's*
Cinquanta
Coming or Going
Common Market Cafe
Cooper's Coffee, Ltd.
Country Club
Dakota Bar & Grill
David Keh's N.R.

Demarchelier
Do Da's
Felix
Fiesta Mexicana
57 Grand St. Cafe*
Flying Fish
Follonico
44 Southwest
Gabriel's
Gian Marino
Grange Hall
Il Nonno
Il–Corallo
Island Spice
Italica*
Itcho
Jean Claude
Jekyll & Hyde
Josephina
Kitchen Club
Kodnoi
Kulu
La Collina
La Topiaire
Le Max
Lipstick Cafe
Lofland's N.Y. Grill
Lolabelle*
Louisiana Comm. Hse.*
Luxe
Manhattan Plaza Cafe
Mappamondo
Maxx*
May We
McFeely's
Mediterraneo
Meli-Melo*
Merchants
Meridiana
Metro C.C.
Millenium Grill
Montebello
Mr. Fuji's Tropicana
Nawab
Nello
Oceana
Oggi Domani*
One Fifth Avenue*
Orson's
Park Ave. Country Club
Park Avenue Cafe
Pastis
Passports
Patric
Pigalle

Pique-Nique*
Pongsri Thai
Portico
Puket
Raymond's Cafe
Regional Thai Taste
Restaurant Daniel*
San Pietro
Scalinatella
2nd Ave. Brasserie
Sequoia
Shabu Tatsu
Shaliga Thai
Shanghai 1933*
Silver Swan
Silverado
1629*
Snaps
Sofia's
Steak Frites
Stick to Ribs BBQ
Sugah's
Sultan
Supper Club
Ta Cocina*
Taliesin
Tartine
Tenth Street Lounge*
Texas Cafe/Grill
Ticino*
Tony's di Napoli
Trois Jean
Valone's
Vespa
Villa Lulu
Vong*
Vong & Kwong
Willie's
Zachary's*
Zip City Brewing Co.
Zocalo
Zoe
Zucchero
(*Not open, looks promising)

**Noteworthy Closings (45)**

Al-Amir
Anatolia
Au Natural
Auntie Yuan
Bernard's & Steve's
Brandywine
Bukhara
Cafe Caramba
Cafe Galette

Cafe Iguana
Cafe Society
Caffe Condotti
Ca'Nova
Carolina
David K's
Delta 88
Espace
Evita Tango Bar
Eze
Fay & Allen's
Gloucester House
Java
Joe's Bar & Brill
John Clancy's
Kikyo
K-Paul's New York
La Camelia
L'Aubiniere
Les Pleiades
Malvasia
Marcello
Marie-Michelle
Maurice
Maxim's
Mondrian
Onda
Phoenix Garden
Raga
Ravelled Sleave
Rex
Saturnia
Tartine (Bklyn)
Trixie's
Vanessa

## Offbeat

Afghan Kebab House
Angelica Kitchen
Barney Greengrass
Bell Caffe
Benito I
Benito II
Boca Chica
Braque
Brother Jimmy's BBQ
Cabana Carioca
Cafe Andrusha
Casa La Femme
Chez Brigitte
Cho-Sen Garden
Chop Suey Looey's
Coming or Going
Copeland's
Dominick's

El Pollo
Frank's
Groceries
Honeysuckle
Hows Bayou
Island Spice
Jai Ya Thai
Jezebel
Karyatis
Kiev
Kom Tang Soot Bul
La Caridad
Las Marcias
La Taza de Oro
La Topiaire
Levee
Lobster Box
Marion's
Mingala Burmese
Mitali East/West
Mocca Hungarian
Mr. Fuji's Tropicana
Mueng Thai
Nosmo King
Perk's Fine Cuisine
Rao's
Red Tulip
Rolf's
Roumeli Taverna
Sammy's Roumanian
Shabu Tatsu
Steak Frites
Stick to Ribs BBQ
Sugah's
Sylvia's
Uskudar
Zen Palate

## Old New York
(Year Opened)

1763 Fraunces Tavern
1836 Delmonico's
1842 Sweets
1854 McSorley's*
1864 Pete's Tavern
1868 Landmark Tavern
1868 Old Homestead
1879 Gage & Tollner
1885 Keens Chop Hse.
1887 Peter Luger
1890 Clarke's, P.J.
1890 Walker's
1894 Old Town Bar
1898 Paddy's Clam Hse.*
1902 Crisci's

| 1905 | Ratner's | Boxers (S) |
|------|----------|------------|
| 1906 | Barbetta | Braque (G) |
| 1906 | Peter McManus* | Brazilian Pavilion (S) |
| 1908 | Grotta Azzurra | Bruno Ristorante (G) |
| 1912 | Frank's | Buckaroo's (G,S) |
| 1913 | Oyster Bar | Busby's (S) |
| 1914 | Cafe des Artistes | Cafe (S) |
| 1919 | Puglia* | Cafe Bel Canto (S) |
| 1920 | Chumley's | Cafe Buon Gusto (G) |
| 1920 | Ye Waverly Inn | Cafe Lucas (G) |
| 1922 | "21" Club | Cafe Metairie (G,S) |
| 1925 | Asti | Caffe Bianco (G,S) |
| 1926 | Palm | Caffe Bondi (G) |
| 1926 | Russian Tea Room | Caffe Cefalu (G) |
| 1927 | Minetta Tavern | Caffe Rosso (G) |
| 1931 | Peacock Alley | Caffe Vivaldi (G,S) |
| 1932 | Copacabana | Caliente Cab Co. (G,S) |
| 1933 | Bill's Gay 90s | Camelback/Central (G,S) |
| 1933 | Gallagher's | Cantina (G) |
| 1934 | Rainbow Room | Capsouto Freres (G) |
| 1941 | Village Atelier | Casalone (G) |

(*Not in *Survey*)

**Outdoor Dining**

(G = Garden,
 S = Sidewalk)

Aglio e Olio (G)
Akbar (G)
Allegria (G)
Amazon Village (G)
American Festival Cafe (G)
Amici Miei (G)
Antico Caffee (G)
Arcobaleno (G)
Arlecchino (G,S)
Arturo's Pizzeria (G,S)
Au Mandarin (G)
Aureole (G)
Azzurro (G)
Back Porch (G,S)
Ballato's (G)
Barolo (G)
Beach Cafe (S)
Becco (G)
Bella Donna (S)
Bella Luna (G,S)
Bell Caffe (G)
Benito I (S)
Benny's Burritos (S)
Bertha's (S)
Bice (G,S)
Black Sheep (S)
Blue Moon Cafe (G,S)
Boathouse Cafe (G)
Boulevard (S)

Chelsea Commons (G)
Chez Jaqueline (S)
Chez Michallet (S)
Chicken Chef (S)
Chin Chin (S)
Chop Suey Looey's (G)
Choshi (G)
Christine's (S)
City Cafe (G)
Ci Vediamo (S)
Ciaobella (G,S)
Cloister Cafe (G)
Coastal (S)
Coconut Grill (S)
Coffee Shop (S)
Collage (G)
Col Legno (G,S)
Coming or Going (G)
Courtyard Cafe (G)
Cowgirl Hall of Fame (S)
Cucina Della Fontana (G)
Cucina di Pesce (S)
Da Silvano (G,S)
Dakota Bar & Grill
Dallas BBQ (G,S)
Duane Park (G)
Due (S)
Ecco-La (G)
El Rio Grande (G)
El Teddy's (S)
Empire Diner (S)
Empire Szechuan (G,S)
Ennio & Michael (G,S)
Ernie's (G,S)

Eva's Cafe (S)
Fagiolini (S)
Fannie's Oyster Bar (G)
Felix (S)
Ferrier (S)
Fiesta Mexicana (S)
Fiorello's (G)
Flamingo East (G)
Flying Fish (G)
Four Winds (G)
Friend of a Farmer (G,S)
Frutti di Mare (S)
Fusillo (G,S)
Gascogne (G)
Giordano (G)
Greek Village (G)
Grove Street Cafe (S)
Harbour Lights (G)
Hasaki (G)
Hatsuhana (S)
Hi-Life Bar/Grill (S)
Honeysuckle (S)
Hosteria Fiorella (G)
Hunan Balcony (S)
Il Cantinori (G)
Il Monello (G)
Il Ponte Vecchio (G)
Indian Cafe (G,S)
Isabella's (G,S)
Isle of Capri (S)
Isola (S)
I Tre Merli (S)
Jackson Hole (G,S)
Japonica (S)
Jean Claude (G)
Jekyll & Hyde (G,S)
Josephina (G,S)
Jour etNuit (S)
Juanita's (S)
Khyber Pass (S)
Kitchen Club (G)
Koo Koo's Bistro (S)
La Bonne Soupe (G)
La Focaccia (S)
La Goulue (G,S)
Laguna (S)
La Petite Ferme (G)
La Ripaille (G,S)
La Strada (S)
Lattanzi (G)
Le Bilboquet (G)
Le Madeleine (G)
Le Pescadou (S)
Le Relais (S)
Lion's Rock (G)

Lobster Box (G)
Louie's Westside (G,S)
Ludlow St. Cafe (G)
Luke's Bar & Grill (G,S)
Mackinac Bar & Grill (S)
Manhattan Chili Co. (G)
Manhattan Plaza Cafe (G)
March (S)
Marnie's Noodle Shop (S)
May We (S)
Maz Mescal (S)
Mediterraneo (S)
Melon, J.G. (G,S)
Meridiana (S)
Metro C.C. (G)
Metropolis Cafe (G,S)
Metropolitan Cafe (G)
Mezzaluna (G,S)
Mezzogiorno (G)
Mickey Mantle's (S)
Miracle Grill (G)
Mme. Romaine (G)
Moreno (S)
Mr. Fuji's Tropicana (G)
Mughlai (S)
Nawab (S)
New Deal (G)
Old Bermuda Inn (G)
101 Seafood (G)
Orson's (G)
Pamir (S)
Pappardella (S)
Paradis Barcelona (G)
Passports (G)
Pasta Place, A (S)
Pasta Presto (G,S)
Pastis (S)
Patriccio's (G)
Patsy's (NYC) (S)
Patzo (G,S)
Pellegrino (S)
Perretti (S)
Petaluma (G,S)
Pete's Tavern (G,S)
Phoebe's (S)
Piccolo Pomodoro (G)
Pierre's (G)
Pietro & Vanessa (G)
Pigalle (G,S)
Poiret (S)
Presto's (G,S)
Provence (G)
Quartiere (G)
Raoul's (G)

Raphael (G)
Remi (G)
R.H. Tugs (G)
River Cafe (G)
Roettelle A.G. (G)
Rose Cafe (S)
Rosolio (S)
Ruppert's (S)
Sabor (G)
Sal Anthony's (S)
Saloon (S)
Sam's Cafe (S)
San Pietro (G)
Sarabeth's (G)
Sawadee Thai (S)
Sazarac House (S)
Sea Grill (G)
Sel et Poivre (G,S)
Sequoia (G)
Sign of the Dove (G,S)
Silver Swan (G)
Sirabella's (S)
Smith & Wollensky (G,S)
Solera (G)
Sotto Cinque (G,S)
Soup Burg (G,S)
S.P.Q.R. (S)
Spring St. Natural (S)
Stage Deli (S)
Stanhope (G,S)
Steamer's Landing (G)
Stick to Ribs BBQ (G)
Sumptuary (G)
Sushi Zen (G)
Symphony Cafe (G,S)
Tang Tang (G)
Tartine (G)
Tavern on the Green (G)
Telephone Bar (S)
Tennessee Mountain (G)
Terrace (G)
T.G.I. Friday's (S)
Third Ave. Cafe (G,S)
Time Cafe (G,S)
Tiramisu (S)
Tiziano Trattoria (G)
Tompkins Park (G)
Tortilla Flats (G,S)
Trattoria Alba (S)
Trattoria dell'Arte (G,S)
Triangolo (S)
Tutta Pasta (G)
Two Eleven (G)
Urbino (S)
Vespa (S)

Via Via (S)
Victor's (S)
Vince & Eddie's (G)
Vinsanto (S)
Vittorio Cucina (G)
Voulez-Vous (S)
Vuccaria (S)
Water Club (G,S)
Water's Edge (G)
West Broadway (S)
White Horse Tavern (S)
Willie's (G)
Wollensky's Grill (G)
Yellowfingers (S)
Ying (G)
Zocalo (G,G)
Zula (G)

**Parties &
Private Rooms**
(Any nightclub or
 restaurant charges
 less at off-hours;
 *indicates private
 rooms available;
 best of the many)

Akbar*
Amazon Village
Ambassador Grill
American Festival Cafe
Aquavit
Arcadia*
Ballroom
Barolo*
Bayamo
Becco*
Bill's Gay 90s*
Black Sheep*
Boathouse Cafe*
Boca Chica
Boulevard*
Bouley
Box Tree*
Bruno Ristorante*
B. Smith's*
Cafe Bel Canto
Cafe des Sports*
Cafe Greco
Cafe Nicholson*
Cal's
Cameos
Capriccio*
Capsouto Freres
Casa La Femme
Casalone*

Century Cafe*
Charlotte*
Chefs & Cuisiniers
Chelsea Commons*
Chez Josephine*
Chez Michallet
Chiam*
China Grill
Chin Chin*
Cite Grille*
Coconut Grill
Copacabana*
Country Club*
Dakota Bar & Grill*
Darbar*
Dawat*
Do Da's
Duane Park
East*
E.A.T.
Ed Debevic's
Edward Moran*
Ernie's*
5 & 10*
Four Seasons*
44*
Frank's*
Fraunces Tavern*
Gabriel's*
Gage & Tollner*
Gallagher's*
Gianni's
Golden Unicorn*
Grange Hall
Harbour Lights*
Hard Rock Cafe
Harry's*
Hi-Life Bar/Grill*
Honeysuckle
Hows Bayou
Hudson River Club*
Il Vagabondo
Indochine
I Tre Merli*
Jockey Club*
Keens Chop Hse.*
Kulu*
La Caravelle*
La Colombe d'Or*
La Grenouille*
La Petite Ferme*
La Reserve*
Laura Belle
Le Bar Bat*
Le Bernardin*

Le Cirque*
L'Ecole
Le Madri
Leopard*
Le Perigord*
Les Celebrites*
Levee
Lobster Box*
Lola*
Lora*
Lucy's
Lutece*
Luxe*
Mackinac Bar & Grill
Manhattan Ocean Club*
Manhattan Plaza Cafe*
March*
Mark's*
Marylou's*
Metro C.C.*
Michael's*
Miracle Grill
Mortimer's*
Mr. Chow*
Mr. Fuji's Tropicana
Nirvana
Nosmo King*
Old Bermuda Inn*
One Hudson Cafe
One if by Land, TIBS*
Palio*
Palm*
Park Avenue Cafe*
Park Bistro*
Pembroke Room*
Pen & Pencil*
Periyali*
Perk's Fine Cuisine*
Peter Luger*
Planet Hollywood*
Positano*
Primavera*
Provence
Rainbow Room*
Regency*
Remi*
Roumeli Taverna
Russian Tea Room*
Sammy's Roumanian*
Sardi's
Sea Grill
Sequoia*
Serendipity 3*
7th Regiment Mess*
Sfuzzi*

Shark Bar*
Sign of the Dove*
Smith & Wollensky*
Solera*
Sonia Rose
Stick to Ribs BBQ
Sugah's*
Sumptuary*
Supper Club*
Sushisay*
Symphony Cafe*
Table d'Hote*
Tatou*
Tavern on the Green*
Tommy Tang's
TriBeCa Grill*
Triple Eight Palace*
Tropica
Tse Yang*
"21" Club*
Water Club*
Water's Edge*
West Broadway*
Wilson's*
Windows on the World*
World Yacht*
Zarela*
Zip City Brewing*

## People-Watching

Alo Alo
America
Aureole
Banana Cafe
Becco
Bertha's
Bice
Boca Chica
Brasserie des Theatres
B. Smith's
Cafe des Artistes
Carmine's
Chez Josephine
Country Club
Dakota Bar & Grill
Elio's
Ferrier
Florent
Four Seasons
44
Gotham Bar/Grill
Harry Cipriani
Jim McMullen
Jour et Nuit
La Grenouille

Laura Belle
Le Bar Bat
Le Bilboquet
Le Cirque
Le Comptoir
Le Relais
Live Bait
Lucy's
Mesa Grill
Mezzanine
Nello
Park Avenue Cafe
Planet Hollywood
Provence
River Cafe
Russian Tea Room
Shelby
TriBeCa Grill
"21" Club
Union Square Cafe
Villa Lulu
West Broadway
Zoe

## Power Scenes

Ambassador Grill
Aureole
Bouley
Four Seasons (lunch)
Gage & Tollner
Hudson River Club
Il Mulino
La Cote Basque
La Grenouille
La Reserve
Le Cirque
Le Perigord
Les Celebrites
Lutece
Manhattan Ocean Club
Palm
Park Avenue Cafe
Peter Luger
Post House
Primavera
Rainbow Room
Regency (breakfast)
Russian Tea Room
Sette Mezzo
Shun Lee Palace
Smith & Wollensky
Sparks
"21" Club

## Pre-Theater Menus
(Call to check prices
and times; also see
pp. 19 and 20)

Aquavit
Assembly
Bellini by Cipriani
Bistro 790
Bistro Du Nord
Bondini
Broadway Grill
BTI
Cafe Botanica
Cafe Greco
Cafe Luxembourg
Camelback & Central
Cameos
Casalone
Chantal Cafe
Chez Michallet
Dolce
Fiori
Florent
44
Gabriel
Giando
Halcyon
Hudson River Club
Il Gattopardo
Jockey Club
Koo Koo's Bistro
L'Acajou
La Cote Basque
La Mediterranee
La Primavera
La Reserve
La Topiaire
L'Ecole
Le Max
Le Quercy
Les Pyrenees
Letizia
Louie's Westside
Manhattan Cafe
Metropolis Cafe
Nawab
Nicole Brasserie
Nirvana
Our Place
Palio
Pen & Pencil
Rainbow Room
Regency
Rene Pujol
San Domenico

Santerello
Sea Grill
Sfuzzi
Shinbashi
Sidewalker's
Small Cafe
Snaps
Stellina
Symphony Cafe
Tatou
Tavern on the Green
Third Ave. Cafe
Top of the Sixes
Townhouse
Trattoria Alba
"21" Club
View
Vinsanto
Vittorio Cucina
Vivolo
Voulez-Vous
Willie's
Windows on the World
Zephyr Grill
Zucchini

## Prix Fixe Menus
(Call to check prices
and times; also see
pp. 19 and 20)

Akbar
Alison
Alo Alo
Ambassador Grill
American Festival Cafe
American Harvest
Amici Miei
Amsterdam's
An American Place
Anche Vivolo
Aquavit
Arcadia
Arcobaleno
Arizona 206
Arriba Arriba
Artie's
Assembly
Au Mandarin
Aureole
Bali Burma
Ballato's
Ballroom
Becco
Bellini by Cipriani
Bienvenue

Bistro Bamboche
Bombay Palace
Bondini
Bouley
Box Tree
Broadway Grill
Bull & Bear
Cafe Crocodile
Cafe de Bruxelles
Cafe des Artistes
Cafe Greco
Cafe Loup
Cafe Nicholson
Cafe Pierre
Cameos
Capsouto Freres
Carlyle Dining Rm.
Cellar in the Sky
Cent' Anni
Cesarina
Chanterelle
Charlotte
Chez Jaqueline
Chiam
Christ Cella
Churchill's
Cinquanta
Cite Grille
Cite Grille
Collage
Coming or Going
Crepes Suzette
Cucina & Co.
Dawat
Delmonico's
Dosanko
Eldorado Petit
Ferrier
1st Wok
Florent
Four Seasons
Gabriel
Gage & Tollner
Gascogne
Giando
Girafe
Halcyon
Harry Cipriani
Honeysuckle
Honmura An
Hourglass Tavern
Hudson River Club
Il Gabbiano
Il Gattopardo
Jean Lafitte

Jo Jo
Jockey Club
J. Sung Dynasty
Jour et Nuit
Koo Koo's Bistro
La Brochette
L'Acajou
La Caravelle
La Colombe D'Or
La Cote Basque
La Grenouille
La Mangeoire
La Mediterranee
La Primavera
La Reserve
La Strada
La Vieille Auberge
Lafayette
Lamarca
Le Bernardin
Le Boeuf a la Mode
Le Chantilly
Le Cirque
L'Ecole
Le Max
Leopard
Le Perigord
Le Pistou
Le Quercy
Le Regence
Le Rivage
Les Celebrites
Lespinasse
Les Pyrenees
Les Sans Culottes
Le Steak
Levana
Lora
Lutece
Mambo Grill
Manhattan Cafe
Man Ray
March
Mark's
Marylou's
Mimosa
Montrachet
Mughlai
Nawab
New Deal
Nicole Brasserie
Nirvana
Nusantara
Oceana
Odeon

Omen
Our Place
Oyster Bar
Palio
Palm
Pamir
Paradis Barcelona
Passage to India
Pasticcio
Patzo
Paul & Jimmy's
Peacock Alley
Pen & Pencil
Petrossian
Pier 25A
Pierre Au Tunnel
Pierre's
Poiret
Prix Fixe
Quatorze
Quatorze Bis
Quilted Giraffe
Raymond's Cafe
Regency
Rendez-vous
Rene Pujol
River Cafe
Roettelle AG
Rogers & Barbero
Rosemarie's
Russell's
Russian Samovar
Russian Tea Room
Sal Anthony's
Sam's Cafe
San Domenico
Santerello
Sardi's
Sawadee Thai
Scarlatti
Scoop
Sea Grill
Shinwa
Sido Abu
Sign of the Dove
Solera
Sonia Rose
Sotto Cinque
Stanhope
Supper Club
Symphony Cafe
Tango
Tavern on the Green
Tempo
Terrace

Terry Dinan's
Third Ave. Cafe
Tommaso's
Tommy Tang's
Townhouse
Trattoria Alba
TriBeCa Grill
Triplet's Roumanian
Tse Yang
T.S. Ma
"21" Club
Two Eleven
Umeda
Urban Grill
Voulez-Vous
Water Club
West Broadway
Windows on the World
Woo Lae Oak
World Yacht
Yankee Clipper
Zona Rosa
Zula

## Pubs

Bill's Gay 90s
Billy's
Boxers
Bridge Cafe
Broome St. Bar
Buckaroo's
Chelsea Commons
Chumley's
Churchill's
Clarke's P.J.
Corner Bistro
Dakota Bar & Grill
Edward Moran
Fanelli
Frank's
Harry's
Hi-Life Bar/Grill
Jim McMullen
Lion's Head
Luke's Bar & Grill
Marion's
McFeely's
Oak Bar
Pete's Tavern
Rao's
Rascals
Sam's Cafe
Telephone Bar
Walker's
White Horse Tavern

Wollensky's Grill
Zip City Brewing

## Quiet Conversation

Adrienne
Algonquin Hotel
Ambassador Grill
American Harvest
Aquavit
Aria
Asia
Aureole
Barbetta
Bistrovia
Bloom's Delicatessen
Box Tree
Brasserie des Theatres
Cafe Andrusha
Cafe Botanica
Cafe Nicholson
Cafe Trevi
Carlyle Dining Rm.
Castellano
Chanterelle
Charlotte
Cinquanta
Cite
Coach House
Cooper's Coffee
David Keh's N.R.
Demarchelier
Edwardian Room
Eldorado Petit
Follonico
Four Seasons
Gabriel's
Garibaldi Ristorante
Giambelli
Gibbon
Grove Street Cafe
Gus' Place
Harlequin
Honmura An
Hudson River Club
Il Monello
Il Tinello
Inagiku
Jockey Club
John Clancy's
J. Sung Dynasty
Keens Chop Hse.
Kitchen Club
La Caravelle
La Collina
La Cote Basque

Lafayette
La Grenouille
La Maison Japonaise
La Reserve
Le Bernardin
Le Chantilly
Le Max
Le Perigord
Le Regence
Les Celebrites
Lespinasse
Lutece
Manhattan Ocean Club
Manhattan Plaza Cafe
Maz Mescal
Meridiana
Mitsukoshi
Mortimer's
Oak Bar
One if by Land, TIBS
Palio
Palm Court
Pembroke Room
Petrossian
Pigalle
Polo
Primavera
Quilted Giraffe
Regency
Russell's
Scalinatella
Scoop
Seryna
Snaps
Solera
Stanhope
Terrace
Terry Dinan's
Time & Again
Tse Yang
Windows on World

## Romantic Spots

Alison
Arcadia
Aureole
Banana Cafe
Barbetta
Black Sheep
Bouley
Box Tree
Cafe Botanica
Cafe des Artistes
Cafe Metaire
Cafe Nicholson

Cafe Trevi
Caffe Vivaldi
Carosello
Chez Josephine
Chez Ma Tante
Chez Michallet
Grove Street Cafe
Hudson River Club
Kulu
La Colombe d'Or
La Goulue
La Grenouille
La Metairie
La Vielle Auberge
Le Bernardin
Le Cirque
Le Pescadou
Le Refuge
Les Celebrites
Lora
Luxe
Mark's
Merchants
Nirvana
One if by Land, TIBS
Pembroke Room
Periyali
Petrossian
Provence
Rainbow Room
River Cafe
Russian Tea Room
Sign of the Dove
S.P.Q.R.
Supper Club
Tavern on the Green
Terrace
Trois Jean
Vivolo
Water Club
Water's Edge
Windows on World
World Yacht

## Senior Appeal

Abe's Steak House
Adrienne
Algonquin Hotel
Aquavit
Asia
Aureole
Barbetta
Becco
Bistro 790
Bistrovia

Bouley
Box Tree
Cafe Botanica
Cafe Metairie
Cafe San Martin
Cafe S.F.A.
Cafe Trevi
Casa di Pre
Charlotte
Cinquanta
Coach House
Dawat
Demarchelier
E.A.T.
Edwardian Room
Four Seasons
Fu's
Gabriel's
Gallagher's
Garibaldi Ristorante
Gian Marino
Halcyon
Hudson River Club
Il Gabbiano
Il Menestrello
Il Monello
Jim McMullen
Jockey Club
John Clancy's
Kulu
La Boulangere
La Caravelle
La Colombe d'Or
La Cote Basque
Lafayette
La Grenouille
La Reserve
Le Bernardin
Le Chantilly
Le Cirque
Le Veau d'Or
Les Celebrites
Lutece
March
Mario's (Bronx)
Mme. Romaine
Nello
Oak Room/Bar
Palm Court
Post House
Primavera
Rainbow Room
Raphael
Romeo Salta
Russell's

Russian Samovar
San Domenico
San Giusto
Scoop
Shun Lee Palace
Sign of the Dove
Snaps
Solera
Tavern on the Green
Terrace
Tina's
Trois Jean
Union Square Cafe
Voulez-Vous
Wilkinson's

## Singles Scenes

Acme Bar & Grill
Alo Alo
Amazon Village
America
Amsterdam's
Antico Caffee
Arizona 206
Aspen Cafe
Automatic Slims
Banana Cafe
Bayamo
Bella Donna
Benny's Burritos
Bertha's
Bimini Twist
Boca Chica
Boom
Boxers
Braque
Brother Jimmy's BBQ
Brother's BBQ
B. Smith's
Cafe Tabac
Canyon Road
Caribe
Carmine's
Casa La Femme
Ci Vediamo
Clarke's
Coconut Grill
Coffee Shop
Dakota Bar & Grill
Do Do's
Edward Moran
Felix
Gulf Coast
Hi-Life Bar/Grill
Honeysuckle

Hows Bayou
Il–Corallo Trattoria
Isabella's
I Tre Merli
Jekyll & Hyde
Jerry's 103
Juanita's
Le Bar Bat
Le Relais
Levee
Lion's Head
Live Bait
Lucy's
Mappamondo
Memphis
Merchants
Mesa Grill
Metro C.C.
Mezzanine
Mr. Fuji's Tropicana
Mulholland Drive
Old Town Bar
Rocking Horse Cafe
Ruppert's
Shark Bar
Silverado
Sugar Reef
Texas Cafe/Grill
Tortilla Flats
TriBeCa Grill
Two Boots
Villa Lulu
Walker's
White Horse Tavern
Wilson's
Zip City Brewing
Zoe

## Sleepers
(Good to excellent
food, but little known)

Appetito
Bistro 36
Boca Chica
Bora
Borsalino
Cafe Botanica
Cafe Word of Mouth
Chikubu
Cho-Sen Garden
Cinquarta
Col Legno
Copeland's
El Pollo
Gabriel's

Gian Marino
Grappino
Hamachi
Il Nonno
Island Spice
Itcho
Jean Claude
Kulu
Kurumazushi
La Barca
Lamarca
L'Auberge du Midi
L'Ecole
Les Friandises
Manhattan Plaza Cafe
Mesa de Espana
Montebello
Nicole Brasserie
Oriental Town
Orson's
Pasta Place
Patsy's
Perk's Fine Cuisine
Piccolo Pomodoro
Pigalle
Pongsri Thai
Regional Thai Taste
Road to Mandalay
Sabor
Stick to Ribs BBQ
Sunny East
Tango
Tartine
Tempo
Totonno Pizzeria
Urbino
Vespa
Villa Berulia
Volare
Vong & Kwong
Woo Chon
Ying

## Teflons

(Get lots of business, despite so-so food, i.e. they have other attractions that prevent criticism from sticking)

Acme Bar & Grill
Albuquerque Eats
Algonquin Hotel
Alo Alo
America
Amazon Village

American Festival Cafe
Amsterdam's
Asti
Barolo
Boathouse Cafe
Boogies Diner
Boulevard
Brasserie
Broadway Grill
Burger Heaven
Busby's
Cafe Botanica
Caliente Cab Co.
Camelback & Central
Cantina
Charley O's
Clarke's P.J.
Dosanko
Elaine's
Empire Diner
Empire Szechuan
Ernie's
Fagiolini
Gonzalez y Gonzalez
Hard Rock Cafe
Houlihan's
Hows Bayou
I Tre Merli
Jackson Hole
La Bonne Soupe
La Fondue
Le Bar Bat
Live Bait
Mamma Leone's
Manhattan Chili Co.
Melon, J.G.
Mickey Mantle's
Mortimer's
Mulholland Drive
Ottomanelli's Cafe
Pizzapiazza
Pizzeria Uno
Planet Hollywood
Saloon
Sam's Cafe
Sardi's
Tavern on the Green
Tennessee Mountain
Tony Roma's
Tortilla Flats
Via Via
Windows on the World
World Yacht

## Sunday Dining – Best Bets

(B = brunch; L = lunch; D = dinner; plus all hotels and most Chinese)

Aggie's (B,L)
Alison (D)
Alo Alo (B,L,D)
Ambassador Grill (B,D)
America (B,L,D)
Amsterdam's (B,L,D)
Anglers & Writers (B,L,D)
Arizona 206 (L,D)
Arqua (D)
Becco (L,D)
Ben Benson's (D)
Bendix Diner (B,L,D)
Benny's Burritos (B,L,D)
Bice (L,D)
Billy's (L,D)
Black Sheep (B,D)
Box Tree (D)
Boxers (B,L,D)
Brasserie (B,L,D)
Brasserie/Theatres(B,L,D)
Brighton Grill (B,L,D)
B. Smith's (L,D)
Busby's (B,L,D)
Cafe des Artistes (B,D)
Cafe des Sports (D)
Cafe Greco (B)
Cafe Luxembourg (B,D)
Cafe Pierre (B,L,D)
Cafe Trevi (D)
Caffe Vivaldi (B,L,D)
Cal's (D)
Capsouto Freres (B,L,D)
Carmine's (L,D)
Chefs & Cuisiniers (L,D)
Chel. Commons (B,L,D)
Chez Michallet (B,D)
China Grill (D)
Cite Grille (L,D)
City Cafe (B,L,D)
Coconut Grill (B,L,D)
Coco Pazzo (D)
Coffee Shop (B,D)
Cornelia St. Cafe (B,L,D)
Cowgirl Hall/Fame (L,D)
Cucina Stagionale (L,D)
Cupcake Cafe (B)
Cupping Room (B,D)
Dakota Bar & Grill (B,D)
Demarchelier (B,L,D)
Dock's (B,L,D)

Dominick's (L,D)
El Rio Grande (B,D)
Elephant & Castle (B,D)
Elio's (D)
Embers (D)
Empire Diner (B,L,D)
Empire Szechuan (L,D)
Fanelli (L,D)
Ferrier (B,D)
Fiorello's (L,D)
Florent (B,L,D)
44 (B,D)
Friend of a Farmer (B,D)
Gage & Tollner (B,D)
Gallagher's (L,D)
Gianni's (L,D)
Gino (L,D)
Good Enough to Eat (B,D)
Gotham Bar/Grill (D)
Grange Hall (D)
Grotto Azzurra (L,D)
Grove Street Cafe (D)
Gulf Coast (B,L,D)
Hi-Life Rest. (B,D)
Honeysuckle (L,D)
Hudson River Club (B,D)
Hulot's (L,D)
Il Monello (L,D)
Indochine (D)
Isabella's (B,L,D)
Island (B,L,D)
Island Spice (B,D)
Jim McMullen (B,L,D)
Juanita's (L,D)
La Colombe D'Or (D)
La Goulue (L,D)
La Luncheonette (D)
La Mediterranee (D)
La Metairie (L,D)
La Mirabelle (D)
La Petite Auberge (D)
La Ripaille (D)
Le Boeuf a la Mode (D)
Le Comptoir (D)
Le Madri (B,D)
Le Relais (L,D)
Les Routiers (D)
Lion's Head (B,L,D)
Lion's Rock (B,D)
Lobster Box (L,D)
Lola (B,D)
Louie's Westside (B,D)
Lucky Strike (D)
Lupe's East L.A. (B,D)
Lusardi's (L,D)

Mackinac Bar & Grill (B,D)
Manhattan Ocean (D)
Manhattan Plaza Cafe (B)
Mappamondo (B,L,D)
Mazzei (D)
Melon, J.G. (B,L,D)
Memphis (D)
Meridiana (L,D)
Mesa Grill (B,D)
Metropolis Cafe (B,D)
Michael's (B,D)
Mi Cocina (B,L,D)
Miracle Grill (B,D)
Mocca Hungarian (L,D)
Mortimer's (B,L,D)
Mr. Chow (D)
Mulholland Drive (B,D)
Neary's (B,D)
Nicola's (D)
Odeon (B,D)
Ollie's (L,D)
107 West (B,D)
One If by Land TIBS (D)
Palm Court (B,D)
Paola's (D)
Park Avenue Cafe (B,D)
Park Bistro (D)
Parma (D)
Pat. Lanciani (B,L,D)
Perk's Fine Cuisine (B)
Peter Luger (L,D)
Petrossian (L,D)
Phoebe's (B,D)
Planet Hollywood (L,D)
Poiret (D)
Polo (B,L,D)
Popover Cafe (B,L,D)
Post House (D)
Primavera (D)
Primola (D)
Prix Fixe (B,D)
Provence (L,D)
Quatorze (D)
Quatorze Bis (L,D)
Ratner's (B,L,D)
Remi (D)
River Cafe (L,D)
Rogers & Barbero (B,D)
Rosa Mexicano (D)
Royal Canadian (B,L,D)
Russian Samovar (D)
Russian Tea Room (L,D)
Santa Fe (B,L,D)
Sarabeth's (B,D)
Saranac (B,L,D)

Sette Mezzo (L,D)
Sfuzzi (B,D)
Shabu Tatsu (D)
Shelby (B,D)
Sign of the Dove (B,D)
Sistina (D)
Smith & Wollensky (L,D)
SoHo Kitchen/Bar (L,D)
S.P.Q.R. (L,D)
Steak Frites (B,L,D)
Stephanie's (B,L,D)
Sylvia's (B,L,D)
Table d'Hote (B,D)
Tavern/Green (B,L,D)
Time Cafe (B,L,D)
Trattoria Dell'Arte (B,D)
TriBeCa Grill (B,D)
"21" Club (L,D)
Twigs (B,D)
Union Square Cafe (D)
Vico (L,D)
Victor's (B,L,D)
Vince & Eddie's (B,D)
Voulez-Vous (B,D)
Walker's (B,D)
Water Club (B,L,D)
West Broadway (B)
Whole Wheat (B,D)
Wilkinson's (D)
Windows on World (B,D)
World Yacht (B,L,D)
Yellowfingers (B,D)
Zarela (D)
Zoe (B,D)

## Takeout – Best Buys

(Almost all ethnics,
BBQs, diners, burger
joints and pizzerias
sell takeout, as do the
following; also see
*Delivers Index*)

Aggie's
Aquavit
Automatic Slims
Azzurro
Bellevues
Ben Benson's
Bendix Diner
Benny's Burritos
Bertha's
Bice
Billy's
Bloom's Delicatessen
Braque

Brasserie
Bright Food Shop
Brighton Grill
Brother's BBQ
B. Smith's
BTI
Bubby's
Cabana Carioca
Cafe Andrusha
Cafe Greco
Cafe Lalo
Cafe Loup
Cafe San Martin
Cafe Word of Mouth
Caffe Rosso
Cal's
Camelback & Central
Campagnola
Caribe
Carmine's
Casa Colombia
Charley O's
Chelsea Trattoria
Christine's
City Cafe
Coming or Going
Common Market Cafe
Corrado
Cottonwood Cafe
Cowgirl Hall of Fame
Cucina Della Fontana
Cucina Stagionale
Cupcake Cafe
Cupping Room
Demarchelier
Divino
Dock's
Donald Sacks
Ed Debevic's
Eighteenth & Eighth
Empire Diner
Ernie's
Eva's Cafe
Fiesta Mexicana
Firenze
Florent
Friend of a Farmer
Frutti di Mare
Gabriel
Gino
Good Enough to Eat
Great Am. Health
Great Shanghai
Gulf Coast
Harriet's Kitchen
Harry's

Health Pub
Hi-Life Bar/Grill
Hosteria Fiorella
Jerry's
Jim McMullen
Keens Chop Hse.
Kiev
La Bonne Soupe
Lamarca
La Sarten
Les Friandises
Lou G. Siegel
Lupe's East L.A.
Mackinac Bar & Grill
Manganaro's Hero-Boy
Manhattan Chili Co.
Manhattan Plaza Cafe
Mappamondo
Marnie's Noodle Shop
Metropolis Cafe
Metropolitan Cafe
Mi Cocina
Mi Tierra
Nawab
Nazareth Restaurant
NoHo Star
Old Homestead
Original Taqueria
Palm
Pamir
Paola's
Patisserie Lanciani
Pete's Place
Peter Luger
Pie
Provence
Quilted Giraffe
Rocking Horse Cafe
Rosa Mexicano
Sarabeth's
Shaliga Thai
Sido Abu
Smith & Wollensky
SoHo Kitchen/Bar
Sultan
Teresa's
Trattoria dell'Arte
Tripoli
Vernon's
Veselka
Viand
Vince & Eddie's
Walker's
White Horse Tavern
Yellowfingers
Zarela

## Teas
(Major hotels and
the following)

Adrienne
Algonquin Hotel
Anglers & Writers
Cafe Botanica
Cafe Lalo
Cafe Pierre
Cafe Word of Mouth
Caffee Biondo
Caffe Bondi
Caffe Vivaldi
Carlyle Dining Rm.
Charlotte
Cornelia St. Cafe
E.A.T.
Jockey Club
La Boulanger
Le Regence
Le Train Bleu
Les Friandises
Mark's
Mayfair Lounge*
Mezzanine
Palm Court
Peacock Alley
Pembroke Room
Regency
Rendez-vous
Russian Tea Room
Stanhope
Village Atelier
(*Not in *Survey*)

## Teenagers & Other
## Youthful Spirits

Acme Bar & Grill
Aggie's
America
Amir's Falafel
Anglers & Writers
Arriba Arriba
Aspen Cafe
Benito I &II
Benny's Burritos
Bertha's
Boca Chica
Boogies
Brasserie des Theatres
Bright Food Shop
Brighton Grill
Broome St. Bar
Brother Jimmy's BBQ
Brother's BBQ

Bubby's
Cafe Lalo
Caliente Cab Co.
Camelback & Central
Cantina
Canyon Road
Carmine's
Carnegie Deli
Coconut Grill
Coming or Going
Corner Bistro
Cucina di Pesce
Cucina Stagionale
Dallas BBQ
Dominick's
Dosanko
E.A.T.
Ed Debevic's
EJ's Luncheonette
Elephant & Castle
El Pollo
El Rio Grande
Empire Diner
Empire Szechuan
Fine & Schapiro
1st Wok
Fisher & Levy
Freddie & Pepper
Good Enough to Eat
Gray's Papaya
Grotta Azzurra
Hamburger Harry's
Hard Rock Cafe
Harriet's Kitchen
Hosteria Fiorella
Hows Bayou
Hunan Balcony
Il–Corallo
Il Fornaio
Jackson Hole
Jerry's
Jim McMullen
John's Pizzeria
La Caridad
Levee
Lupe's East L.A.
Manhattan Chili Co.
Manhattan Plaza Cafe
Mappamondo
Mary Ann's
Maryland Crab House
Mezzaluna
Mickey Mantle's
N.Y. Deli
NoHo Star

Original Taqueria
Ottomanelli's Cafe
Papaya King
Pasta Lovers
Patsy's (Bklyn)
Pedro Paramo
Pig Heaven
Pizzeria Uno
Planet Hollywood
Rosa Mexicano
Ruppert's
Sarabeth's
Second Ave. Deli
Serendipity 3
Shun Lee Cafe
Sidewalker's
Silverado
Sotto Cinque
Steak Frites
Stick to Ribs BBQ
Sugah's
Sugar Reef
Szechuan Hunan
Szechuan Kitchen
Tavern on the Green
Texas Cafe/Grill
Tony Roma's
Tortilla Flats
Tutta Pasta
Two Boots
Villa Lulu
Vinnie's Pizza
Wolf's 6th Ave. Deli
Yellowfingers
Zarela
Zona Rosa

## Trips to Country
(Reviewed in our
*Tri-State Restaurant
Survey*)

LONG ISLAND
Glen Cove
  Nicola's
Great Neck
  Navona
  Peter Luger
St. James
  Mirabelle
Westhampton Beach
  Starr Boggs
NORTH OF NYC
Banksville
  La Cremailliere

Granite Springs
  Maxime's
Piermont
  Xaviar's in Piermont
Rye
  La Panetiere
White Plains
  Livanos
CONNECTICUT
Centerbrook
  Fine Bouche
New Canaan
  L'Abbee
New Haven
  Frank Pepe's
  Robert Henry's
  Sally's Apizza
Westport
  Da Pietro's
NEW JERSEY
Bergenfield
  Chez Madeleine
Oakland
  Ruga
Ramsey
  Cafe Panache
Saddle River
  Saddle River Inn
Westfield
  Chez Catherine

## Visitors on
## Expense Accounts

Aquavit
Arcadia
Aureole
Bouley
Brasserie des Theatres
Cafe des Artistes
Carnegie Deli
Cellar in the Sky
Chanterelle
Chiam
Chin Chin
Da Umberto
Dawat
Four Seasons
Gotham Bar/Grill
Hatsuhana
Hudson River Club
Il Mulino
Il Nido
Jo Jo
La Caravelle
La Cote Basque

La Grenouille
La Reserve
Laura Belle
Le Bernardin
Le Cirque
Le Madri
Le Perigord
Les Celebrites
Lespinasse
Lutece
Manhattan Ocean Club
March
Mesa Grill
Montrachet
One if by Land, TIBS
Oyster Bar
Palm
Park Avenue Cafe
Periyali
Peter Luger
Petrossian
Planet Hollywood
Post House
Primavera
Prix Fixe
Provence
Quilted Giraffe
Rainbow Room
Remi
River Cafe
Russian Tea Room
Sea Grill
Shun Lee Palace
Sign of the Dove
Smith & Wollensky
Sparks
Supper Club
Sushisay
Tatou
Tavern on the Green
Terrace
TriBeCa Grill
Trois Jean
Tse Yang
"21" Club
Union Square Cafe
West Broadway
Windows on the World
World Yacht

**Wheelchair Access**
(Check for bathroom
access; almost all hotels,
plus the following)

Aggie's
Albuquerque Eats

Alison
Alo Alo
American Festival
Amici Miei
Amsterdam's
An American Place
Andiamo
Angelica Kitchen
Anglers & Writers
Arlecchino
Au Mandarin
Auntie Yuan
Aunt Sonia's
Automatic Slim's
Azzurro
Barney Greengrass
Barolo
Basta Pasta
Bell Cafe
Bendix Diner
Benny's Burritos
Bernard & Steve's
Billy's
Bimini Twist
Bistro 790
Bistro 36
Bistrovia
Boogies
Bright Food Shop
Brighton Grill
Brasserie des Theatres
Broadway Grill
B. Smith's
Busby's
Cafe
Cafe Bontanica
Cafe des Artistes
Cafe Luxembourg
Cafe Melville
Cafe Pierre
Cafe S.F.A.
Cafe St. John
Cafe Trevi
Caffe Biondo
Caffe Bondi
Cal's
Can
Caribe
Carmine's
Carnegie Deli
Carnegie Hill Cafe
Casa di Pre
Castellano
Cellar in the Sky
Chanterelle
Charlotte

Chefs & Cuisiniers
Chez Jacqueline
Chez Michallet
Chiam
Chicken Chef
China Grill
Cho-Sen Garden
Christ Cella
Cite
Cleopatra's Needle
Coach House
Coastal Cafe
Coffee Shop
Corner Bistro
Cowgirl Hall of Fame
Cucina & Co.
Dakota Bar & Grill
Darbar
Da Tommaso
Dawat
Day-O
Divino
Dock's Oyster Bar
Dolce
Duane Park
Ed Debevic's
Eden Rock
Edward Moran
EJ's Luncheonette
Eldorado Petit
Embers
Ernie's
Eva's Cafe
Ferrier
Franks
Friend of a Farmer
Frutti di Mare
Fusillo
Gage & Tollner
Gallagher's
Grand Central Oyster
Grand Dairy
Grange Hall
Halcyon
Hamburger Harry's
Harry Cipriani
Hasaki
Haveli
Health Pub
Hudson River Club
Hunan Garden
Il Cortile
Il Giglio
Il Monello
Il Mulino

Isabella's
Istanbul Cuisine
Japanese on Hudson
Jerry's
Jewel of India
Jim McMullen
John's Pizzeria
JoJo
Karyatis
Katz's Deli
Kikyo
Kulu
La Boulangere
La Caravelle
La Chandelle
Lafayette
La Goulue
La Petite Auberge
La Primavera
La Reserve
Le Bernardin
Le Madeleine
Le Pactole
Le Regence
Le Relais
L'Escale
Lespinasse
Les Routiers
Lexington Ave. Grill
Lola
Ludlow Street Cafe
Luma
Lum Chin
Mananaro's Hero-Boy
Marcello
March
Mark's
Mazzei
Mesa Grill
Mezzogiorno
Mickey Mantle's
Mi Tierra
Mocca Hungarian
Mondrian
Monreale
Montrachet
NoHo Star
Nusantara
Odeon
Odessa
Old Homestead
Old Town Bar
Olio
One Hudson Cafe
Oriental Pearl

Ossie's Table
Osso Buco
Oyster Bar
Palio
Pandit
Paper Moon
Paradis Barcelona
Paris Commune
Park Bistro
Parma
Pasta Roma
Peacock Alley
Peter Luger
Planet Hollywood
Plaza Oyster Bar
Poiret
Polo
Primavera
Prix Fixe
Quatorze Bis
Quilted Giraffe
Ratner's
Rectangle's
River Cafe
Ronasi
Rosa Mexicano
Rosemarie's
Roumeli Taverna
Royal Canadian
Russell's
Sambuca
Sam's Cafe Restaurant
San Domenico
Sant Ambroeus
Satrunia
Sawadee Thai
Scarlatti
Sea Grill
Sfuzzi
Shelby
Shun Lee Cafe
Shun Lee Palace
Shun Lee West
Smith & Wollensky
Snaps
Solera
Symphony Cafe
Tang Tang
Taormina
Tatou
Tavern on the Green
Temple Bar
Terrace
Texas Cafe/Grill
Time Cafe

Tirami Su
Top of the Sixes
Townhouse
Trattoria Alba
Trianglo
TriBeCa Grill
Tropica
Twigs
Two Boots
Vanessa
View
Village Atelier
Vinnie's Pizza
Vinsanto
Voulez-Vous
Water Club
Water's Edge
West Broadway
Westside Cottage
White Horse Tavern
Windows on the World
Winter Garden Cafe
World Yacht
Zen Palate
Zinno
Zip City Brewing Co.
Zocalo
Zoe

## Winning Wine Lists

An American Place
Aureole
Barbetta
Chiam
Cite
Felidia
Four Seasons
I Tre Merli (Italian)
Lafayette
Le Cirque
Levana (kosher wine)
Lora
Lutece
Manhattan Ocean Club
Michael's
Montrachet
Nicola Paone (Italian)
Oyster Bar (Am. white)
Palio
Park Avenue Cafe
Post House
Quilted Giraffe
Rainbow Room
River Cafe
San Domenico

Smith & Wollensky
Sparks
Tommaso's
Union Square Cafe
Windows on World
 (Ask for mimeo list)
Wollensky's Grill

**Young Children**
(Besides the normal
fast-food places)

Aggie's
America*
Bayamo*
Bendix Diner
Benihana of Tokyo
Bistro 790*
Bloom's Delicatessen
Boathouse Cafe*
Boulevard*
Broadway Diner
Brother Jimmy's BBQ*
Burger Heaven
Cafe S.F.A.*
Carnegie Deli
Chop Suey Looey's
Cite Grille*
Coastal*
Coffee Shop*
Coming or Going
Conservatory Cafe*
Cowgirl Hall of Fame*
Cucina*
Dallas BBQ
E.A.T.
Ed Debevic's
Edward Moran*
EJ's Luncheonette*
El Pollo
Embers*
Empire Diner
Empire Szechuan
Freddie & Pepe
Friend of a Farmer
Gabriel*
Gage & Tollner*
Good Enough to Eat
Hamburger Harry's*
Harbour Lights*
Hard Rock Cafe
Houlihan's*
H.S.F. (Chinatown)
Jackson Hole
Jim McMullen
Jockey Club*

John's Pizzeria
Josephina*
Katz's Deli
La Bonne Soupe
La Mirabelle*
Leopard*
Lexington Ave. Grill*
Lobster Box*
Lupe's East L.A.
Mamma Leone's*
Manhattan Chili Co.*
Manhattan Plaza Cafe*
McDonald's*
Mingala West Burmese*
Nick & Eddie*
N.Y. Deli
Original Taqueria
Palm Court*
Parker's Lighthouse*
Pasta Lovers
Pasta Presto
Patisserie Lanciani
Peacock Alley*
Peretti
Pete's Place
Phoebe's
Piccolino
Pier 25A*
Pig Heaven
Pizzapiazza*
Planet Hollywood
Popover Cafe*
Royal Canadian*
Rumpelmayer's*
Saloon*
Saranac*
Second Ave. Deli
Serendipity 3
7th Regiment Mess
Stage Deli
Stick to Ribs BBQ
Sylvia's*
Tang Tang
Tartine*
Tennessee Mountain*
T.G.I. Friday's*
Tony Roma's*
Tortilla Flats*
Tutta Pasta*
Two Boots*
Whole Wheat 'n Berrys*
Wilson's*
Wolf's 6th Ave. Deli
World Yacht
Zarela
(*Children's menu available)

# WINE VINTAGE CHART 1981-1991

These ratings are designed to help you select wine to go with your meal. They are on the same 0–to–30 scale used throughout this *Survey*. The ratings reflect both the quality of the vintage and the wine's readiness to drink. Thus if a wine is not fully mature or is over the hill, its rating has been reduced. The ratings were prepared principally by our friend Howard Stravitz, a law professor at the University of South Carolina.

| WHITES | 81 | 82 | 83 | 84 | 85 | 86 | 87 | 88 | 89 | 90 | 91 |
|---|---|---|---|---|---|---|---|---|---|---|---|
| **French:** | | | | | | | | | | | |
| Burgundy | 15 | 20 | 15 | 11 | 28 | 29 | 13 | 23 | 27 | 20 | 14 |
| Loire Valley | — | — | — | — | 17 | 18 | 14 | 19 | 25 | 24 | 15 |
| Champagne | 23 | 29 | 23 | — | 25 | 24 | — | — | 26 | 25 | — |
| Sauternes | 25 | — | 28 | — | 21 | 26 | — | 27 | 26 | 23 | — |
| **California:** | | | | | | | | | | | |
| Chardonnay | — | — | — | 18 | 22 | 25 | 19 | 26 | 22 | 28 | 25 |

| REDS | 81 | 82 | 83 | 84 | 85 | 86 | 87 | 88 | 89 | 90 | 91 |
|---|---|---|---|---|---|---|---|---|---|---|---|
| **French:** | | | | | | | | | | | |
| Bordeaux | 23 | 29 | 25 | 14 | 28 | 24 | 22 | 24 | 26 | 24 | 19 |
| Burgundy | — | 18 | 25 | — | 28 | 13 | 22 | 24 | 24 | 26 | 23 |
| Rhône | 16 | 16 | 25 | — | 25 | 21 | 14 | 25 | 24 | 23 | 17 |
| Beaujolais | — | — | — | — | 18 | 17 | 18 | 22 | 25 | 23 | 24 |
| **California:** | | | | | | | | | | | |
| Cabernet/ Merlot | 22 | 23 | 16 | 27 | 26 | 25 | 25 | 17 | 20 | 24 | 23 |
| Zinfandel | — | — | — | 18 | 18 | 17 | 20 | 15 | 16 | 19 | 19 |
| **Italian:** | | | | | | | | | | | |
| Chianti | 14 | 16 | 13 | — | 25 | 15 | — | 23 | — | 24 | — |
| Piedmont | 13 | 25 | — | — | 25 | 12 | 17 | 20 | 25 | 22 | 11 |

Bargain sippers take note—some wines are reliable year in, year out, and are reasonably priced as well. These wines are best bought in the most recent vintages. They include: Alsatian Pinot Blancs, Côtes du Rhône, Muscadet, Bardolino, Valpolicella and inexpensive Spanish Rioja and California Zinfandel.